WRO

...ed and tells the story from obscure beginnings to the present, with some surprising discoveries on the way.'

Evening Standard

'Hosken does an excellent job of sorting out the American reaction, the failure of the Iraqi leadership in the form of Nouri al-Maliki and others, and how IS has becomes the richest terrorist group in the world. A tremendously useful, insightful study of the frightening spread of a culture of death.'

Kirkus, starred review

'It's a bloody, violent tale, told here with compassion and a quest for understanding. Hosken explores these historical roots with depth and clarity; readers will come to understand a more focused version of what motivates the Islamic State.'

Publishers Weekly

'Veteran BBC correspondent Andrew Hosken ably chronicles and thoroughly documents the rise of ISIS and its leaders – as well as explaining how the group managed, in a few short months, to threaten everything Americans and others fought and paid dearly to establish in Iraq from 2003 to 2011.'

Christian Science Monitor

'Of all the recent crop of books about the Islamic State, this is the best. It is well-written and superbly researched by someone who knows his subject intimately; if you want an authoritative, well-researched but above all readable account of this foul but for many all too appealing organisation, look no further – *Empire of Fear* is that book.'

Frank Ledwidge, author of Losing Small Wars
and Investment in Blood

'Andy Hosken is a brilliant investigative reporter with an unerring eye for a story. The rise of the Islamic State is an event as seismic as it is widely misunderstood, and *Empire of Fear* is an essential contribution to fathoming the truth of what is currently happening in the Middle East.'

Tom Holland, author of *Persian Fire* and *In the Shadow of the Sword*

About the Author

Andrew Hosken is one of the BBC's most experienced correspondents. He reported on the 9/11 attacks from New York and on the 7/7 attacks from London. Over the course of his career he has covered a number of Middle-Eastern conflicts and their aftermaths, including the Arab Spring, the fall of Gaddafi, and the rise of the Islamic State. In 2003, he won the One World Media Award for his series on Algerian terrorism.

Empire of Fear
Inside the Islamic State

Andrew Hosken

ONEWORLD

A Oneworld Book

First published in North America, Great Britain and
Australia by Oneworld Publications, 2015
This updated edition published 2016

Copyright © Andrew Hosken 2015, 2016

Map artwork copyright © Laura McFarlane

ISBN 978-1-78074-823-8
eISBN 978-1-78074-933-4

Printed and bound in Great Britain by Clays Ltd, St Ives plc

Oneworld Publications
10 Bloomsbury Street
London WC1B 3SR
England

Contents

List of illustrations

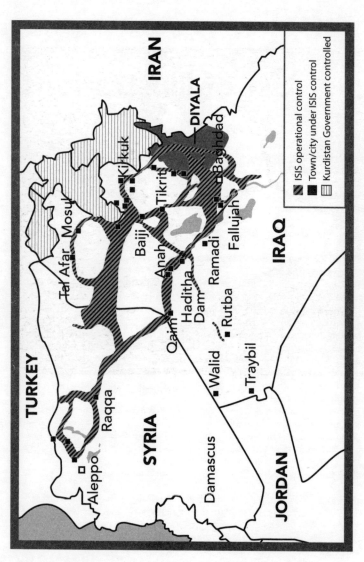

The tentacle-like nature of Islamic State, July 2014

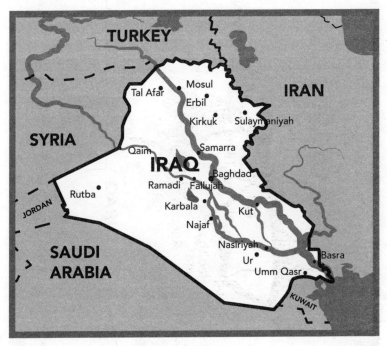

The key battleground

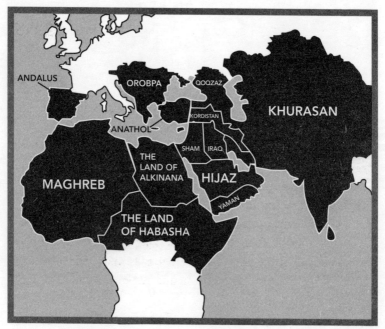

A new world order, as conceived by Islamic State

Introduction

2015

No one predicted Islamic State's astonishing blitzkrieg in the June of 2014 that created a caliphate roughly the size of Britain in the Middle East and presented the world with its greatest security challenge of recent times.

I asked Dr Azzam Tamimi, the prominent and sometimes controversial British Palestinian scholar and activist, the question everyone wants the answer to: 'What is Islamic State?' He was clear: 'ISIS is a very desperate insane response to a very deep crisis.'[1]

But what exactly is the crisis and why such a terrifying response? What do they want and what happens if they get it? What drives their utter relentlessness? In the immortal words of Butch Cassidy and the Sundance Kid about the indefatigable posse pursuing them, 'Who are those guys?'

To many people, Islamic State (IS) and its caliphate had appeared from nowhere and that is because most people had lost interest in Iraq and the seemingly never-ending tide of violence ebbing and flowing over the country. The Iraq War had not been popular and had dragged on too long. Besides there were other serious distractions, such as the Arab Spring of 2011 or the war in Ukraine, where I spent some time in early 2014 before IS launched its stunning military campaign.

IS had not come from nowhere. Its roots go back to the US-led invasion of 2003 and even further back to older conflicts in Afghanistan. When you investigate the organization's terrible history you realize that in fact the US has been at war with IS in its various incarnations for twelve years now, which is almost four times as long as its fight against Japan and Nazi Germany. There appears no end in sight. Other dangerous extremist jihadist groups, such as Boko Haram in Nigeria, have pledged allegiance to IS and by early 2015, the group managed to establish a murderous presence amid the chaos of Libya.

For me as a BBC reporter, the phenomenon of militant Islamism has clearly been one of the big stories of our times. It had taken me to New York to report on the attacks of 9/11, and to London for the suicide bombings of 7 July 2005. I was in Libya when it started to take root there and have seen it wreak death and destruction in Iraq. In early 2015, I was in Paris in the wake of the attacks on *Charlie Hebdo* and the Hyper Cacher kosher supermarket.

In November 2015 I was dispatched again to the continent in the wake of the deadly attacks by Islamic State on Paris, this time to investigate the jihadi cells, based in the Molenbeek district of Brussels, that had planned the assault. During 2015, the group claimed responsibility for a string of attacks, including the massacre of 39 tourists at Sousse in Tunisia in June and the downing of the Russian airliner Metrojet 9268 in late October over Sinai, which killed 224 passengers and crew. But it was the November attacks on Paris involving suicide bombings and mass shootings that brought the full panoply of IS horror to Europe, killing at least 129 people and wounding more than 300. The attacks brought home to many people in the West the full scale of the threat posed by the group.

INTRODUCTION

Despite the enormous publicity, there is still so much we don't know about IS and the violent men who control it. We have been learning more and more about life within the so-called caliphate itself. For a journalist, security considerations have made Iraq an extremely difficult place to work in. There has been a persistent kidnap risk and of course the danger of suicide and car bombings. Much of Syria has become a virtual no-go area for the Western media. IS has brutally murdered brave journalists like Kenji Goto, James Foley and Steven Sotloff who got too close.

I wanted to investigate IS to try to understand its history, its savagery and the ruthless men who have created it. I have spoken to people in Iraq and elsewhere in the Middle East as well as in the UK and the US. I have interviewed a wide range of people, from experts and politicians in the West and the Middle East, to the US military strategists who tried to eliminate the group, and other important eyewitnesses. There is also a treasure trove of important documents, from the secret cables of the US embassy in Baghdad to the documents and letters discovered at the home of al-Qaeda leader Osama bin Laden by the US Navy Seals who killed him. I even got information from leaks that US intelligence believes emanated from within the leadership of Islamic State itself. All of this helps paint a harrowing picture of the rise of IS and the people and circumstances that helped it happen.

Since its inception as a small violent gang of jihadi extremists called al-Tawhid wa'l Jihad, IS has gone through no fewer than five name changes. Many people still prefer to call it ISIS; President Barack Obama decided on ISIL; to the BBC it is the 'so-called Islamic State' or IS. In the Middle East, it is known simply by the acronym Da'esh, Islamic State of Iraq and the Levant. To avoid confusion, I have simply decided to call the group whatever it was calling itself at the time or 'the group'. All of these name changes are important because they reflect how the group saw itself at the time.

Another problem is aliases. All the leading terrorists and other jihadis had anything up to three aliases, or *noms de guerre*. This was done, mainly successfully, to confuse their enemies. I will try not to add to the confusion. Where possible, I will also give their real names and then stick to the *noms de guerre* by which they are known.

Problems also arise with language and words such as 'Islamist' and 'Islamism'. Many Islamists believe in democracy and it is possible to be an Islamist extremist and not engage in violence. There are Salafis and Wahhabis who oppose IS and those who support them. Even terms such as 'terrorism' and 'terrorist' can be loaded and problematic. Again, in an attempt to be helpful, I use the word 'Shia' for all people and things Shia, although I appreciate that strictly speaking, 'Shiite' is the adjective. Otherwise, I will try to be as exact as possible.

1

The face that launched a thousand hits

Baghdad, 5 July 2014

He was either dead or seriously wounded, or so they told us. It had all just happened during an attack by Iraqi security forces on a town called al-Qaim on the Syrian border. For me, working behind the concrete blast walls and barbed wire of the Baghdad office, it all sounded too incredible to be true even in those astonishing days of June and July 2014. But the Iraqi interior ministry was adamant when we called it – the world's most dangerous man was possibly out of action, and for good.

Within a few weeks, Abu Bakr al-Baghdadi seemed to transcend his shadowy role as one of the world's most wanted terrorists to become a force of nature. Like an avenging fire, he and his thirty thousand jihadis had roared east across the border from Syria into Iraq. They had seized territory that then stretched around 415 miles from eastern neighbourhoods of Aleppo in Syria to the Iraqi town of Sulaiman Bek, which lies just 60 miles from the Iranian border. In a breathtaking move that stunned the world, Mosul,

Iraq's second-biggest city, had fallen to Baghdadi. Thousands of Iraqi troops and civilians had been massacred and thrown into shallow graves. Baghdadi now marched on Baghdad itself.

Only six days earlier, on 29 June, Abu Mohammed al-Adnani, Baghdadi's bloodthirsty media spokesman, had issued an alarming proclamation. The Islamic State of Iraq and Syria was no longer. ISIS would now be known simply as Islamic State, an entity no longer constrained by the borders of Syria and Iraq. An Islamic empire known as a caliphate was declared and Baghdadi would be the caliph, or *khalifah*. He was not just some sort of Islamic pope-emperor but the true descendant of Muhammad, second only to the Prophet himself.

Baghdadi's full *nom de guerre* was Abu Bakr al-Baghdadi al-Husseini al-Qurayshi; his real name was also known. He was really Ibrahim Awwad Ibrahim Ali al-Badri al-Samarrai, but with a critical addition. As with his alias, he was also 'al-Qurayshi', meaning 'from the Qurayshis'. This meant al-Baghdadi was claiming lineage from the tribe of Muhammad's own family, known as the Qurayshis, considered by many Islamic scholars and clearly by Islamic State as an essential requirement to be caliph.

This was made by clear by the IS media guru Adnani, who declared:

The *khalifah* Ibrahim (may Allah preserve him) has fulfilled all the conditions for *khilafah* [caliphate] mentioned by the scholars… His authority has expanded over wide areas in Iraq and Sham [Syria and Lebanon]. The land now submits to his order and authority from Aleppo to Diyala. So fear Allah, O slaves of Allah! Listen to your *khalifah* and obey him! Support your state, which grows every day – by Allah's grace – with honour and loftiness, while its enemy increases in retreat and defeat.[1]

For Muslims there are few more loaded words than *khalifah*. The historic caliph is regarded as by far the greatest and most important sovereign institution in the history of Islam and the word appears several times in the plural forms, *khulafa* and *khala'if*, and is translated as 'successors' or 'heirs'.[2] Following the death of Muhammad in 632 AD, the first acknowledged caliph was Abu Bakr, called *Khalifatu Rasul Allah*, the 'Deputy of the Prophet of God'.[3] In Islam, to any mortal man – and there could be no other kind of man – there could be no greater honour than to be Muhammad's heir.

As we hit the phones to try to confirm what had happened to Baghdadi, the man himself suddenly and dramatically appeared on our television screens. He was attired in the black cloak and turban of the Prophet as he limped his way up the steps to the *minbar*, Muslims' version of a pulpit, at the great mosque of al-Nuri in Mosul. At the top, he greeted his audience of mainly young men in jeans and T-shirts and then sat down and flossed his teeth while waiting for the muezzin to finish the call to prayer.

This was the first time Baghdadi had shown himself to the world on his own terms. Until then all anyone had was the image of a resentful glowering face peering from a prison mug shot. The Iraqi interior ministry, which can often be relied upon for the odd comic touch during many a dark moment, issued a statement, asserting that this baffling figure was 'indisputably' not Baghdadi. Brigadier General Saad Maan, the ministry's well-meaning spokesman, stated confidently, 'We have analysed the footage… and found it is a farce.'[4] No farce this, but a recording of Baghdadi made the previous day.

The confusion was perhaps understandable. Despite the terror inflicted by Baghdadi during the last four years, few people knew who he was or what he looked like. It was said he even wore a mask, earning him the nickname 'the Invisible Sheikh'.[5]

Until then, the world had only two mug shots of Baghdadi,

taken during his ten months of captivity in a US prison camp,[6] but the face beneath the straggly, greying beard, with its thick black Groucho Marx-style eyebrows and cold brown eyes, was unmistakable. It was 'indisputably' Abu Bakr al-Baghdadi, so far one of the biggest killers of the twenty-first century. Yes, this really was the face that launched a thousand hits and more than 6,800 bombings during the course of 2013 alone, according to the grisly annual report called *Al-Naba* ('The Report') he had published a few months earlier.[7] In fact, to be exact, Baghdadi boasted, 6,876 bombings and 1,083 targeted assassinations for the year. This was a man who had not only killed thousands of people; he liked to catalogue his murders and massacres meticulously, for posterity.

From his *minbar* he called on the *Ummah*, the term for Muslims around the world, to pay him their allegiance, or *bay'ah*: 'I am the *wali* [leader] who presides over you,' he said, 'though I am not the best of you, so if you see that I am right, assist me. If you see that I am wrong, advise me and put me on the right track, and obey me as long as I obey God in you.' As he spoke, Baghdadi's eyes scanned his audience slowly and warily from left to right and back again like searchlights on a prison watchtower.

Since the fifteenth century the sultans of the Ottoman Empire had claimed the title of caliph. In November 1922, a new Turkish assembly dismissed the last sultan and abolished the sultanate, but by a constitutional quirk the title of caliph went to the crown prince, Abdülmecid Efendi, an accomplished artist and avid butterfly collector. Abdülmecid was the 101st Sunni Muslim to claim the caliphate since the death of the Prophet Muhammad in 632 AD. On 3 March 1924, the assembly abolished the caliphate, and on the following day officials of the new Turkish republic escorted Abdülmecid to Istanbul railway station, in what has been described as a 'humiliating manner', and bundled him onto the Orient Express to Paris and permanent exile.[8] He died in the

French capital twenty years later just as the Nazis were expelled.[9] The contrast between the last recognized caliph of the Islamic world and this apparition in Mosul could not have been greater.

Baghdadi had declared a caliphate stretching from the Pyrenees to Indonesia with himself as emperor and head pontiff, effectively world domination, yet the thing that attracted most ridicule from the Western media was his watch, which was either an Omega Seamaster, 'as worn by James Bond', or a Rolex worn by anyone with £8,000 or so to spare.[10] His hatred for Western values clearly was not all-consuming, but despite this unusual PR glitch, Baghdadi did not cut a ludicrous figure – far from it. By then, the TV screens had shown terrifying images of the massacres committed in his name.

Until he launched his war on the world, the Iraq conflict had been a distant memory and the terrible ensuing carnage all too awful to contemplate; the crowds had gone home and so had the foreign troops. For many people in the West, Baghdadi appeared almost as a goblin from a half-forgotten horror story.

For Baghdadi and his predecessors, and for nearly twenty years, the caliphate had been the ultimate goal all along and the reason for all the extraordinary violence they employed against their many enemies. Every atrocity, torture, assassination and theft was simply a means to one overpowering obsession – to destroy nation states, seize territory and build a caliphate from the ashes.

Baghdadi had come a long way. In a little more than four years, he had taken a broken gang of jihadis from the brink of complete defeat to the dream they had long cherished: a caliphate at the heart of the Muslim world, governed by Islamic Sharia law and with access to the region's vast oil supplies. Baghdadi had hijacked sectarian uprisings either side of the Syria–Iraq border to create his caliphate, and the United States, the UK and governments in the Middle East had been powerless to prevent it. 'Therefore, rush O Muslims to your state!' he exhorted Muslims. 'Yes, it is your state. Rush, because Syria is not for the Syrians, and Iraq is not for the Iraqis. The earth is Allah's.'[11]

In the words of IS, this land had been taken by the sword[12] and by June 2014 its territories had assumed many of the characteristics of a state. At the time of writing, more than six million people live in the 'Islamic State' and are subject to Sharia law as interpreted by Baghdadi. I have communicated with people in the twin IS capitals of Raqqa in Syria and Mosul in northern Iraq. They have provided eloquent testimony to the fear many normal decent people have of living under the harsh and unforgiving rule of IS.

Islamic State is said to be the richest terror organization in history thanks to its control of people and territory. It has robbed banks. In Mosul, the group was accused of stealing some $425 million from the central bank, although the bank's deputy governor refused to confirm or deny the money had gone.[13]

The group's seizure of oil wells and refineries, particularly in Syria, has helped make IS fabulously rich, possibly to the tune of $4.5 billion, although no one really knows the full extent of its wealth. Control of important border posts has allowed it to smuggle oil into Turkey and elsewhere and trade it on the black market. In the first two weeks of July 2014, IS was said to be earning $1 million a day from the sale of black market oil alone,[14] although it could be three times that figure.[15]

Huge revenues have also been generated for the caliphate through hostage ransoms, the sale of antiquities, extortion and taxation of the people captive in their territories, fuelling its expansion and terror. Primarily, that terror has been exercised in the territory of the caliphate itself. I have spoken to people in Raqqa who have witnessed many beheadings. Gay men have been thrown to their deaths from tower blocks in the northern

Iraqi territory of Nineveh and in Raqqa; women stoned to death for adultery; Christians crucified; and young Kurdish boys tortured and killed. Men have been beheaded for 'sorcery'; a young Jordanian pilot has been burned alive in a cage.[16] The Yazidi people, who suffered from the IS onslaught on Sinjar in northwestern Iraq in late summer 2014, saw their wives and children, in the words of Islamic State's own glossy magazine, *Dabiq*, 'divided according to the Shari'ah amongst the fighters of the Islamic State who participated in the Sinjar operations'.[17] Baghdadi's media guru, Abu Mohammed al-Adnani, warned everyone else, probably most people reading this book, that they would be next: 'We will conquer your Rome, break your crosses, and enslave your women, by the permission of Allah, the Exalted. This is His promise to us; He is glorified and He does not fail in His promise. If we do not reach that time, then our children and grandchildren will reach it, and they will sell your sons as slaves at the slave market.'[18]

Many of us who reported from Baghdad during those dangerous hot fetid weeks of June and July 2014 found it uncomfortable, to say the least, knowing that the forces of Baghdadi and his mouthpiece Adnani were trying to fight their way into the capital. To the west, Islamic State fighters were supposed to be contesting the towns of Ramadi and Abu Ghraib. They were also around a hundred miles to the north fighting around Tikrit. In this strange sprawling conflict, IS were trying to seize Kirkuk in the northern Kurdistan region and Baqubah, north-west of Baghdad, in an attempt to encircle the Iraqi capital. It had become a nasty multi-front war. Before I had set out for Baghdad, several BBC colleagues bet me I would have to be whisked to safety by helicopters to escape advancing IS fighters just like they had seen in the old footage of the fall of Saigon to the Vietcong in 1975. There was an evacuation plan but thankfully it would not be needed. The march of IS had been stalled on the western and northern approaches to the capital.

In July 2014, with the enemy at the gate, Baghdad was a frontline city, but then it had been since the jihadis began their assault on the capital eleven years previously. As we sizzled in temperatures of more than 50°C, the relentless grind of bombings and shootings continued, thanks to Baghdadi's killers. We had all been told about the coming 'Zero Hour'. More than 200 IS terror sleeper cells would rise up inside Baghdad and support the fighters pushing in from the west of the capital. More than 1,500 IS fighters would intensify their bomb attacks on key targets and try to penetrate the 'Green Zone', the heavily fortified city within a city housing key government ministries and the vast US embassy.[19] But Zero Hour did not come then or on subsequent visits. It may never come. For Baghdadi, the Iraqi capital would remain the objective, the future hub of his caliphate. After all, his *nom de guerre* means 'from Baghdad'.

This caliphate had been helped into being by a toxic combination of factors. These included the 2003 US-led invasion of Iraq and the bungled occupation of the country, along with the Syrian Civil War; rampant corruption, particularly in the army; the sectarian divide between Sunni and Shia Muslims, both in Iraq and Syria; and the failure of Iraq's predominantly Shia-led governments to behave fairly and sensibly towards the country's desperate Sunni minority. All these terrible failures played their part in the rise of IS. But to give credit where it is due, it was also down to the ability of Baghdadi and his forebears to exploit all these factors to their own advantage, along with their ruthless ambition to establish the caliphate come what may.

Zarqawi and the big bad idea

Islamic State began life back in 1999 as a training camp for jihadis in Afghanistan called Tawhid wa'l Jihad. Its name means 'Monotheism and Jihad',[20] monotheism being the fundamental belief in Allah as the one God and jihad the means to establish his law, Sharia, on earth. In charge of the camp near the city of Herat was a Jordanian man called Abu Musab al-Zarqawi, who would help bring chaos and death to Iraq and become one of the world's most feared terrorists.

Zarqawi established the virulently intolerant ideology that is the foundation of Islamic State today. Zarqawi's driving obsession was also the establishment of a caliphate and his methods were virtually the same as Baghdadi's, give or take the odd burning alive of a captured pilot, although his bombs would burn many thousands of men, women and children in his three-year-long frenzy of terror. Abu Bakr al-Baghdadi rightly considers Zarqawi the true founding father of Islamic State. Richard Barrett, a former senior British intelligence officer and now a security analyst with the US think-tank the Soufan Group, said, 'It's interesting looking at Islamic State because al-Baghdadi and the Islamic State propaganda really hold up Abu Musab al-Zarqawi as being the guy, the founder, and even more important than Osama bin Laden himself.'[21]

Like Baghdadi, Zarqawi was obsessed with the media and how to project himself and his message to a disbelieving world. Then there is the astonishing violence that both men used against their fellow Muslims, mainly the Shia, their most hated enemy, as well as their supposedly fellow Sunnis, whom they claimed to represent. Zarqawi also kidnapped Western hostages and filmed them as he personally cut their heads off with a knife; Baghdadi was content to let others carry out such tasks, albeit under his direction.

It was Zarqawi who would first reveal to an outside world the timetable by which the jihadists hoped to dominate the globe. He would lead a short brutal life and brutally cut short the lives of countless innocent people. His legacy has been the deaths of thousands more. I spoke to Dr Alaa Makki, an important Iraqi Sunni parliamentarian, about Zarqawi, and asked him to compare Zarqawi, the first so-called emir, with Baghdadi. 'Let me put it this way in the terms of a computer system,' said Makki: 'if al-Baghdadi is Windows 10, then Zarqawi was more like Windows 1 or 2. Musab al-Zarqawi was the leader of small armed groups, a local militia leader, who killed mainly Shia Muslims and also many Sunnis. But Abu Bakr al-Baghdadi has many fighters and made his caliphate and announced himself to be caliph, and demands loyalty from all Muslims. That was a very dangerous announcement. That is the very obvious difference.'[22]

Unlike Baghdadi, about whom so little is known, Zarqawi is no mystery. By all accounts, he was a street thug and a bully before falling under the influence of religious Islamist extremists. Zarqawi was born on 20 October 1966 in a house overlooking a cemetery in the Jordanian town of Zarqa,[23] hence his later *nom de guerre* al-Zarqawi, 'from Zarqa'. His real name was Ahmad Fadil al-Nazal al-Khalayleh, and his family were originally Bedouin Arabs of the al-Khalayleh clan, a branch of the Banu Hassan tribe. After dropping out of school at the age of seventeen, he worked in a series of dead-end jobs, including in a paper factory.[24] He was drinking heavily and getting into fights. He would be accused of drug dealing, and even pimping. He was known as the 'Green Man' because of his many tattoos, which he would later try to erase with hydrochloric acid.[25] Zarqawi was squat and well built and struggled with his weight. Photos and film of the Jordanian down the years show a big, puffy, sometimes gelatinous-seeming face, often curtailed by a beard and moustache.

Zarqawi started to become radicalized in prison after being convicted of drug possession and sexual assault.[26] It is not hard to understand why Zarqawi would become infected with Islamist extremism in prison. He was a troubled man living in a troubled country. In September 1970, King Hussein of Jordan went to war with the Palestinian Liberation Organization (PLO), a conflict that led to the expulsion of thousands of refugees and PLO fighters. In the following decades, political Islam in the shape of the transnational organization the Muslim Brotherhood became increasingly prominent in Jordan, taking over universities and other important institutions. According to Zarqawi's biographer Jean-Charles Brisard, one offshoot of the Brotherhood infiltrated Palestinian enclaves in Jordan while another, the Islamic Action Front, became a real power in the land. 'Thus the Jordanian political context in the 1990s was like a nutritious broth in which Islamist organizations and radical currents proliferated.'[27]

Towards the end of the 1980s Zarqawi attended mosques for religious instruction, principally the al-Husayn Ben Ali mosque in the Jordanian capital, Amman. He then took the fateful decision to travel to Afghanistan, where he came in contact with the Mujahidin, and al-Qaeda and its charismatic leader, Osama bin Laden. Zarqawi was a Johnny-come-lately as far as the real fighting against the Soviets was concerned. The Soviet Union, considered to be made up of infidels and crusaders by the Mujahidin, had decided to end its disastrous intervention in Afghanistan and was pulling out. At the start of the 1990s in Afghanistan Zarqawi is believed to have met bin Laden for the first time, and so began the often fraught, up-and-down relationship between al-Qaeda and the Zarqawi network which later became Islamic State. But it was his meeting in the Pakistan city of Peshawar with an obscure Islamist scholar that would have significant ramifications.

Born in 1959, Abu Muhammad al-Maqdisi became one of the most influential Islamist scholars in the Middle East. (His real name is Isam Muhammad Tahir al-Barqawi.) To many jihadis, Maqdisi has been an extremely important spiritual leader and ideologue. Eighteen publications by Maqdisi were found among the effects of Mohammed Atta, the leader of the 9/11 attacks on New York and Washington.[28] He made his name in the early 1980s when he published *The Creed of Abraham*, revered as a textbook by Islamist extremists around the world. More than any other scholar, Maqdisi is responsible for the ruthless and intolerant ideology followed by IS, although even he had become a fierce critic of the group by 2014.[29] Maqdisi also helped make Zarqawi the monster he became, Jean-Charles Brisard describing him as 'a thousand times more dangerous than Zarqawi'.[30]

Maqdisi introduced an impressionable twenty-three-year-old Zarqawi to an extremely puritanical form of Islam known as Salafism. Salafis believe in the cleansing from Islam of what they see as the contamination and corruption caused by the colonization of the Middle East by European powers such as Britain and France. Salafis like bin Laden also added the 'far enemy' of the US and the effects of American influence to the list of contaminants. Men should revert more than 1,300 years to the time of the Prophet Muhammad when Islam was purest and God, or Allah, was the source of all power.

Modern Salafis see Western civilization as extremely dangerous to Islam, a destructive threat most powerfully articulated by a second fundamentalist Islamist scholar and one of the most important of his age, Sayyid Qutb. In his hugely influential book of 1964, *Milestones*, Qutb, an Egyptian, argued for jihad, a holy war not just in defence of Islam but ultimately as the way of establishing Sharia law throughout the world, or in his own words 'as a means of establishing the Divine authority…to be carried throughout the earth to the whole of mankind, as the object of this religion is all humanity, and its sphere of action is the whole earth'.[31] So, Qutb's project clearly included all non-Muslims as well as Muslims. He mentioned the elevation of man to the position of *khalifah*, caliph, as Allah's regent on earth, as 'an essential requirement for attaining the leadership of mankind' and 'an essential condition of our very existence and Islam itself'.[32]

Qutb argued that 'Western man' was no longer capable of leading humanity because he was 'unable to present any healthy values for the guidance of mankind'.[33] Only Islam and Sharia law could do that but first the Muslim community 'must be restored to its original form'. The community must return to the seventh century and the days of the Prophet Muhammad and the first generation of Muslims, whose only guidance was the Holy Koran. In those days there was a true Islamic system governed by Sharia. 'No other generation of this calibre was ever again to be found,' wrote Qutb,[34] who was eventually hanged after being convicted for his alleged part in an assassination attempt on Egypt's President Gamal Abdel Nasser.[35]

Salafism is derived from the Arabic expression *al-salaf al-salih*, which refers to the 'pious forebears'[36] of the seventh century, in other words the generation of Muhammad and the two that followed him. Like Qutb, the modern Salafis are ultraconservative Sunnis who believe the first Muslims and the immediate successors of Muhammad exemplify most perfectly what it means to be a virtuous Muslim and demand that later generations must emulate them. Islam must be purged of any impurities and shorn of any ambiguity or sentimentality about other religions. If it was a highly evolved luxury car, it would revert to the first model and then stripped down so all working parts could be on display.

Concepts such as democracy are alien to Salafis. The answer must be an Islamic state where the only law is God's law, or Sharia. This had long been espoused by the Wahhabis, the extreme Islamist sect that is often described as synonymous with Salafism. Bankrolled by the Saudi royal family, to whom they give legitimacy, the Wahhabis had spread their fundamentalist and intolerant message far and wide across the Middle East with enormous consequences for the region and the world.

'Democracy is a religion. But it is not Allah's religion,' wrote Maqdisi. Even implementing legislation was heresy. Legislators, including members of parliament, were apostates, guilty of *kufr*.[37]

Kufr, or unbelief, is the ultimate sin of apostasy, committed by people turning away from pure Islam as interpreted by the Salafis. Apostates were beyond the pale and should be stripped of social rights and excluded from the economy.[38] For Baghdadi and Zarqawi before him, *kufr* was applied to everyone, non-Muslims as well as Muslims, who did not agree with this extremely narrow interpretation of Islam, and it became a death sentence resulting in the genocidal slaughter of many thousands of Shia Muslims, Yazidis and Christians. Apostates, or *kuffar*, deserved to die. 'Islam never was for a day the religion of peace,' Abu Bakr al-Baghdadi declared in 2015. 'Islam is the religion of war. Your Prophet (peace be upon him) was dispatched with the sword as a mercy to the creation. He was ordered with war till Allah is worshipped alone.'[39]

Maqdisi and Zarqawi became unlikely friends, the star ideologue and intellectual and the one-time hoodlum and drunk. Together they proved to be a lethal concoction of ideology and extreme brutality. According to another Zarqawi biographer, Loretta Napoleoni, the ideology mixed with the anger running through Zarqawi's veins horribly simplified the world for him: '*Takfir* [the act of declaring someone an unbeliever] was his response to the consumerism and rapid modernization that had destroyed the Bedouin way of life. *Takfir* was how he attacked those who had forced upon him a life of misery, of socioeconomic marginalization, of endless humiliation.'

Salafism had long proved to be a dangerous ideology, but Zarqawi would take it to its logical conclusion. To this violent and unstable man, that meant the physical destruction of the guilty apostates, the *kuffar*, according to his limited and twisted perception of his own religion and the world around him. *Takfirism* was the most extreme form of Sunni Islam so far and it would become a justification for genocide against other Muslims, particularly the Shia, as well as against 'errant' Sunnis. It also demanded the extermination of non-Muslims, particularly the Christian and Yazidi minorities of Iraq, a 'policy' that was still being driven relentlessly by Abu Bakr al-Baghdadi during his lightning conquests of large swathes of Iraq in 2014. *Takfirism* gave Zarqawi all the excuse he needed to indulge his monstrous inner demons and let them loose on the world.

2
Seven steps
1996–2003

In 1996 it probably didn't feel like a huge scoop, which is probably why the Jordanian reporter Fouad Hussein would not publish it for another decade. But his exclusive story, a blueprint for the establishment of an Islamic caliphate revealed to him in part by Abu Musab al-Zarqawi, looks increasingly disturbing as time goes by.

Hussein's journalism had got him in trouble with the Jordanian authorities and he had become a political prisoner in the al-Suwaqah jail. The reporter was imprisoned in the cell next door to Zarqawi and Abu Muhammad al-Maqdisi,[1] who were just one year into fifteen-year sentences for the possession of bombs and mines. In addition, Zarqawi had confessed to using a forged passport.[2]

Hussein managed to gain the trust of both men when Zarqawi was incarcerated in solitary confinement for arguing with a guard. Maqdisi asked Hussein to join in a prison protest to get his friend released and Hussein readily agreed. 'The protest was effective, the prison director promised to release Zarqawi. When he was released and heard what I had done for him, he warmed to me,' Hussein said later.[3]

Soon Maqdisi and Zarqawi would reveal to him the Seven

Steps plan, drawn up by al-Qaeda strategists sometime in the early 1990s. It is clear Zarqawi would adopt this strategy as his own, and adapt it as he and his successors believed they were eclipsing al-Qaeda. Hussein would turn this revelation first relayed to him in jail into his 2005 book, *Zarqawi: Al-Qaeda's Second Generation*. To say the least, the plan looks uncannily prescient.

Step 1: 'The Awakening', 2000–3

This phase of the strategy would provoke the US into declaring war on the Islamic world, thereby resulting in the 'awakening' of Muslims. The revelation was of course five years before the September 11 attacks and the US-led invasion of Afghanistan. Hussein spoke to other al-Qaeda bosses later for his book. 'The first phase was judged by the strategists and masterminds behind al-Qaeda as very successful,' he wrote. 'The battlefield was opened up and the Americans and their allies became a closer and easier target.' The terrorist network was satisfied that its message could now be heard 'everywhere'.

Step 2: 'Opening Eyes', 2003–6

In this phase, the jihadists hoped to make the West aware of the 'Islamic community'. Hussein believed this was a phase in which al-Qaeda wanted an organization to develop into a global movement. The network hoped to recruit young men during this period. Iraq should become the centre for all global operations, with an 'army' set up there and bases established in other Arabic states. Again, at the time of the revelation to Hussein, the invasion of Iraq was still seven years off.

Step 3: 'Arising and Standing Up', 2007–10

There would be a series of attacks across Turkey and the Middle East, including Israel. 'There will be a focus on Syria,' prophesied

Hussein, based on what his sources told him. The attacks would also help al-Qaeda's global branding as the main jihadi franchise. Hussein further believed that countries neighbouring Iraq, such as Jordan, were also in danger.

Step 4: 'Fall of the Regimes', 2010–13

Hussein revealed that al-Qaeda aimed to bring about the collapse of hated Arab governments across the Middle East. The forecast was that the 'creeping loss of the regimes' power will lead to a steady growth in strength within al-Qaeda'. Again this seems to predict the Arab Spring of 2010 and 2011, which in truth had little to do with al-Qaeda, although Islamic State has certainly benefitted from it, particularly in Syria and later apparently in Libya. At the same time attacks would be carried out against oil suppliers and, through cyber terrorism, the US economy.

Step 5: 'Declaration of the Caliphate' or Islamic State, 2013–16

At this point, an Islamic state, or caliphate, could be declared. By this time, Western influence in the Islamic world would be so reduced and Israel weakened so much that resistance would not be feared. Al-Qaeda hoped that by then the Islamic state would be able to bring about a new world order.

Step 6: 'Total Confrontation', 2016–

As soon as the caliphate had been declared, the 'Islamic army' would instigate the 'fight between the believers and the non-believers'.

Step 7: 'Definitive Victory'

The ultimate victory by the Islamic state is certain because the rest of the world will be so beaten down by the 'one and a half billion

Muslims'. Hussein writes that, in the terrorists' eyes, the caliphate will undoubtedly succeed. This phase should be completed by 2020, although the war shouldn't last longer than two years.[4]

The last two steps appear 'somewhat fanciful'[5] to many experts now but that is probably little comfort. Back in 1996, the whole blueprint would have struck any rational person as utterly implausible. It could not have been possible then to foresee the approaching tumult. But it leads to a central question: is Islamic State an offshoot of al-Qaeda, as is commonly believed, or was it always something separate and even more sinister from the beginning? The groups have been loosely affiliated in the past, but from the beginning they would argue bitterly over methods and ideology. In 2004, Zarqawi took on the al-Qaeda brand in Iraq largely for pragmatic reasons but the evidence strongly suggests that both groups had different priorities and strategies. Both believed in the caliphate but they always had different aims, particularly around who to kill. That is why the story of Zarqawi is important to our understanding of IS now.

According to experts, the caliphate was always a distant hope for al-Qaeda, something bin Laden hoped he could help bring about by creating the necessary conditions. Professor John Esposito, one of the world's leading Islamic studies scholars, based at Georgetown University in Washington, said, 'Inspirationally al-Qaeda was sort of saying, "We're going to take over the world, and we're going to take back everything, including Spain." But it was a case of *Insha'Allah*, in other words, God willing and God knows. Only God knows when it's going to happen.'[6]

Al-Qaeda saw itself very much as the special 'vanguard' of Muslims that the influential Islamist scholar Sayyid Qutb said was necessary for the revival of Islam, and for the return of God's sovereignty on earth. Both communism and capitalism were but 'a corollary of rebellion against God's authority and the denial of dignity of man given to him by God'.[7] Qutb called on this vanguard to wage 'Islamic Jihad', in order to establish an 'Islamic state' where 'Sharia is the authority and God's limits are observed'.[8] The rest of the world was 'the home of hostility' and there were only two possible relations with it, peace by treaty or war.[9] Qutb did not use the word 'caliphate', although his call for an 'Islamic state' resonated with many groups such as al-Qaeda that regarded the abolition of the Ottoman caliphate as evidence of Islam's decline, and even harboured nostalgic sentiments for the Ottoman caliphs who would send their fleets and armies 'to defend any threatened Muslim areas'.[10]

The Seven Steps plan shows that Zarqawi and at least some senior strategists in al-Qaeda had a timetable as well as a desire to bring about the caliphate through savagery and chaos. Step 6 is emphatic about the wider aims beyond the caliphate. Once established the caliphate would then go to war with the non-Muslim world; as the leading terrorism expert David Kilcullen once said, 'it is clear that the *Takfiri* aim is first to overthrow and control power structures in the Muslim world, and only then turn against the West'.[11] Zarqawi announced to the world his obsession with a caliphate in Iraq in 2004 after the US-led invasion had toppled Saddam Hussein. 'There will be a caliphate that follows the guidance of Prophethood remaining with you for as long as God wills it to remain,' he declared in his vainglorious speech of October 2004.[12] Zarqawi and his successors did not just want to wage jihad and destroy their enemies; they wanted to conquer territory and hold it.

Zarqawi and Maqdisi would serve only four years of their sentence in prison before being released through a general amnesty in 1999, but it was during this period that Zarqawi moulded further his terrifying character, recruited followers and prepared for a life of jihad. In retrospect, it seems astonishing that the Jordanian authorities placed all the Islamists in one block, creating something of an 'emirate behind bars'.[13] If this really was the case then Zarqawi was considered the 'emir' of the prison. His allure rested mainly on his reputation as one of the Mujahidin, the victorious Arab warriors in Afghanistan. For years, some commentators believed that Zarqawi's reputation as a war-hardened mujahid was a little threadbare, as it seemed probable that he had neither 'participated in any battle nor killed any single individual'.[14]

However, fellow jihadis later claimed that Zarqawi was in Afghanistan between 1989 and 1993 before returning to Jordan. Apparently at first, the Jordanian worked as a reporter for a small jihadist magazine called *Al-Bonian al-Marsous*. Huthaifa Azzam, the son of an important Mujahidin leader, got to know Zarqawi well after greeting him at Peshawar airport in Pakistan in 1989. 'He was an ordinary guy, an ordinary fighter, and didn't really distinguish himself,' Azzam would say later, adding that Zarqawi fought in the war waged by the Mujahidin against the communist Kabul government, formerly supported by Moscow, following the withdrawal of Soviet forces. 'Zarqawi doesn't know the meaning of fear,'[15] Azzam said, also claiming that Zarqawi was injured several times in battle and witnessed the bloody capture of Kabul by the Mujahidin in 1992. He may even have witnessed the gruesome end of the Communist president Mohammad Najibullah, whose bloody body was hanged from a traffic control box after he was castrated and dragged to his death on the streets behind a truck driven by a mujahid.[16]

Fouad Hussein later described the Zarqawi of al-Suwaqah prison to fellow journalist Abdel Bari Atwan as a 'a cool, self-contained person who would speak only when addressed'.[17] But Zarqawi also menaced the authorities and individual prisoners. On several occasions he tried to organize uprisings[18] and on another he threatened a prisoner he caught reading *Crime and Punishment* by Dostoyevsky. Zarqawi asked the prisoner, Abu Doma, 'Why are you reading this book by a heathen?' Later Doma received a letter from Zarqawi in poor Arabic ordering him to stop reading 'Doseefsky'.[19]

Zarqawi is likely to have been further brutalized by his prison experience. He probably suffered torture during his incarceration; fellow prisoners reported that all the Jordanian's toenails were removed and at one stage he was placed in solitary confinement for eight and a half months.[20] He seemed to require little company and his aloofness and strangeness soon earned him the nickname al-Gharib, 'the Stranger'.[21]

'Zarqawi was the muscle, and al-Maqdisi the thinker,' said fellow prisoner Abdullah Abu Rumman, a journalist and editor.[22] 'Through sheer force of personality, Zarqawi controlled the prison ward, Abu Rahman went on, 'He decided who would cook, who would do the laundry, who would lead the readings of the Koran. He was extremely protective of his followers and extremely tough with prisoners outside his group. He didn't trust them. He considered them infidels.'[23]

During this time, other inmates noticed the friction between Zarqawi and his ideological master, Maqdisi, possibly due to the recognition afforded the dangerous theologian.[24] Later, during Zarqawi's killing rampage in Iraq, Maqdisi would repeatedly condemn the extremism and violence of his former disciple. In particular, he would emphatically reject Zarqawi's assertion that Shia Muslims were apostates and even non-Muslims. He would also criticize the use of violence against civilians and mosques.[25] It is highly likely these differences started to play out during the long tedious months behind bars. Maqdisi must have seen the possible threat to the whole concept of jihad that was being posed by Zarqawi's genocidal approach to the so-called *kuffar*, or unbelievers.

The scholar made his feelings bitterly clear in 2004 and 2005 when he strongly criticized Zarqawi's targeting of the Shia,[26] and much later with his repeated condemnations of the excesses of Abu Bakr al-Baghdadi and his 'deviant organization'.[27] At that time, long before Zarqawi's war on the world, Maqdisi may not have believed himself to be a Dr Frankenstein but he may well have felt uneasy about the conclusions the Jordanian had drawn from his teachings.

When not arguing with Maqdisi or memorizing the 6,000-plus verses of the Koran,[28] Zarqawi spent time developing the body of the fighter he wanted to become by lifting makeshift weights made from cans or buckets of rocks.[29] In 1997 he was moved to the prison of al-Salt before being finally transferred to a high security jail at Jafar, evidence of the danger he still posed.[30] But he would be released within months, despite the deep concerns harboured by the Jordanian security services.

In February 1999 King Hussein of Jordan died and the Muslim Brotherhood and various other Islamist organizations prevailed on his successor, King Abdullah II, to announce a general pardon for three thousand prisoners. The royal decree was approved by the Jordanian parliament on 18 March 1999. The amnesty was supposed to exclude prisoners convicted of crimes such as rape, murder and terrorism, which should have kept Zarqawi and Maqdisi behind bars. However, several Islamist groups in the Jordanian parliament lobbied hard for the release of the 'Afghans' and Zarqawi was discharged on 29 March 1999.[31] Within five years he would become the world's deadliest terrorist.

Zarqawi on the loose

In the summer of 1999, Zarqawi returned to Peshawar in Pakistan and towards the end of the year crossed the border into Afghanistan, then largely controlled by the Taliban. Later he met Osama bin Laden at the Government Guest House in the southern city of Kandahar. According to later reports, the two men did not get on.[32] Apparently bin Laden was highly suspicious of the reasons behind Zarqawi's release and believed that he might have been an agent for Jordanian intelligence. Like Maqdisi, bin Laden was also said to be disturbed by Zarqawi's professed hatred of the Shia Muslims.[33] Bin Laden's mother, Alia Hamida al-Attas, was said to be a Shia, from Syria. Certainly, the issue of the Shia would cause friction between Zarqawi and al-Qaeda over the following years. For Zarqawi and those who followed him, including Abu Bakr al-Baghdadi, Shia Muslims became the main target of their violence. This continued to be the case even when Zarqawi finally agreed to take on the al-Qaeda franchise in Iraq in 2004.

Zarqawi wanted to build a jihadi army he could lead anywhere but he needed the help and support of al-Qaeda. Ultimately, he was given £5,000 by al-Qaeda and allowed to set up his desert training camp near Herat, Afghanistan's third-biggest city. It was called Tawhid wa'l Jihad, the Organization of Monotheism and Jihad. This would be the formal name of Zarqawi's murder machine in Iraq from 2003 onwards, the forerunner to ISIS and Islamic State. According to a former bodyguard of bin Laden, Tawhid's initial mission statement included the overthrow of the government of Jordan as well as the annihilation of Jews all over the world.[34]

Al-Qaeda appointed one of its senior commanders, Saif al-Adel, to keep an eye on Zarqawi. Adel was a former colonel in the Egyptian army and believed to have been one of the masterminds behind the assassination of President Anwar Sadat in October 1981.[35] He is also listed by the FBI as one of its 'most wanted terrorists' for his alleged part in the 1998 bombings of the US embassies in Kenya and Tanzania.[36] The Egyptian was impressed by how Zarqawi had built his militia from the dozen or so who were with him at the start to hundreds over the following year. By the time of the attacks of 11 September 2001 the number of fighters and their families was estimated to be between two and three thousand.[37]

Zarqawi demanded that his recruits pledge an oath of allegiance, or *bay'ah*, to him personally, a requirement of jihadi commanders including Baghdadi and bin Laden.[38] Although Zarqawi kept in contact with al-Qaeda he did not pledge his allegiance to bin Laden.[39] This may have been down to the alleged antagonism between the pair but it is more likely Zarqawi wanted to be his own man.

Increasingly during 2001, bin Laden became focused not only on the forthcoming attacks of September 11th but also on the inevitable consequences. He knew the US would strike back. With this in mind bin Laden looked at Iraqi Kurdistan, now an autonomous region, as a possible bolthole for jihadis in the event of the anticipated US attack on Afghanistan. It seemed perfect for the job. As an autonomous region of northern Iraq since the first Gulf War, it was out of the reach of Saddam Hussein, then still president of Iraq. At the time of bin Laden's intervention, it was under the control of an important nationalist Kurd political party called the Patriotic Union of Kurdistan, or PUK.

Zarqawi's first caliphate

Under Saddam, it would have been impossible for Islamist militants to take over towns and villages within Iraq itself, but small groups of Salafi militants had established themselves in autonomous Iraqi Kurdistan long before bin Laden saw this area as a possible safe haven for jihadis in the wake of September 11th. It is not known how much Zarqawi knew about 9/11 prior to the attack. Probably not much, according to some sources that say he was dismayed with bin Laden's decision to attack the US because it destroyed the security the jihadis had enjoyed in Afghanistan,[40] the closest they had at the time to their own 'Islamic State'. But without 9/11 there would have been no invasion of Iraq and no Zarqawi legend.

On 1 September 2001, under the auspices of bin Laden and Zarqawi, two Kurdish jihadi groups merged to form a new jihadi group called Jund al-Islam, 'Soldiers of the Levant'. This was soon renamed Ansar al-Islam fi Kurdistan, or 'Partisans of Islam in Kurdistan'. Soon the group's enclave of ten or so villages began to receive and host Zarqawi's fighters. It was later claimed that bin Laden gave the group $300,000.[41] Violence and murder would follow in the jihadis' wake.

In mid September 2001 it was reported that some fifty-seven 'Arab-Afghan' fighters of various nationalities, almost certainly belonging to Zarqawi, had entered Iraqi Kurdistan via Iran earlier in the month, around the time of the 9/11 attacks.[42] All the evidence suggests that Zarqawi remained in Afghanistan as it came under attack by the US-led coalition but that he later escaped to Iraqi Kurdistan via Iran around April 2002. By then the influence of bin Laden and Zarqawi's fighters from al-Tawhid wa'l Jihad had had a profound impact on both Ansar al-Islam and Iraqi Kurdistan.

I unearthed an old report by the charity Human Rights Watch published in February 2003 about what Ansar al-Islam got up to in Iraqi Kurdistan under the influence of Zarqawi and the backing of al-Qaeda and it makes sobering reading. Essentially Ansar al-Islam declared war on the ruling Patriotic Union of Kurdistan, or PUK, and sought to inflict its own rigid and extreme version of Islam on the people in the territory it sought to control. A caliphate was declared in these territories and what happened next sounds eerily similar to life under Islamic State more than a decade later in Iraq and Syria.

In its 2003 report, Human Rights Watch said that on 8 September 2001, three days before the 9/11 attacks, Ansar al-Islam

issued decrees including the obligatory closure of offices and businesses during prayer time and enforced attendance by workers and proprietors at the mosque during those times; the veiling of women by wearing the traditional '*abaya*' [loose over-garment or robe]; obligatory beards for men; segregation of the sexes; barring women from education and employment; the removal of any photographs of women on packaged goods brought into the region; the confiscation of musical instruments and the banning of music both in public and private; and the banning of satellite receivers and televisions.

Some villagers had witnessed the fate of PUK fighters captured by Ansar:

Some prisoners' throats had been slit, while others had been beheaded; some of the bodies were mutilated, including by having their sexual organs severed. They were apparently found with their hands tied behind their back. Photographs taken by the PUK of the victims' bodies were shown on the party's satellite television channel, KurdSat, on September 26.

The group also announced that it would apply Islamic punishments of amputation, flogging and stoning to death for offences such as 'theft, the consumption of alcohol and adultery'.[43]

The alleged atrocities followed the declaration of a caliphate in the Kurdish towns of Biara and Tawela[44] by Ansar al-Islam's religious guru or emir; the ebullient Kurdish Salafi Mullah Krekar would be the caliph, but increasingly Zarqawi became the strong man. Krekar would later turn up in Norway claiming asylum.[45]

At this time Zarqawi also began his campaign to destabilize neighbouring Jordan. On 28 October 2002 Laurence Foley, a sixty-year-old American diplomat, was shot dead outside his home in the Jordanian capital, Amman.[46] Zarqawi was determined to oversee the planning and preparation of the murder, and supplied Foley's two killers[47] with more than $50,000 in funds and the murder weapon, a 7-millimetre pistol.[48]

Zarqawi established another training camp near the town of Khurmal in the north-eastern province of Halabja. Here, allegedly, he also established a laboratory for the manufacture of chemical and biological weapons. Later the US would claim Zarqawi's camp and presence in Iraqi Kurdistan as evidence of Saddam Hussein's complicity in the manufacture of weapons of mass destruction.

Zarqawi was named no fewer than twenty-one times by US secretary of state Colin Powell as he outlined to the United Nations the case for war against Saddam on 5 February 2003. In his now notorious speech,[49] Powell said, 'Iraq today harbours a deadly terrorist network headed by Abu Musab al-Zarqawi, an associate and collaborator of Osama bin Laden and his al-Qaeda lieutenants,' and claimed that Saddam had placed an agent in 'the most senior levels of the radical organisation, Ansar al-Islam'.[50] Powell also showed aerial photographs of the camp at Khurmal. He added that Zarqawi's network was 'teaching its operatives how to produce ricin and other poisons. Let me remind you how ricin works. Less than a pinch – imagine a pinch of salt – less than a pinch of ricin, eating just this amount in your food, would cause shock followed by circulatory failure. Death comes within seventy-two hours and there is no antidote, there is no cure. It is fatal.'

Six weeks later another US-led coalition would be at war with Iraq. That war would be over quickly with the fall of Baghdad and

Saddam Hussein. Other wars would then follow, starting with the long insurgency waged by the deposed Sunni Muslim minority. The most terrible conflict would be Zarqawi's campaign of ultra-violence, a war of savagery to cleanse Iraq of the non-believers and apostates and prepare the way for the caliphate. That war would start in the summer of 2003 and still rages today.

3
Chaos theory and fact
2003

Firdos Square in Baghdad is not really a square; it is a roundabout and more often than not it is clogged with traffic. The roads running off Firdos are lined with concrete bomb-blast walls sheltering some embassies and the homes of ordinary Iraqis that cower behind them. On one side of the square is a large mosque with a beautiful blue dome, and on a plinth in the middle stand two metal boots, providing one of the more incongruous sights in the Iraqi capital. The boots belonged to the statue of Saddam Hussein which once stood in the square with right arm held aloft in salutation, a sixty-fifth birthday present from a grateful nation, until the invading American army arrived on 9 April 2003.

Most of the international media corps were staying in the Palestine Hotel opposite the mosque and various new teams stood on the flat roof of the hotel's extension to get a good view of the toppling of the statue. Andrew Gilligan was there for BBC Radio and had a front-row seat for what remained the iconic moment of the Iraq War. First the Iraqi wrestler Kadhem Sharif attacked the plinth with a sledgehammer before American soldiers used a recovery vehicle to pull the statue down. Gilligan said:

I was standing on the roof of the hotel which overlooked Firdos Square watching them do it and giving a live commentary on one of the networks. The Iraqis couldn't get the statue down so the Americans gave a hand and a scream of joy went up when the statue came down.

We then went for a drive around the city to do some reporting. You could see that there was a lot of joy and jubilation that day, but the looting had already started. It really got underway in earnest the following day. The 10th of April was madness. The streets were full of people in trucks and minibuses with anything they could carry, just crammed into these vehicles. They even used the red British double-decker buses Baghdad had in those days; you could see them being driven all over the road, erratically all over the road, and when you got closer to them I could see they were rammed with looted goods. There were no police at all.[1]

However, the jubilation soon dissipated and the atmosphere deteriorated rapidly. 'It started turning nasty, lots of people's houses were being broken into and people being attacked in their homes,' said Gilligan. 'Also there was no electricity. We had electricity back at the Palestine Hotel from the generator and we also had security courtesy of the Americans. We also had the only electricity equipment still with its original owners.'

Two days later, Gilligan reported on the mounting chaos for Radio Four's *Today* programme, saying that Iraqis were probably 'living in more fear than they have ever known', which brought an angry response from the British government. The junior defence minister Adam Ingram accused the BBC of 'trying to make the news rather than report the news'.[2] Within two months of course Gilligan found himself at the centre of a huge political storm after running a story alleging that the British government had deliberately 'sexed up' a pre-war dossier on Iraq's supposed weapons of mass destruction (WMD) to justify war with Saddam.

Senior US officials also seemed to be in a state of denial, with US Defense Secretary Donald Rumsfeld claiming that TV images of isolated acts of looting and violence were being played over and over again by the networks for sensational effect. 'It's the same picture, of some person walking out of some building with a vase,' Rumsfeld said dismissively.[3]

The weeks following the fall of Baghdad are crucial to understanding the rise of Abu Musab al-Zarqawi and later Islamic State. The post-invasion mayhem and looting would soon be compounded by decisions taken by the new interim bodies that would run Iraq on behalf of the US-led coalition, decisions that would prove disastrous for years after they were taken.

The initial failure to provide sufficient security has been blamed on an institutional failure in Washington and London to understand the scale of the task following the military campaign. Allegedly, the coalition leaders made few plans for how to deal with Iraq once victory was won. From the start American and British leaders expected the occupation to be short and that the main challenge would be dealing with war damage.[4]

'I saw no evidence of any particular planning for post-war operations,' a senior British general, Major General Tim Cross, would say later.[5] He added, 'The paradigm effectively was the plan is we do not need a plan. The plan is that once we have moved into Iraq, then the Iraqi people, generally speaking, will welcome us and we will move very quickly on to establishing ministries and some form of democracy, but that pretty quickly, as in six months, we will downsize the military commitment and we will have secured this issue.'[6]

At the time of the invasion, Clare Short was the secretary of state for the UK's Department for International Development.

She thought the war reckless and resigned shortly after the invasion. She told me the failure to plan for the post-invasion period was all wrapped in the flawed case put forward for the war by the US and UK governments, which was based on the false claim that Saddam Hussein had WMD. She said, 'The deceit explains the failure afterwards. The American neo-cons[7] convinced themselves that they were going to be made so welcome with flowers in the streets and all that; they threw away all the preparations that had been made in the State Department, which were extensive. Also there had been links made with the main players in humanitarianism. All that was thrown away.'[8]

Short claimed that until late in the day, both governments still maintained the pretence that war could be averted if Iraq complied with their pre-war demands over WMD. She said that that explains the failure to properly prepare for post-invasion reconstruction, adding:

> The US didn't listen to any of the experience and advice we had in the international system about how to go about these things because the deceit that led to war meant they couldn't share planning with all the responsible bodies. The American people were lied to when they were told that the attack on the Twin Towers came out of Iraq and the British people were lied to in different ways – that Britain was going to stick with the United Nations and that it was all about bringing democracy to Iraq, but in reality Tony Blair [UK prime minister] had given promises to the US that he would go along with it and he believed that America was such a powerful country that its preparations would be good enough, and the tragedy goes on.

The large-scale looting inflicted terrible harm on an infrastructure already ravaged by years of economic sanctions imposed by the West following the 1990–1 Gulf War. It also destroyed the capacity of any government to provide many essential services. Seventeen of Iraq's twenty-three government ministries were completely ransacked,[9] often it seems at the organized instigation of the country's own civil servants.

'The objectives were manifold, and included sowing the seeds of administrative chaos and disorganization,' wrote Ali Allawi, a future Iraqi government minister. 'In many ministries, individual managers were responsible for organizing and directing the theft and burning of their departments.'[10] So much copper electricity wiring was being stripped out of the walls and melted down for scrap that it created a surplus and metal prices in Iraq and neighbouring Kuwait plummeted.[11]

On top of that, after thirty-three years of misrule by Saddam, Iraq's infrastructure was already in an advanced state of dilapidation. Eighty percent of the country's schools were falling down, and none of Baghdad's sewage treatment plants were operational, which meant some 500,000 tons of untreated sewage were being pumped into the Tigris and Euphrates rivers every day.[12] The availability of drinking water had dropped by sixty percent during the 1990s.[13]

De-Ba'ath time

That was bad enough, but within a month of the fall of Baghdad, the US-led coalition would make two catastrophic decisions which essentially acted as recruiting sergeants for Zarqawi and other violent insurgent groups: the two decrees aimed at destroying the Iraqi army and Saddam's ruling Ba'ath Party. At the core was the fault line between Iraq's Shia and Sunni communities that had lain dormant for years. Later I will explain what has separated the

Sunni and Shia for more than 1,300 years and why it is so central to the rise of Zarqawi and later Islamic State.

Only fifteen percent of the world's estimated 1.6 billion Muslims are Shia, but their influence far outweighs their numbers in many countries in the Middle East, and they make up the majority in a few. Crucially, in Iraq, the Shia account for up to sixty-five percent of the population, and in Iran to the east they make up ninety-five percent of the population.[14] Iraq is the true heart of Shia Islam. It is where the schism between Sunni and Shia took place – back in the days following the death of the Prophet Muhammad in 632 AD – and it is where the most important Shia shrines are located and the most significant Shia imams are buried. At the time of the invasion, the Shia had been a persecuted majority in their own country, constituting considerably more than half the population; the dominant Sunnis made up around forty percent.[15]

For hundreds of years, under the Ottoman Empire and later under the Ba'ath Party from the late 1960s onwards, the Sunnis had been primarily in charge, although they were in the minority. Established in the 1940s, the Ba'ath was a radical Arab national-istic, supposedly socialist, movement – *ba'ath* means 'resurrection' in Arabic.[16] The party believed in one-party rule by itself, in other words dictatorship. The Ba'athists consolidated their power over Iraq with two coups, the first bloody revolt occurring in 1963, after which they ruled for just nine months.[17] The second coup in 1968 established the Ba'ath dictatorship for more than thirty-four years, ending with Saddam's overthrow in 2003. In a democracy, the majority Shia seemed certain to dominate the country, its government and an increasingly embittered Sunni minority.[18]

Under Saddam, the Ba'ath Party had progressively hollowed out and ingested all important state, political and civil society institutions[19] and party membership was the key to advancement, privileges and power. Naturally, at first, membership was extremely exclusive. In the mid-80s there were only thirty thousand members, representing a pitiful 0.2 percent of the Iraqi population.[20] Benefits of party membership included bonus points for children's secondary school examination results, vehicles and greater ease of access to government jobs and promotion. High-ranking members even enjoyed extrajudicial powers over their fellow Iraqis. Some members received a monthly stipend of $250, potentially a life-saver as Iraq suffered terribly from the sanctions imposed by the international community in the wake of the First Gulf War.[21] Ba'athists could be paid up to fifty times the pitiful wage rates prevalent in the public sector. A non-Ba'athist primary school teacher would be paid around $3 a month whereas a Ba'athist in the same post would expect $150.[22]

Saddam clearly needed more friends after his disastrous wars with Iran and over Kuwait so he opened up Ba'ath Party membership to more and more people. By the time of the invasion of 2003, membership was estimated at around 600,000,[23] of which an estimated 15,000 to 40,000 were considered to be 'senior members'.[24]

A key objective of the invasion, as far as the US was concerned, was not only the removal of Saddam Hussein but the purging from Iraqi society of the Ba'ath Party, the force that had sustained him in power for so long. The Americans and the British saw the Ba'ath, rightly in many ways, as Saddam's instrument of terror against his own people. As events turned out, there proved to be three big problems with this. First, many ordinary people who may have hated the regime had clearly felt pressured into joining the Ba'ath Party to get on in Iraq; and second, it was not possible to get a job with the military or security forces without the recommendation of a member.[25] 'People join for party benefits – jobs, access to places in the university – or merely to avoid suspicion of disloyalty,' wrote one keen observer of the Ba'ath.[26]

The third and most lethal problem was that members of Iraq's Sunni minority were disproportionately represented in the Ba'ath upper ranks.[27] In particular, senior posts in the military and the security services, as well as other top government jobs, were populated 'overwhelmingly' by Sunnis. Saddam Hussein himself was a secular Sunni Muslim. Zarqawi was a different kind of Sunni altogether and one who already believed Shia Muslims were 'evil scorpions',[28] although they represented less than two percent of the population in his native Jordan.[29] Zarqawi was a Sunni Muslim from an overwhelmingly Sunni country determined to wage jihad against the newly dominant Shia of Iraq to achieve his caliphate, and his partners in crime would be the embittered remnants of Saddam's Ba'ath. These remnants would form the nucleus of ISIS and Islamic State.

The US military had already officially 'disestablished' the Ba'ath Party on 16 April 2003 with an initial proclamation by General Tommy Franks,[30] but it was the so-called 'de-Ba'athification proclamation' issued by the new Coalition Provisional Authority on 16 May 2003 that would prove so devastating.

The new man in charge of both Iraq and the Coalition Provisional Authority (CPA) was an American diplomat called L. Paul Bremer III, known to his family and friends as 'Jerry'. As CPA administrator and presidential envoy, Bremer's task was to promote the development of a functioning democracy that could be returned as soon as possible to the Iraqis. Like some feudal monarch, Bremer possessed full executive, legislative and judicial power.[31] On his arrival in Baghdad, on 12 May 2003, Bremer announced almost immediately that he would purge senior Ba'ath Party members and disband the army.

The de-Ba'athification decree declared that senior party

members 'are hereby removed from their positions and banned from future employment in the public sector'.[32] In addition, any Ba'ath Party member with a job in the top three management layers of any government ministry and any other government institution or affiliated corporation would be automatically fired. That included staff in universities, institutes and hospitals.[33]

Bremer thought the order would affect around 20,000 Iraqis but as many as 85,000 people were driven out of their jobs, including '40,000 teachers who had joined the Ba'ath to keep their jobs'.[34] This mass firing took place when Iraq's unemployment rate already stood at around fifty percent.[35]

Clearly, America's model was the policy of de-Nazification used by the Allies to remove all influences of the Nazi Party from Germany.[36] Bremer would later repeatedly compare Saddam and the Ba'ath party to the Nazis.[37] On one occasion, in May 2003, an evidently emotional Bremer visited a mass grave containing the Shia victims of a Saddam massacre that had been discovered near the central Iraqi town of al-Hillah, not far from the ancient ruins of Babylon. 'It's like the Einsatzgruppen during the Holocaust,' Bremer remembered telling a possibly perplexed young US marine, before explaining, 'Hitler's mobile killing squads, army, and police massacred over a million people at isolated places like this...Jews, Gypsies, prisoners of war, Catholic clergy.'[38]

Bremer's policy of de-Ba'athification simply burrowed far too deep into Iraqi public and private life and seriously inflamed rising tensions between the Shia majority and Sunni minority. The senior British general at the time, Sir Mike Jackson, said later the deteriorating situation was 'exacerbated' by the decision to 'de-Ba'athify right down to a very low level, even talking about the privatization of the state industries, in particular oil, at a time when Iraq had gone through this extraordinary trauma of invasion and defeat'.[39]

At least two senior US government officials stationed in Iraq, Bremer's immediate predecessor, Lieutenant General Jay Garner, and the local CIA station chief, were appalled when they read the proposed decree. The CIA station chief pleaded with Bremer to reconsider, reminding him that the people he was targeting understood the country's tatty infrastructure from electricity to water. Furthermore, he warned, 'By nightfall, you'll have driven 30,000 to 50,000 Ba'athists underground and in six months you will really regret this.'[40] Bremer refused to back down and has always insisted that President George W. Bush and in particular his immediate boss, Defense Secretary Donald Rumsfeld, had given him his 'marching orders' to carry out the purge.[41]

Bremer's second decree was also to have far-reaching consequences that are still being felt today. On 23 May 2003, Provisional Order Number 2 proclaimed the 'dissolution of entities' that included the army and all armed services, associated militias, three government ministries involved with security, including the ministry of defence, as well as all intelligence bodies. It was a breathtaking dismantling of Iraq's security and intelligence infrastructure, and it involved the wholesale dismissal of thousands of military officers and security officials. One section read, 'Any military or other rank, title, or status granted to a former employee or functionary of a Dissolved Entity by the former Regime is hereby cancelled.' All conscripts were released from their service obligations. Conscription was suspended indefinitely, subject to decisions by future Iraq governments. Every soldier or defence security official was dismissed 'effective of 16 April 2003'.[42]

Among those thrown out onto the streets with little prospect of work were some eleven thousand embittered army generals, and that's according to Bremer's own estimate.[43] As Bremer pointed out, that compared to just three hundred generals in the US army![44] Also out of work was a corps of several hundred thousand mostly Sunni officers.[45] Most senior officers were threatened with poverty. Anyone above the rank of colonel would be 'deemed a Ba'ath Party member' unless they could prove otherwise and 'no payment, including a termination or pension payment will be made to any person who is or was a Senior Party Member'.[46] One of the most extraordinary documents I unearthed from those times is a list of military officers whom the Americans disqualified from future service in the Iraqi military. Running to 278 pages, it lists some 8,697 officers from lieutenants to lieutenant generals, forever barred from being in the military.[47]

In total, more than 700,000 people were fired, including 385,000 Iraqi armed forces personnel and nearly 300,000 interior security staff.[48] Many well-armed, experienced and angry army officers and other ranks joined the various insurgency groups and would later follow Zarqawi and his successors. Given their training and skills set, it is hard to see who else would have employed former Ba'athist soldiers and security officials in Iraq at that time. After all, they knew how to torture people, use guns and make bombs.

The Ba'athists and the jihadis had much in common, both ideologically and in their shared belief in rule through terror and violence. In late 2002, almost a year after the 9/11 attacks and six months before the invasion of Iraq, the American writer Paul Berman wrote with great prescience that the Ba'ath and the Islamists were 'two branches of a single impulse which was Muslim totalitarianism'.[49] Berman described this instinct for totalitarian rule as the 'Muslim variation on the European idea' of fascism and Nazism. Above all Zarqawi's movement, and ultimately Abu Bakr al-Baghdadi's 'caliphate', constituted the consummation of a marriage of convenience between a terror organization and a terror apparatus. The savagery and crimes of IS become that much more comprehensible when you remember that under Saddam the Ba'ath slaughtered thousands of Kurds and Iranians with poison gas and thousands more Shia by mass shootings. When it comes to killing, both the Ba'ath and the jihadis often display great relish. Apparently, one of the Ba'ath's favourite ways of dispatching dissidents was to feed them feet first through giant shredders or wood chippers.[50]

By 2014, the top ranks of Islamic State were filled with former Ba'athist officers such as Abu Muslim al-Turkmani, ex-leader of the IS provisional council, a former intelligence colonel. There was also Abu Ayman al-Iraqi, member of the IS governing *shura* council. A former Ba'ath party member in Saddam's time, Ayman served in air defence intelligence. Abu Ahmad al-Alwani, who sat on IS's military council, was also in Saddam's army. Perhaps most important of them all was Haji Bakr, once a brigadier general in Saddam's notorious intelligence services, who was eventually killed in Syria in January 2014.[51] Later, according to authoritative leaks probably from within the IS hierarchy itself, Bakr, whose real name was Samir Abd Muhammad al-Khlifawi, acted as kingmaker to Baghdadi in 2010 and helped him liquidate his internal enemies to secure the future 'caliph' leadership of the group.[52] Documents recovered from Bakr's home after his death also showed him to have been the architect of the intelligence and terror structure of ISIS/IS. Who better than a former senior Saddam spy?[53] These dangerous men would provide IS with the military expertise and know-how to fight their common enemies, and take over territory. They had helped Saddam Hussein terrorize and oppress the Iraqi people and they would do the same for Abu Musab al-Zarqawi and Abu Bakr al-Baghdadi.

I interviewed Dr Ali Makki, a senior Sunni member of Iraq's parliament, about Bremer's decision to disband the army. He said:

A high percentage of Islamic State fighters and advisers are previous Iraqi army officers, who had very good training and are professional and [proved] very capable.

The decision by the US to get rid of the army was a disaster; it insulted the situation in Iraq. It was really the cornerstone of what we describe [as] the national resistance to [the] Americans. Paul Bremer made some very bad decisions.[54]

The promise to create a new army outlined in the decree cut little ice with many of the officers dismissed because Bremer's first decree had banned Ba'ath party members from future employment in the public sector.[55] In any event, Bremer envisaged a much smaller new army of around forty thousand personnel with no tanks or artillery.[56] Soon thousands of angry soldiers were protesting in the streets of Baghdad.[57]

Even senior Shia politicians regret the decisions taken immediately after the US military had declared 'Mission Accomplished'.[58] Saad al-Muttalibi, a senior Shia politician, who has advised two Iraqi Shia prime ministers, told me:

A series of mistakes took place but I don't think the Iraqis are innocent in all this because if they wanted they could have stopped Ambassador Bremer, or they could have advised him at least otherwise.

We knew and we were talking to Bremer and other people at that time. Many times Bremer mentioned that the dissolving of the army was to please Masoud Barzani [a senior Kurdish politician and president of Iraqi Kurdistan since 2005]. It was done at the insistence of Barzani that the army must be dissolved. The de-Ba'athification was done to please other people. So the Iraqis are not innocent of the mistakes that were made. Those [that] were close to Ambassador Bremer and involved in politics at the time, they share the same responsibility.

De-Ba'athification was a mistake because it was a political tool not a legal tool. The actual bad Ba'athists managed to stay in power, or were in jail. But the poor Ba'athists who weren't real Ba'athists…who had to join the Ba'ath Party for whatever reasons, social or economic, they were kicked out. So it was used selectively.[59]

The years following the invasion witnessed attempts mainly by the US to mitigate the effects and extent of de-Ba'athification, but these often met with stiff resistance from powerful and often sectarian-minded Shia politicians who had suffered persecution and exile at the hands of the Ba'athists under Saddam Hussein.[60] The bungled de-Ba'athification project added to the chaos of post-invasion Iraq and would do irreparable damage to attempts at a national reconciliation for years to come. This serious failure would help fuel the coming insurgency and particularly the ferocious campaign of violence begun by Abu Musab al-Zarqawi within months of the beginning of the occupation. For the US, vengeance on Saddam and his apparatus of oppression would not be sweet, as would soon become clear. There is no better example of the 'law of unintended consequences'. Observing the wreckage of his country's disastrous retribution on Iraq, the former US navy secretary John Lehman later observed, 'We provided revenge, which felt good after 9/11, but [it] has sown more dragons' teeth.'[61]

4
The management of savagery
2003–2005

Few cities can have suffered as much carnage and terror as Baghdad since 2003. When you are there, you try as much as possible to avoid certain mosques or markets and other public places at certain times, but of course the bombers know that as well. 'Death can come at any time,' one woman I met in Baghdad's main shopping mall in the Mansour district told me.[1]

So you soon become used to hearing explosions from suicide bombings and car bombs. At a distance of a few streets away there is the strange almost muffled bang, followed by first the car alarms and some moments later the sirens. Then a black column of smoke and fire belches furiously into the air. Sometimes what is called 'a secondary device' will go off, aimed at killing the emergency services or nosey bystanders. After half an hour or so the interior ministry phones in the casualty figures like some grisly football score – how many dead and how many injured. Few people phone back later to enquire how many of the injured have perished from their injuries, although sadly many do die. By that time there are more bombings and more shootings to report and tragically the attack is soon forgotten, except of course by the many widows and widowers, orphans and grieving relatives. The victims are guilty of nothing more than being in the wrong place at the wrong time, which is what makes the horror so random, almost as if people were being incinerated in cars and cafés for sport by some casually psychopathic dragon. It all seems so crazy and pointless.

Now we know that these massacres were being carefully chronicled by bureaucrats working for Abu Bakr al-Baghdadi, the leader of Islamic State, so an accurate annual report called *Al-Naba* can be presented to the world.[2] This document details every car bomb, every 'improvised explosive device' (IED), every assassination by gun or knife. There are also the beheadings of hostages or the burning of a Jordanian pilot in a cage – all carefully choreographed and directed by IS. Caliphates don't just happen by accident. There is a conscious attempt to manage all this savagery – a 'method to the madness'. Behind it, there is even a textbook.

Believe it or not, *The Management of Savagery* is the actual title of an online book that appeared in 2004 and it eerily describes the terror strategy used by Baghdadi and his predecessors including Abu Musab al-Zarqawi. Essentially, it is a terror manual that will most probably never be read by most Western consumers of news and current affairs. Its 268 pages detail how to bring about an 'Islamic state' or caliphate through the use of extreme violence and brutality.

A state of extreme savagery is still better than rule by apostates or *kuffar*, argues the book: 'the most abominable of the levels of savagery is [still] less than stability under the order of disbelief by [several] degrees'.[3] Strewn with historical and religious references, the writing is often puzzling and arcane, as is often the way with jihadi texts, but certain sections jump out at you with shocking clarity, particularly chapter 2, 'The path for establishing an Islamic State'.

The book argues that the enemy should be ground down and defeated through the '"the power of vexation and exhaustion" by means of groups and separate cells in every region of the Islamic world'.[4] Attacks by these groups would continue 'until the anticipated chaos and savagery breaks out in several regions'.[5]

The US would then be drawn into conflict because of not only this strategy but also attacks directed against it. The 'Crusader-Zionist' enemy (the US) must then be attacked 'in every place in the Islamic world, and even outside if possible, so as to disperse the effort of the alliance of the enemy and thus drain it to the greatest possible extent'.[6] The book adds, 'The inevitable result of this escalating sequence is the fall of American prestige among the masses and among the elites of the world in the armies of apostasy.'[7]

Islamic target countries would be chosen based on 'the weakness of the ruling regime and the weakness of the centralization of its power'.[8] Iraq must have gone to the top of the list! The savagery would continue relentlessly until 'the public will see how the troops flee, heeding nothing. At this point, savagery and chaos begin and these regions will start to suffer from the absence of security.'[9] This mayhem or *tawahush*[10] would lead to the Islamic State. In many ways *The Management of Savagery* feels like a focused and analytical companion volume to the Seven Steps.[11]

For a long time no one knew who had written it until it was discovered the author was probably one Abu Bakr Naji,[12] an Egyptian, who was thought to have been an important al-Qaeda strategist, possibly even its one-time 'head of external relations'. In August 2006, al-Qaeda's current leader, Ayman al-Zawahiri, introduced Naji as such to the world in an al-Qaeda video.[13] (His real name was Muhammad Hasan Khalil al-Hakim.) Ironically in

October 2008, Naji was to succumb to a rather hi-tech piece of savagery management himself when a US Predator drone struck his car as he drove through the jihadist badlands of North Waziristan in Pakistan.[14]

Zarqawi would follow the textbook to the bloody letter and deploy extreme savagery for the first three years of the US-led occupation of Iraq. His campaign would be devastating, not only against the US and important international agencies, but against his principal target, the Shia majority of Iraq.

By the summer of 2003, Zarqawi was preparing his onslaught on his enemies. He would have extraordinary success in Baghdad but his stronghold from where he would draw his support and strength and where he would make his car bombs would be in the so-called 'Sunni Triangle', the densely populated and predominantly Sunni area of central Iraq. Roughly speaking, the base of the triangle stretches some 120 miles from the east of Baghdad westwards to a point just past the city of Ramadi in Iraq's vast Anbar province, with the apex just north of the city of Tikrit. The city of Fallujah, an important future base for Zarqawi and his successors, lies just above the base almost halfway between Ramadi and Baghdad.[15] The 'Sunni Triangle' and the towns and cities within it would play a key role in the Sunni insurgency and in the later success of Islamic State in 2014.

In 2003, Zarqawi and his group of jihadis in Tawhid wa'l Jihad was just one of a plethora of terrorist groups emerging in Iraq at the time, although it was markedly different in its objectives to all the others. In truth, Zarqawi was never part of the real Sunni insurgency against the US-led occupation and the Americans' Iraqi allies. Zarqawi would of course target Americans and their allies but above all he wanted to wage his genocidal war against the Shia and drag them into a conflict with the Sunni, and so bring about the collapse of the state necessary for the caliphate.

The alien and sinister nature of Zarqawi's war took time to emerge in the chaos and violence of post-invasion Iraq. His group would stand out for its sheer savagery but even other insurgents were slow to realize that Zarqawi, who was after all a Jordanian, was using their revolt as cover for his own brutal jihad. An Iraqi insurgent sheikh, Osama al-Jadaan, later murdered on Zarqawi's orders, would sum it up shortly before his death:[16] 'We realised that these foreign terrorists were hiding behind the veil of the noble Iraqi resistance. They claim to be striking at the US occupation, but the reality is they are killing innocent Iraqis in the markets, in mosques, in churches, and in our schools.'[17]

The other groups were mainly true insurgents, for example, those ex-Ba'athist soldiers and leaders who were determined to defeat the occupying forces and restore what they saw as the true order of things, in other words, the old order with Sunnis like them in charge. Perhaps the most prominent Ba'athist group formed in 2003 was the Army of the Men of the Naqshbandi Order. At the head of the Naqshbandi Order was the extraordinary figure of Field Marshal Izzat Ibrahim al-Douri, Saddam's former vice president and the deputy chairman of his ruling Revolutionary Command Council. At the time of the invasion, US troops were given packs of playing cards showing the fifty-two most wanted Iraqi leaders so they could identify and arrest them. Saddam was the ace of spades; Douri was the king of clubs.[18] Known as 'the Hidden Sheikh',[19] the red-haired field marshal would elude capture for more than a decade. Douri would go on to fight alongside Baghdadi in June 2014, and played a critical role in supporting his capture of Iraq's second-biggest city, Mosul.[20] When Saddam was executed at the end of 2006, former Iraqi Ba'ath functionaries appointed Douri as head of the Ba'ath Party.[21] Douri was at large for twelve years until he was reportedly killed near Tikrit in April 2015.[22]

Other groups would play an important role in the Sunni insurgency in the years to come. They included the 1920 Revolution Brigades, essentially a hotchpotch of nationalists and Salafis. They were founded in July 2003 and organized themselves into several combat brigades. Their name refers to the failed 1920 Iraqi uprising against British colonial rule. They were also closely associated with Sunni political parties and groups involved in the faltering political process in Baghdad.[23] The Revolution Brigades targeted mainly US troops with bombings, shootings and kidnappings, although they would later join the US in a war against Islamic State of Iraq, a precursor to ISIS and Islamic State.[24] Jamaat Ansar al-Sunna (Assembly of the Helpers of the Sunni People) was another important insurgent group, primarily made up of Sunni Kurds, determined to establish a Salafi Islamic state governed by Sharia.[25] Its members were also exponents of deadly roadside IEDs, mainly against coalition troops. Like Zarqawi, Jamaat Ansar al-Sunna would kidnap and behead hostages, but neither it nor the 1920 Brigades targeted fellow Muslims, Sunni or Shia, in the way Zarqawi and his successors did, or used anything like the remorseless mass casualty violence.

To many in the West these groups would always remain obscure. The Ba'athists and nationalists fought the occupation by targeting US forces in particular. Almost at the start, and in no small way thanks to Colin Powell's pre-invasion speech to the United Nations, Zarqawi became the face of the Sunni insurgency and that's how he wanted it. For the Jordanian, the insurgency was always the cover for the destruction of the Shia and the ultimate creation of the caliphate. His notoriety also helped attract recruits and funding. By the end of the summer of 2003, Zarqawi had destabilized Iraq with a string of devastating attacks on a range of high-profile targets.

The Zarqawi terror

Zarqawi opened his account of death with a car bomb attack on the Jordanian embassy in Baghdad on 7 August 2003. At least a dozen people were killed and another fifty were injured. Many of the victims were found in burning cars in front of the building. According to some eyewitness reports, a mob of Iraqis then stormed the building. One man emerged with a photo of King Hussein of Jordan that he then smashed to 'loud cheers' from the assembled mob. It would be another half an hour before US troops turned up to restore order.[26] The following day, 'Jerry' Bremer's Coalition Provisional Authority (CPA) issued a press release, 'Results in Iraq: 100 Days toward Security and Freedom', in which it claimed, 'Most of Iraq is calm and progress on the road to democracy and freedom not experienced in decades continues. Only in isolated areas are there still attacks.'[27] Much worse was to follow.

On 19 August, a suicide cement truck loaded with high explosives slammed into the Baghdad headquarters of the United Nations, killing twenty-two people and injuring another seventy. Sergio de Mello, the head of the UN mission to Iraq, survived the initial blast but died several hours later after being trapped upside down in the rubble.[28] Nesri Tehayneh, once a close associate of Zarqawi's, said later in a TV interview, 'Zarqawi told me he needed to hit a big target to recruit followers. Zarqawi said that the UN was a nest for secret services and American spies. He said he needed to attack the UN and kill that criminal Sergio.'[29] A month later, the UN suffered another bomb attack. The attacks were brutal but extremely effective. Eight hundred UN personnel pulled out, leaving behind only a skeleton staff of fifteen. Other international agencies including the charity Oxfam were already pulling out people[30] by the time another Zarqawi suicide bomber attacked the headquarters of the International Committee of the Red Cross (ICRC).

On 27 October, approximately thirty-four people were killed in the ICRC bombing and other attacks, which included the bombing of a police station. At the time, one US spokesman said the attacks bore hallmarks of 'foreign fighters' while others started to mention al-Qaeda.[31] For the first time, someone was practising what was preached in *The Management of Savagery*.

These attacks stunned the world and many ordinary Iraqis. On 19 August 2003, a 24-year-old woman blogger going by the name Riverbend wrote:

> The UN explosion is horrible…terrifying and saddening. No one can believe it has happened…no one understands why it has happened. For God's sake these people are supposed to be here to help. I'm so angry and frustrated. Nothing is moving forward – here is no progress and this is just an example. The media is claiming al-Qaeda. God damn we never had al-Qaeda before this occupation.[32]

In an opinion poll taken in Baghdad in early autumn of 2003, ninety-four percent of people said their capital was a more dangerous place than before the invasion.[33]

Before Zarqawi's campaign began, there had been a brief flickering false dawn of hope, remembered Caroline Hawley, the Baghdad correspondent for the BBC at this time. She said:

> It became a frightening place. In the very early days [of the occupation] it was amazing because you could speak to people for the first time and they could answer openly, and all the mass graves

were being discovered and people could tell you about that. It all felt like this huge cathartic moment for a country because all this repressed torment was bursting into the open. In the early days you could do anything and go anywhere.

People could speak for the first time, which was incredible to be able to be there and to listen to all that. Then there were bombs and then everybody started to feel afraid because you felt you could be unlucky and be hit [by a bomb attack or shooting] anytime.[34]

Over the next three years, Zarqawi would continue to target the Iraqi government and US troops and anyone who supported them. He would personally behead hostages and post the footage on the web. Within a year, Zarqawi would be the most wanted terrorist on earth with a $25 million reward on offer from the US government.[35] To put that in context, the US offered the same bounty for information leading to the arrest or conviction of Osama bin Laden.[36] However, the US state department never offered more than $10 million for the Islamic State 'caliph' Abu Bakr al-Baghdadi.

Zarqawi's main target remained Iraq's majority Shia Muslims. In this campaign of slaughter he would stop at nothing; he would even turn a Shia youth with Down's syndrome into a walking bomb to use against his own people. Not even his associates in al-Qaeda like Osama bin Laden could prevent Zarqawi from carrying out his genocide against the Shia. Zarqawi's jihad against Iraq's Shia majority was always a complete departure from the true jihad for al-Qaeda, whose main targets remained the 'far enemy' (the US) and the 'near enemy' (the interim Iraqi governing institutions). The differing objectives and strategies of Zarqawi and al-Qaeda provided the source of continuing friction between the two groups for years to come.

Zarqawi had nothing but contempt for the 'Crusader' Americans. 'We consider it a certainty that the armed forces of these Crusaders will disappear in short order,' he wrote in 2004. 'These, as you know, are the most cowardly of God's creatures. They are easy prey, God be praised. We ask that God allow us to kill and capture them, so we can sow panic among those who support them.'[37]

In a letter,[38] apparently sent to Osama bin Laden[39] in January 2004,[40] Zarqawi was clear in his main aim: to bring about a civil war between the Shia and the minority Sunni Muslims. To Zarqawi, Shia Muslims, or Shiites, were 'the insurmountable obstacle, the prowling serpent, the crafty evil scorpion, the enemy lying in wait, and biting poison'.[41]

He said, 'Our fight against the Shi'ites is the way to draw the nation [of Muslims] into battle...our only option is to strike at the Shi'ites, attacking their religious, military and other personnel, coming at them relentlessly until they yield to the Sunnis.' Zarqawi also extended his genocidal wrath to Iraq's more than five million Kurds, around fifteen to twenty percent of the population,[42] saying they 'are a foreign body that is strangling us and a wound of which we have yet to rid ourselves. They are the last on the list, even if we did everything we could to get at some of their figureheads, with God's help.'

On 29 August 2003, just ten days after his lethal attack on the UN, Zarqawi struck at the very heart of Shia Islam and killed one of its most senior religious leaders and politicians. Ayatollah Muhammad Baqir al-Hakim was leaving Friday prayers[43] at the revered shrine of Shia's first Imam, Ali, in, the holy city of Najaf when a suicide car bomber detonated his device, killing Hakim and more than ninety others. The bomber was said to be one Yasin Jarad, Zarqawi's own father-in-law.[44]

Hakim was not only a cleric of great significance but also the religious leader of the main Shia political party, the Supreme

Council for Islamic Revolution in Iraq, or SCIRI. Hakim had returned from exile a little more than three months earlier[45] and for the US he was probably the most important Iraqi ally. On hearing the news, Paul Bremer, the administrator of the Coalition Provisional Authority, almost broke down.[46]

For Zarqawi this was a huge coup, but it was just the start. Over the following years he continued to pound relentlessly on the sectarian divide between Shia and Sunni Muslims. On 2 March 2004, Zarqawi's suicide bombers attacked Shias in Baghdad and the second holy city of Karbala. The attacks took place among crowds of worshippers taking part in the so-called Ashura religious ceremonies.

At the Imam Musa al-Khadim shrine in Baghdad's Kadhimiya district, three bombers struck. The first blew himself up in the crowds outside the mosque while the second detonated his device among the pilgrims inside the shrine. As people ran screaming through a pair of big doors a third suicide bomber standing at the doorway struck. 'Streaks of blood and bits of flesh clung to the tiled walls and floors of the Imam Musa al-Khadim shrine,' a newspaper correspondent described later.[47] The total death toll was estimated conservatively at more than 140. In December 2004, Zarqawi's bombers hit both Karbala and Najaf once again, killing more than sixty.[48] Zarqawi and his successors would attack these holy Shia cities time and again over the years.

Zarqawi and the Iraqi Sunni insurgents quickly shattered US hopes of a quick victory followed by a flower-strewn victory march through Baghdad or a ticker-tape parade down Wall Street. Instead another Vietnam-type fiasco started to loom large and there was confusion about how to deal with this new and unexpected stage of the war. A young Iraqi American called Ali Khedery was an important front-row witness to the events in Iraq over a decade. From the invasion of 2003 onwards, Khedery acted as personal adviser to five successive US ambassadors to Iraq as well as three successive US army commanders. He is very critical about the way the US military tried to deal with the insurgency at first. He said:

Some of us learned the hard way that you were never going to crush this thing by force. So we went into Iraq in 2003, and Baghdad, and the regime crumbled.

The fourth infantry division tried to kill their way out of the insurgency when in fact all they did was make it worse. The divisional commander, General Ray Odierno, who was then a two-star general, was based in Tikrit and he had virtually the entire Sunni central area of the country; he was in charge of it and all he did was make it much worse – he hid behind his tactics.

Folks like General David Petraeus, who was also then a two-star commander in Mosul at the time in charge of the 101st Airborne Division, adopted a 'counter-insurgency approach', as [General George] Patton did in Germany after World War Two, in that he was willing to let Ba'athists continue [in] various civil servant positions, to keep the power going and to keep security going and that's why Mosul in the first year was totally pacified. Petraeus embraced the Ba'athists like Patton did with the Nazis as Germany was falling.

So the insurgency got worse across most of the country thanks to Ambassador Bremer's various ridiculous edicts like suspending the military and then putting the de-Ba'athification commission under the control of sectarian Shia politicians. By 2005 myself and a couple of other colleagues were convinced we had to reach out to the Sunnis and to see if we could broker a deal with them.[49]

The US general David Petraeus, whose actions so impressed Khedery in Mosul, would be the man to take on Zarqawi's organization in 2007 and 2008 and almost destroy it.

Two attacks in 2004 and 2005 revealed just how far Zarqawi was prepared to go in his war on the Shia. On 30 September 2004 crowds had gathered for a government-sponsored celebration to inaugurate a new sewage plant in the predominantly Shia western Baghdad neighbourhood of al-Amel. US troops were handing out candy to children when three bombs exploded nearby. A BBC TV crew was on the way to the scene after news of the first bomb at the sewage works ceremony, but Zarqawi had made some stories too dangerous to report. Patrick Howse, the BBC producer with the crew, remembers, 'We were on our way when the second bomb went off. When we heard the bang, it was clearly quite close. Immediately, our security adviser made a circular motion with his finger and we decided to turn back after without getting out of the car.'[50] Among the forty-two dead were thirty-five children. There were pitiful scenes according to one reporter: 'Grief-stricken mothers wailed over their children's corpses, as relatives collected body parts from the street for burial and a boy picked up the damaged bicycle of his dead brother.'[51] The bombing had not only been about punishing families and children for daring to fraternize with the US, it was also aimed at the coalition's attempt to rebuild Iraq, to get the country the infrastructure it desperately needed. For Zarqawi, the al-Amel attack had all the perfect ingredients, slaughtering Shia children and US troops while they were celebrating, of all things, a new sewage plant that would have helped make their difficult and dangerous lives just a little more tolerable. Above all the attack was text book management of savagery, striking at the foundations of a still fragile state and security infrastructure, and destroying people's faith in the protection offered by the new order.

On 1 February 2005, a nineteen-year-old youth called Amar Ahmed Mohammed approached a polling booth in the al-Askan district of Baghdad. The bomb strapped to his body was supposed to kill his fellow Shias as they took part in Iraq's first election. He detonated the device some distance away from his target, killing only himself. Amar had Down's syndrome and apparently had the mental age of a four-year-old. He had been abducted by Zarqawi's men, who turned him into a human bomb by strapping him into a suicide belt.[52] His cousin said of young Amar later, 'He was mindless, but he was mostly happy, laughing and playing with the children in the street. Now, his father is inconsolable; his mother cries all the time.'[53] It would not be the last time that the group would use wholly innocent people with Down's syndrome as bombs.

Amar Ahmed was murdered around the time Zarqawi's child bride, fourteen-year-old Israa, gave birth to their baby boy Abdul Rahman. They had been married the previous year when Zarqawi was thirty-seven and Israa was only thirteen. It was reportedly Israa's father, Yasin Jarad, who was the suicide bomber in the deadly attack in Najaf in August 2003. Her marriage would end up killing her and her son. Zarqawi was said to have had two wives and four children during his short life.[54]

Whenever there was a huge mass-casualty attack in Iraq, Zarqawi was always at the top of the list of suspects. On 28 February 2005, one of his suicide bombers, a fellow Jordanian, Raed Mansour al-Banna, drove a car packed full of explosives into a crowded bazaar at a recruitment centre in the predominantly Shia town of al-Hillah around sixty miles south of Baghdad. Banna detonated his bomb, killing at least 166 people and injuring another 146.[55] Many of the victims were Shia men hoping to be recruited as policemen. It was the biggest mass casualty suicide attack since the invasion. The attacker, Banna, was a law graduate who had lived in the US and loved 'motorcycles, women and partying', an American friend said later, until he returned from a long trip to his native Jordan seemingly 'indoctrinated'.[56]

On 17 October 2004, Zarqawi and his Tawhid wa'l Jihad group issued an online statement in the usual flowery language of the jihad pledging allegiance to al-Qaeda and its commander Osama bin Laden. Tawhid wa'l Jihad was no more; henceforth Zarqawi's group would be called al-Qaeda in the Land of the Two Rivers, or al-Qaeda in Iraq for short, or shorter still, AQI. 'Praise be to God who has untied the ranks of Mujahideen and disperses the forces of the infidels,' Zarqawi announced, 'and praise be to God who said, "Hold fast to the rope of God and you shall not be divided."'

It was a marriage of convenience for both groups. In hiding from the US following the 9/11 attacks, bin Laden and his deputy Ayman al-Zawahiri would again suddenly appear horribly relevant as a force in global jihad; for Zarqawi, it was a chance to boast possession of the most famous terrorist franchise in the world as well as access to al-Qaeda's private donors and logistical and recruitment networks.[57] Zarqawi and his successors would be referred to as 'al-Qaeda in Iraq' long after they had dropped the title; often it was used as a shorthand to describe what was an even more sinister and dangerous movement. For the next ten years, the association with Zarqawi and his successors would cause al-Qaeda much embarrassment as well as angst over the harm they did to the image of jihad. The final break-up, after years of bickering, would be brutal and apparently final.

Richard Barrett was a former British diplomat as well as a senior intelligence officer with the agencies MI5 and MI6 in the UK. For almost a decade, he headed the United Nations' specialist team that monitored both al-Qaeda and the Taliban. He is now senior vice-president of a respected US-based think-tank, the Soufan Group. He said:

From the very start, Abu Musab al-Zarqawi was not really a follower of Osama bin Laden. Certainly he took his money. Sure, overall they were sharing objectives but even then Zarqawi thought doing stuff in the broader Levant [this area includes Jordan, Syria and Lebanon] was much more important than worrying about what the Americans were doing in Iraq. So they had a difference of opinion there.

And then when Abu Musab al-Zarqawi was so successful from 2003 in Iraq, Zawahiri [then deputy leader of al-Qaeda] in particular thought, 'Well, this is a bit poor; here's the biggest battle ever in our lifetimes going on against the West and we're not even represented.' So he was eager to sign up Abu Musab al-Zarqawi as an al-Qaeda person and Zarqawi was prepared to accept that deal on the basis they wouldn't interfere with him too much and, by having a label, he would get more money and recruits and more prestige and prominence.[58]

The two groups would soon fall out, not over the strategy of savagery for a caliphate, but over Zarqawi's 'methods', particularly the Jordanian's war on the Shia.

Zarqawi introduced various innovations still being used a decade later by Islamic State. He established a 'media department' to issue press releases and speeches as well as to post online the macabre snuff movies in which hostages were dressed up in Guantanamo-style orange jumpsuits and beheaded with a knife.[59] The same style of jumpsuit would be used by Islamic State for its hostage victims. For Zarqawi, as with ISIS/Islamic State, the media battle was an essential part of the jihad and it was important the jihad had a public face. He once said, 'Our fight must have a face or every battle we win will be lost in obscurity.'[60]

On 11 May 2004, a video was posted online entitled 'Abu Musab al-Zarqawi Slaughters an American'. Nick Berg, a

26-year-old radio tower repairman, could be seen in his orange jumpsuit seated in front of five masked men. Following a statement, two men held a screaming Berg down while Zarqawi cut off his head with a knife.[61] The head was then placed on the body just the way Islamic State does now after a decapitation, whether the murder takes place in its stronghold of Raqqa or on a beach in Libya. Zarqawi had personally threatened contractors, or 'betrayers', that if they continued working for US forces 'you will be dead and this is a final warning to you from the leader of al-Qaeda in Mesopotamia [Iraq], if you ever enter an American base or work with them anymore, you and all with you will be killed'.[62] Other beheading victims were to follow, including the British civil engineer Kenneth Bigley and his fellow captives, Jack Hensley and Eugene Armstrong, both US contractors.

Caroline Hawley, the BBC's Baghdad correspondent, said:

> It was already bad when the hostage takings began. Then it became a whole different proposition to be working there. It became so dangerous. It wasn't just the danger that you might face by going out and about, which our security people worried about, but it's the danger you put people [Iraqis] in by [them] associating with you. It was then a problem of how to get into someone's house without anyone seeing a foreigner visiting them.[63]

By the summer of 2005, it was clear that even al-Qaeda Central had tired of Zarqawi's excesses of ultra-violence, his mismanagement of savagery. They had become convinced that he was harming the image of jihad as well as the overriding objective of creating a caliphate in Iraq. On 9 July 2005, Ayman Zawahiri, who would be bin Laden's eventual successor, wrote to Zarqawi reminding him of the first three stages of the strategy: 'expel the Americans from Iraq; establish an Islamic authority or emirate, then develop it and support it until it achieves the level of a caliphate…the third stage: extend the jihad to the secular countries neighbouring Iraq'.

Zawahiri warned Zarqawi that his war against the Shia had appalled ordinary Muslims: 'My opinion is that this matter won't be acceptable to the Muslim populace however much you have tried to explain it, and aversion to this will continue.'[64]

The al-Qaeda deputy leader also raised the thorny issue of the hostages. 'Among the things which the feelings of the Muslim populace who love and support you will never find palatable also are the scenes of slaughtering the hostages. You shouldn't be deceived by the praise of some of the zealous young men and their description of you as the sheikh of the slaughterers, etc.'[65]

For Richard Barrett, this falling out was inevitable. By then it was obvious that Zarqawi was out of control and would not even listen to his supposed al-Qaeda paymasters. 'By 2005, we have these letters which are very instructive,' said Barrett. 'You can see both in the tone of the letters and what they've said where the fault lines were.'[66]

By this time it was clear that al-Qaeda in Iraq was al-Qaeda in name only; Zarqawi would manage savagery in his own way and he would have his terrible civil war between Sunni and Shia.

5
632 and all that
632–2006

There are many deadly things housed within the Imperial War Museum in London; the place is full of old killing machines that have earned an honourable discharge from military service. From the ceiling hang decommissioned fighters and missiles and elsewhere, placed at strategic points near children eating crisps, you can see the other paraphernalia of war, including tanks and field guns. The exhibits look so polished and pristine it is hard to believe they have seen any conflict, with one exception: the rust-covered car wreckage on the ground floor.

The car melted in the blast of a bomb that destroyed Baghdad's famous book market in al-Mutanabbi Street on 5 March 2007. The street and bookshops were devastated utterly by the bombing that broke the capital's cultural heart. At least thirty-eight people died. The attack took place as the terrible civil war caused deliberately by Abu Musab al-Zarqawi burned hot.

The conceptual artist Jeremy Deller obtained one of the cars destroyed in the bombing and exhibited it mainly in the US under the title *It Is What It Is*. Eventually the New Museum in New York exhibited the car before gifting it to the Imperial War Museum.

Tragically the car bomb has become the deadliest weapon of our age, slaughtering countless thousands in Iraq. Kathleen Palmer, the Imperial War Museum's head of art, said, 'The idea that we should have things on display that had been destroyed or damaged was really important in our thinking. We are very aware that the nature of conflict is evolving very quickly and very obviously in the last ten years or more.' She added, 'If a car ends up in that kind of wrecked state just by being within the blast area then you can only imagine what might happen to people.'

By the time of the bombing Zarqawi was dead but the men who followed him were proving themselves if anything even more deadly. Al-Mutanabbi Street was just one of many massacres that year. The street has now been rebuilt and you can see professors and poets shuffling down the road with newly acquired tomes under their arm or rummaging through the books displayed on the pavement.

In November 2013, I visited the centrepiece of the street, the famous Café al-Shabandar. It too had been destroyed in the bombing but it had since been beautifully restored. Sepia photos of old Baghdad hung from the walls, and writers and old sheikhs drank little cups of muddy coffee, smoked their hookah pipes and played backgammon. The proprietor, Mr Muhammad Khish Ali, then seventy-four, sat by the door where I saw displayed the photos of the four sons and a grandson he lost in the bombing. I congratulated him on the restoration of his café. 'What else could I do?' he said gesticulating to the photos of his slaughtered family as he gazed sadly past me to somewhere in the middle distance. 'I have four widows and twelve grandchildren to support.'[1]

The al-Mutanabbi Street bombing was just one of the many atrocities and massacres in the two-year civil war finally brought about by Zarqawi. After almost three years of provocation, the Jordanian finally pushed the long suffering Shia into a grisly conflict with an assault on one of their holiest places. At dawn on

22 February 2006, around a dozen men entered the al-Askariya shrine in the city of Samarra. They tied up the four security guards and then planted bombs in the golden onion-shaped dome. At a safe distance they detonated the devices.[2]

Sixty miles to the south in the Baghdad BBC bureau, the senior news producer Patrick Howse had just sat down for breakfast when the call came in. Howse was the bureau chief at the time and he remembered the day Abu Musab al-Zarqawi destroyed the exquisite shrine at Samarra as if it were yesterday. He said:

> The phone rang and our very good local producer, Samir, a former army officer, was there and he was standing up as he took the call and I was looking at him as he did and he went white, I remember thinking all the colour had gone from his face. He sat down heavily in the chair and gripped the phone and started taking notes. He put the phone down and said that this shrine had been blown up. I had a vague understanding about what he was talking about but I didn't really have any idea other than his reaction that this was something huge.
>
> I assumed that lots of people had been killed but Samir said he didn't think there were any dead. He then said this is one of the holiest sites in Shia Islam and 'this will be war'.

With his genius for savagery and mayhem, Zarqawi had at last suceeded in igniting the fuse to civil war. Most Shia Muslims believe twelve divinely appointed imams succeeded Muhammad after the Prophet's death in 632 CE.[3] Imams number ten and number eleven, the father and son Ali al-Hadi and Hassan al-Askari, are buried in the shrine at Samarra. According to the Shia, imam number twelve, Muhammad al-Mahdi, went into hiding near the shrine and the Shia believe he will return before the day of judgement to return justice to the world.

As the BBC's bureau chief, Howse had to decide whether to send a reporter with a TV camera crew to Samarra. Already thousands of Shia, many armed with machetes and clubs, had taken to the streets of Samarra and other cities to demand revenge. Initially, the BBC news bosses back in London wanted Howse to dispatch a team, but the situation was just too dangerous. He said:

> We had a request from London to go to Samarra to 'get colour' and I told them we would either be shot by gunmen on the way or we'd be torn to shreds by the mob if we got there. The atmosphere in Baghdad itself quickly became very tense; at the end of our street at one point there was a checkpoint manned by Shia militia from the Mahdi Army. They would drag people out of their cars and cut their throats if they weren't Shia.

Samarra did prove lethal for one team of journalists who courageously drove there. Zarqawi had chosen his most senior Samarra-based thug, Haitham al-Badri, to lead the attack on the shrine.[4] Badri had been a government official under Saddam Hussein and later became Zarqawi's 'emir' for Samarra. Later that day Badri became incensed by a live TV report from Samarra presented by a brave female correspondent called Atwar Bahjat, who worked for the Al Arabiya station.[5] 'Whether you are Sunni or Shia, Arab or Kurds, there is no difference between Iraqis,' she said during her live report on camera.[6] Badri and a henchman found the TV crew and abducted them. First the cameraman and engineer were shot. Then Bahjat was raped and murdered. For good measure a few days later, Bahjat's funeral procession was attacked – presumably by Zarqawi – as it made its way through Abu Ghraib west of Baghdad. Three people died when gunmen opened fire and a roadside bomb exploded.[7] By now, this outrage scarcely merited a mention on the news.

At Samarra, Zarqawi had not just attacked a shrine; he had struck at the so-called Twelvers themselves, the bedrock of Shia Islam. The reaction was swift and violent. As 22 February 2006 drew to a close, Shia mobs had attacked twenty-seven mosques in Baghdad alone and killed three Sunni imams.[8]

The next two years of civil war between Shia and Sunni was a catastrophe. The country would now witness murder, chaos and ethnic cleansing on an unprecedented scale. In the three murderous years following the invasion, an estimated 40,000 civilians were killed in Iraq.[9] In the two years following the Samarra bombing, nearly 55,000 are estimated to have died by bomb, bullet and a wide variety of gruesome methods.[10] In Iraq after Saddam, religion and politics became inextricably enmeshed. For Shia militias, often working for powerful Shia figures in the Iraqi government, the electric drill was often the execution weapon of choice as they hunted down suspected jihadis and ferociously 'cleansed' whole districts and neighbourhoods of Sunnis. Over the next two years, the violence would turn ten percent of Iraq's thirty million population into internal refugees.[11]

Patrick Howse would risk the odd jog alongside the river Tigris in Baghdad. 'It was clear that it was a very violent place,' he said. 'There was an eerie quiet but at the same time you could hear shootings and bangs; lots of people were being killed and for months afterwards, bodies were being washed up in the reeds of the Tigris. Often they were people who had been abducted, had their hands tied behind their back and killed by having an electric drill put through their forehead.'

Howse used to run along the Tigris accompanied by an armed security adviser. On one occasion he saw people drag a body out of the reeds and lay it on the ground. Howse added, 'The man had been killed in this way; he'd had a hole drilled right through his forehead. That image stayed with me for a very long time and it featured in nightmares and so forth.'

So many corpses would end up in the Tigris that people were being advised against eating the famous Iraqi dish *masgouf*, smoked carp.[12] An apparently respected Shia imam in Najaf issued a fatwa, a pronouncement on a point of Islamic law, warning of the danger of carp in the Tigris being infected by rotting bodies. The fatwa said, 'As a bottom feeder this fish is especially susceptible to diseases from the water.'[13] Now throughout the Middle East, the long-dormant sectarian split between Shia and Sunni Muslims has become a dominant source of strife and war. In Syria, a Sunni majority seeks to overturn a Shia minority in power; in Bahrain, a Shia majority has risen up against a Sunni minority.

In Iraq after the US-led invasion in 2003, the Shia came to power simply through strength of numbers after centuries of disenfranchisement and oppression by the Sunni, from the Ottomans through to the Ba'ath and Saddam Hussein. In 2014, after the fall of Mosul to Abu Bakr al-Baghdadi, the allegedly anti-Sunni policies of senior Iraqi Shia politicians, including de-Ba'athification, would be blamed for fuelling the rise of Islamic State.

How it all began

Iraq was where Shia and Sunni went their separate ways in 661 CE but the schism was caused almost thirty years earlier in 632 CE with the death of the Prophet Muhammad and the dispute over the succession. None of Muhammad's sons had survived so the succession for the job as caliph, exercising the authority of the Prophet following his death, was unclear.

One faction supported Muhammad's close friend and adviser Abu Bakr for caliph while another group of Muhammad's followers argued that the rightful successor was Ali bin Abi Talib, the Prophet's cousin and son-in-law.[14] Ali's followers became known in Arabic as *Shi'atu Ali*, or Shia for short. The word Sunni comes from the Arabic *ahl as-sunnah wal jama'at*, or 'the people of the tradition of Muhammad and the consensus of the Ummah [worldwide Muslim community]'.

Abu Bakr was chosen as caliph, defeating Ali and his *Shi'atu Ali*; they had to wait for the deaths of Abu Bakr and his two successors, caliphs two and three, before Ali became the fourth caliph in 656 CE. In 661, Ali was assassinated, struck by a poison-coated sword while at prayer in the Great Mosque of the Iraqi city of Kufa. Ali's son Hassan succeeded him but he was swiftly deposed as caliph by Muawiyah of the Umayyad dynasty. On the death of Muawiyah, the Shia saw another opportunity to win the caliphate through another son of Ali, Hussein, although it had already gone to Muawiyah's son, Yazid.

Yazid defeated the Shia at the Battle of Karbala in modern-day Iraq in October 680. Hussein was beheaded and his companions and family also killed, including his six-month-old son. The Shia commemorate Hussein's death and that of his baby boy, Ali al-Ashgar, with a ten-day-long act of remembrance known as Ashura. This includes pilgrimages to Karbala and the stupendous shrines holding the remains of Ali's sons Hussein and Hassan. Pilgrims at such commemorations have often been sitting ducks for Zarqawi and his successors.[15]

After Karbala, the Sunni followed their caliphs and the Shia revered their twelve imams, six of whom are buried in Iraq. Imam number one, Ali, is buried in the great shrine of Najaf, numbers two and three, Hassan and Hussein, at Karbala, and number seven, Musa al-Kadhim, at the al-Kadhimiya Mosque, again a favourite Zarqawi target.[16] And of course, imams ten and eleven were interred at Samarra.

Shias and Sunnis agree about the basic tenets of Islam. They believe in God, Allah, and that his messenger was the Prophet Muhammad. Both sects also fast during the holy month of Ramadan and conduct daily prayers. There are, however, important differences, particularly on the issue of religious authority. For Sunnis, this authority derives from the Koran and the traditions of Muhammad. Sunni scholars exert much less influence over their Muslims than that exercised over the Shia by their complex priesthood structure of imams, ayatollahs and grand ayatollahs.

Zarqawi was not alone in viewing the Shia as heretics. The Wahhabi sect from Saudi Arabia take the view that many Shia beliefs contradict Islam. Classic Sunni religious texts are full of allegations against the Shia that their devotion to Caliph Ali, also the first of the twelve imams, essentially amounted to awarding him 'divine status' and that therefore they are guilty of the ultimate sin of polytheism, the belief in more than one god. The Shia are accused of reviling the first caliphs and companions of Muhammad, and the 'Twelvers'' devotion to the twelve imams sets them alongside or even above the Prophet.[17] The Wahhabis have gone so far as to accuse the Shia of being a Jewish fifth column who should be confined to 'the lowest rank of Hell'.[18]

As the majority in Iraq, the Shia represented by far the gravest threat to the rule of Saddam Hussein and he would show them no mercy when he felt threatened by them. He would slaughter them by the tens of thousands and murder their most important clerics. He savagely put down two attempted uprisings, the first following the Iranian Revolution that had brought the Shia cleric Ayatollah Ruhollah Khomeini to power. Around two hundred were executed and membership of the main Shia political party, Dawa, was made punishable by death.[19] The second uprising, in 1991, followed Saddam's defeat in the first Gulf War and his withdrawal from Kuwait. This time Saddam's executioners killed an estimated 100,000 Shia men, women and children.[20] In 1980 Saddam had hanged the founder of Dawa, Grand Ayatollah Muhammad Baqir al-Sadr, along with his sister Bint al-Huda. It was claimed later that the torturers had hammered a nail into Baqir's head and raped his sister before their executions.[21] Baqir al-Sadr's first cousin and fellow grand ayatollah, Mohammad Sadeq al-Sadr, succeeded him. In 1999, Saddam gunmen in Najaf assassinated him and two of his sons. The two Sadr martyrs are known as 'Sadr 1' and 'Sadr 2' and their portraits can be seen everywhere in parts of Baghdad, and Shia cities such as Najaf and Basra. The firebrand cleric Muqtada al-Sadr is the surviving son of 'Sadr 2'.

The fall of Baghdad in 2003 witnessed the return from exile of many Shia politicians, including the controversial future Iraqi prime minister Nouri al-Maliki. Maliki and his allegedly anti-Sunni policies would be blamed for helping to foment support for ISIS/Islamic State more than a decade later. Other Shia returnees to Iraq following the fall of Saddam included Mohammad Baqir al-Hakim, soon to meet his end at the hands of Zarqawi.[22]

The path to evil, and good intentions

The United States wanted Iraq to be a democracy, and democracy inevitably meant a transfer of power from the minority Sunni elite to the majority Shia, estimated at around sixty percent of Iraq's population.[23] Both Shia and Kurds had suffered terribly at the hands of Saddam and his Sunni-dominated government and army, and both peoples were determined to assert themselves in the new Iraq.

Ali Khedery, an influential young Iraqi-American adviser at the time, told me:

There was Saddam's ruinous war against Iran and just when people started breathing again, there was the ruinous war in

Kuwait; the sanctions imposed by the West after Kuwait destroyed the middle class and the 2003 war was the final nail in the coffin.

So I completely understand the Shias' situation. They were massacred, not by the tens of thousands, but by the hundreds of thousands; they were brutalized and raped and tortured and pushed into exile and into Iran's lap and Iran was only too happy to exploit them. I understand the Kurds' perspective as well, that they were also massacred by the hundreds of thousands and fought for decades. What we tried to do was to create a truly representative and truly federal government in Baghdad during the constitution drafting and hoped that people would [live by] the spirit [of the constitution,] and America would become the guarantor of the Iraqi constitution as we were specifically tasked to do. Or the decision could have been 'This isn't going to work, let Iraq be a confederacy or even partitioned.'

The Sunnis' new subordinate role became clear very early on when the US established Iraq's first formal representative authority, made up of leading Iraqis who would provide advice and leadership. The newly formed Iraqi Governing Council, or IGC, was supposed to give the US the democratic credentials it needed until it could hand over sovereignty to the Iraqi people during 2004 and help pave the way to democracy. On paper, the new council's twenty-five members seemed to reflect the religious and ethnic make-up of Iraq of mainly Shia, Sunni and Kurd, but that is not how some critics saw it.

The United States had 'fundamentally altered the political balance of power in Iraq in favor of both the Shiites and the Kurds', argued a report by the Middle East Research and Information Project think-tank. The Project's analysts argued that the new council was deeply flawed because Shia politicians who were determined above all to promote Shia interests dominated the new council, in other words they were 'sectarian'. The report said, 'Fourteen IGC members are Shiite – five of whom represent parties that are overtly sectarian – and a further five are Kurdish politicians who favor policies with a clear ethnic bias. Only four members are Sunni Arabs, and in contrast to their Shiite and Kurdish counterparts, none are members of organizations that espouse palpably sectarian or ethnic platforms.'[24]

In addition there was 'the US propensity to equate Sunnis with Ba'athists and the latter with "Saddam loyalists"'. The report had this prophetic warning: 'All this has exacerbated fears among Sunni Arabs that they are being purposely marginalized, something that could encourage the community to organize on a sectarian basis in the future and to provide at least tacit support for violent resistance.'[25] Ominously, in its first statement on 13 July 2003, the IGC prioritized 'de-Ba'athification and uprooting of Ba'ath ideology from Iraqi society'.[26]

By the end of 2003, Shia politicians also dominated another newly created organization that was purging many thousands of Sunnis from their jobs. The so-called De-Ba'athification Commission would vastly expand the scope of the purge to prevent Ba'ath suspects getting good jobs in the new state bureaucracy, media, politics and civil institutions.[27] The commission also established de-Ba'athification committees for each government ministry. Nouri al-Maliki, the future prime minister, was making his name as a deputy chairman of the commission and was seen as a strong de-Ba'athification supporter.[28] Increasingly Sunnis saw de-Ba'athification as 'de-Sunnification' and increasingly they began to withdraw from politics.[29]

In Baghdad, I spoke to Hana Edward, the human rights activist who was courageous enough to campaign against human rights abuses during the time of Saddam. She blamed both Shia and Sunni politicians for the growing strife between the two sects, adding, 'All parties played this role, trying to deepen the sectarian feelings among the Sunnis and among the Shia for the purpose of divide-and-rule. The British did it during colonial times [1920–1958] and it was still used by so many actors in Iraqi politics.'

Sunni alienation became clear during 2005 when Iraq held three crucial elections. In January, the Sunnis largely boycotted Iraq's first parliamentary elections, either voluntarily because they deemed the process illegitimate or out of fear of violence.[30] The boycott left them significantly under-represented in the new transitional government;[31] consequently they then felt 'largely excluded' from the crucial process of drawing up the new constitution.[32] A delay in forming the government left the constitutional committee just three months to write the constitution.

In the October 2005 constitutional referendum, two thirds of voters in the all-important Sunni regions of Anbar, west of Baghdad, and Saladin, to the north of capital, scorned the referendum by refusing to participate in it. Just before the vote a report by an important non-governmental conflict prevention group argued that 'a rushed constitutional process has deepened rifts and hardened feelings' and warned, 'Today the situation appears to be heading toward de facto partition and full-scale civil war.'[33]

By the time of the second parliamentary elections in December 2005, just two months before the Samarra bombing, the situation on the ground was deteriorating fast. In addition to Zarqawi and the other insurgents, US troops had already confronted two serious uprisings by both Sunni and Shia that began simultaneously in spring 2004.

On 31 March 2004, in the mainly Sunni city of Fallujah, Iraqi insurgents ambushed a convoy and killed four US contractors working for the Blackwater company. A mob then set fire to the bodies and dragged them through the streets. Then they hung the charred corpses from a bridge over the river Euphrates.[34]

In the heart of the so-called 'Sunni Triangle', Fallujah was also a stronghold for Zarqawi although he was not thought to be present for the battle that followed the Blackwater killings.[35] Days later, the US launched an assault on the town. By the time a ceasefire was announced on 1 May approximately eight hundred Iraqis were dead.[36] After the battle, Fallujah once again fell under Zarqawi's influence and became his base of operations for attacks on Baghdad as well as a place where he could hold and behead hostages.[37]

US-led coalition troops including British and Iraqis renewed their offensive on a largely abandoned Fallujah again in November 2004; only 400 of the 250,000 civilians remained, the rest having fled to safety. The second battle of Fallujah was a determined attempt to kill Zarqawi and his estimated five thousand fighters. During ten days of heavy fighting, coalition troops discovered twenty-six bomb factories, including two for car bombs.[38] They also claimed to have killed or captured three thousand jihadis.[39] Critically, they did not find Zarqawi, who was rumoured to have escaped Fallujah dressed as a woman. Fallujah would fall under the sway of the jihadis again and again over the years and would provide Abu Bakr al-Baghdadi with his foothold in Iraq for his full-scale invasion of the country in 2014.

Dr Afzal Ashraf was a senior RAF officer in Iraq at the time. He is now a terrorism expert with the Royal United Services Institute, the leading UK-based defence and security think-tank founded by the Duke of Wellington. He had long concluded that the strategy for dealing with Zarqawi and other insurgents was not working and the repeated failure to keep them out of Fallujah made that obvious. He said:

When it came to Fallujah in November 2004, it took the entire capability of the American army and on top of that, there was also the Black Watch [Royal Highland Regiment]. It was a big desert with an infinite number of routes in and out of the town so that's why it was a surprise that we managed to clear it. Fallujah was hermetically sealed; the smart insurgents left and they left the dumb guys in there so was a bit of Darwinian clearing out from our point of view. Every single house was cleared; every single room was cleared; a lot of buildings were demolished. There was a lot of reconstruction costing millions of dollars and yet the insurgents came back in not once but two and three times, so the point was, it [the counter-insurgency strategy] didn't work. The evidence that it was failing on a daily basis was obvious.[40]

The US also had to face down an uprising by a Shia militia called the Jaish al-Mahdi, better known as the Mahdi Army. The firebrand Shia cleric Muqtada al-Sadr, the only surviving son of the murdered Grand Ayatollah 'Sadr 2', led the revolt. Sadr's power base was Sadr City, the vast sprawling slum predominantly occupied by poor disaffected Shia. Sadr opposed the US-led occupation and repeatedly demanded the withdrawal of all foreign troops. He also demanded the establishment of a new Iraqi government free of the taint of Ba'athism.

The Mahdi Army uprising of early spring 2004 followed two decisions taken by Ambassador Bremer as Sadr started to stoke the flames of revolt: first to close down the cleric's newspaper, al-Hawza, on 26 March on the grounds of inciting violence, and second to arrest Sadr's senior aide Mustafa al-Yaqubi on 3 April. Soon Sadr's fighters were in a full-pitch battle with the US troops in and around Najaf. The extraordinary Shia cemetery Wadi al-Salaam, 'Valley of Peace', became a principal battleground. At the end of April fighting stopped after the US backed down from its threat to disband the Mahdi Army and arrest Sadr.[41] Both man and militia were to remain ominous influences on Iraq. By April 2007, Sadr's followers would control six government ministries[42] while the Mahdi Army would help rule the streets.

The Shia militia, principally the Mahdi Army and another more powerful organization called the Badr Brigade, still hold sway in Iraq and have long enjoyed the power of life and death over ordinary Iraqis. Often they are connected to powerful senior politicians. In 2014, when Iraqi troops and police melted away, it was mainly the Shia militias that prevented Baghdad falling to Islamic State. Even before Samarra, there were credible allegations that these militias were acting as death squads, and that young Sunni men were the main targets.

In November 2005, US troops discovered a bunker holding 173 malnourished and badly beaten predominantly Sunni men and teenage boys. Reliable sources also reported the discovery of torture implements including saws to cut off prisoners' limbs and razors to peel their skin. What was even more shocking was that the bunker was part of a detention facility owned by the Iraqi interior ministry and that it was being run by ministry-trained and recruited 'special commando units'. Interior minister, Bayan Jabor, a former commander of the Badr Brigade, strenuously denied allegations of cruelty.[43] This denial was seriously challenged by John Pace, a senior human rights official for the United Nations in Iraq around the time of Samarra in February 2006, who accused the interior ministry of acting as 'a rogue elephant within the government'.[44] That was putting it mildly. Even worse human rights abuses by the ministry of interior against Sunnis, ensnared in its regular round-ups, would come to light later.

After Samarra the Shia militias intensified their campaign of ethnic cleansing and killing. Corpses were turning up all over Baghdad and other cities. One study published at the time said, 'Bodies often show signs of torture – drill holes in soft body parts, joints and faces, burns, acid burns, heavy beating.'[45] Death squads often used 'police cars, equipment and ID cards but [wore] civilian clothes under police vests'.[46] A key Shia killer was Abu Dura, a commander in the Mahdi Army. He was so brutal that he was actually known as the 'Shiite Zarqawi'. He ran extortion, kidnapping and assassination rings. He was known to use a power drill to torture and kill his victims.[47] In the aftermath of Samarra, Shia death squads were killing eight times as many people as Zarqawi and the other Sunni insurgents.[48]

6
The forgotten caliph
2006

Zarqawi had proved to be the world's most dangerous man long before the bombing at Samarra. In 2006, he still remained at large despite the $25 million reward[1] and a determined manhunt to catch him. In 2005, he was very nearly captured by the British; he escaped thanks to a spectacular piece of bungling. The fiasco would remain a secret until the emergence of a confidential cable five years later.

On 17 March 2005, British military intelligence in Iraq learned that Zarqawi was travelling along Route 6 from Amarah in south-eastern Iraq towards the southern city of Basra. At 2.45 p.m., according to the secret military cable, G3 passed this hot titbit on to Danish coalition troops stationed along the route but not before dispatching a Lynx helicopter to take a closer look. Within minutes, the chopper crew spotted 'a suspect vehicle' which had stopped by the road some seven miles south of the nondescript desert town of al-Qurnah. The Lynx hovered over 'the target area' for fifteen minutes before running low on fuel. As extraordinary as it sounds, the helicopter had to return to base to refuel, leaving the 'area of interest' unobserved for between twenty and thirty minutes, more than enough time for Zarqawi to make his getaway.[2]

Troops arrived from a reserve company of the UK's Duke of Wellington's Regiment and established an 'inner and outer cordon' around the area where the car was last seen, followed by a search lasting seven hours or so. Two buildings, including a Shia mosque, were found to contain only civilians and the hunt was abandoned around 10.15 p.m. Iraq's grisly bird of prey had flown.

Zarqawi had become so deadly that he could kill without even lifting a finger. On 31 August 2005, around a million Shia pilgrims were marching through Baghdad on their way to the al-Kadhimiya mosque, the scene of Zarqawi's horrific attack the previous year.[3] Earlier that day seven people had died in a mortar attack by a group of Sunni insurgents, so many pilgrims were already fearful.[4] Later that day someone in the massed crowds cried out that they had seen a suicide bomber. In the ensuing panic on the al-Aaimmah bridge around one thousand people died, either drowned in the Tigris or trampled to death.[5]

Zarqawi's terror was no longer confined to Iraq. In April 2004, Jordanian authorities had unearthed an astonishing plot that would have dwarfed the death toll of the 9/11 attacks. Zarqawi and his followers planned to launch a series of chemical weapon attacks against the Jordanian capital, Amman. If the plot had succeeded security officials believe it would have created a toxic gas cloud with a mile radius across the city, killing an estimated eighty thousand people and wounding twice as many again.[6] Jordan's special forces raided the hideout of Zarqawi's cell and discovered explosives and twenty tons of toxic chemicals, including sulphuric acid and cyanide salts. The ringleader, Azmi al-Jayyousi, admitted reporting directly to Zarqawi.[7] On conviction seven men were sentenced to death[8] and three including Zarqawi were charged *in absentia*.

The BBC's Baghdad correspondent Caroline Hawley was caught up in another Zarqawi atrocity, again in Jordan. She had stopped over briefly in Amman on her way back to Baghdad when Zarqawi's suicide bombers struck three hotels in the Jordanian capital, including her own, the Hyatt, on 9 November 2005. There was a terrible twist at the Radisson SAS Hotel when a husband and wife suicide team attacked a wedding party while it was in full swing. The wife bomber, Sajida Atrous al-Rishawi, failed to detonate her suicide belt but her husband, Ali Hussein al-Shamari, managed to explode his bomb, killing thirty-eight wedding guests including the fathers of the bride and groom. The dead numbered 59 and the injured 115. Hawley said:

> I was just in the Hyatt, which was down the road from the Radisson, and eating dinner and we suddenly heard this huge explosion and we saw this giant fireball coming down the Hyatt's spiral staircase. The bomber had blown himself up on the ground floor about sixty yards from us. There was shattered glass in the restaurant and a few people were bloodied and ran out.
>
> We went back inside because we knew there had been a bomb and that's when we saw this vision from Hell with a waiter who had just been killed being brought out on a tablecloth and bodies everywhere.[9]

Rishawi was arrested, tried and sentenced to death. For nearly a decade she languished on death row hoping to get her sentence overturned on appeal. In early 2015 Rishawi would again make the news when Islamic State demanded her release by Jordan after its capture of the Jordanian pilot Moaz al-Kasasbeh, suggesting an exchange might be possible. Abu Bakr al-Baghdadi then decreed that Kasasbeh be put in a cage and burned to death. IS posted a video on the web showing the highly orchestrated murder on 3

February 2015, and the Jordanians hanged Rishawi the following morning.[10]

From time to time, there were reports that Zarqawi had been injured or killed.[11] Any doubts about whether he was dead or alive were dispelled in April 2006 when a thirty-four-minute tape was released by the US showing the Jordanian in a number of heroic poses, either stooped over maps with his commanders or shooting an array of assault rifles. In one scene mocked by a US military spokesman during a press conference,[12] Zarqawi is seen having a problem clearing a jam in an M249 machine gun.

Killing or catching Zarqawi was always going to be difficult because he behaved like the hunted man he was, constantly on the move between safe houses. He and his men did not use mobile phones, knowing that the US could easily trace them. Instead they used satellite phones, which were much more difficult to track.

Eventually hubris and cumulative intelligence cost Zarqawi his life in June 2006; the April videotape had helped identify his likely whereabouts but the critical information came from one of the Jordanian's closest lieutenants. Finally, Zarqawi was betrayed.

At the end of May 2006, Iraqi forces raided a house and arrested three senior Zarqawi men in Baghdad's northern Adhamiya district.[13] One of the men, Kassim al-Ani, was a senior Zarqawi aide and one of the most wanted men in Iraq. It seems clear that it was Ani who provided the key piece of intelligence – the identity of Zarqawi's spiritual leader, Sheikh Abdul-Rahman al-Iraqi.

US military intelligence began trailing Abdul-Rahman with a remotely controlled aircraft,[14] hoping he would lead them to their quarry. He did. Eventually he drove to an isolated house in a grove lined by date palms on the outskirts of Hibhib, a village thirty-five miles to the north of Baghdad. The drone filmed Abdul-Rahman being greeted by a man dressed all in black, later described by a US general as Zarqawi's 'signature look, the Johnny Cash look'.[15]

Half a dozen commandos from the US Delta force hid among the palms and waited, and watched the house. In the early evening, Zarqawi along with his family and friends sat down for their dinner. As dusk approached, the leader of the small reconnaissance unit attached to the Delta team started to fret that the ever-elusive Zarqawi might suddenly leave, and so he radioed his superiors to request an air strike.[16]

In the early evening of 7 June 2006, two American F-16 fighters took off. At 6.12 p.m., the first jet struck the house with a 500-pound laser-guided bomb; the second dropped a satellite-guided bomb, 'to ensure the target set was serviced appropriately,' an air force general helpfully explained later.[17]

When US troops arrived at the flattened building twenty-three minutes later they found the bodies of two men, including Abdul-Rahman, and three women. Among the dead were Israa, the sixteen year-old wife of Zarqawi' and their eighteen-month-old baby, also named Abdul Rahman after the group's spiritual adviser lying nearby.[18] Zarqawi had survived, but with massive internal injuries, particularly to his lungs.[19] The US would later release the autopsy report to refute allegations reported by two media outlets that Zarqawi had been taken out of the ambulance by US troops who then beat and stomped him to death.[20]

'He obviously had some kind of visual recognition of who they were because he attempted to roll off the stretcher, as I am told, and get away, realizing it was US military,' the US military spokesman, Major General William Caldwell, told a news conference.[21] Zarqawi was declared dead fifty-two minutes after the strike. No one received the $25 million reward.[22]

Iraqi prime minister Nouri al-Maliki announced the death at a news conference and the news was greeted by celebratory shouts and joyful cries to the Prophet Muhammad of 'peace be upon him'.[23] In truth there was little to celebrate. The killing and ethnic violence would continue and deteriorate much further over the next eighteen months. For his followers Zarqawi was going to be a very hard act to follow, but they were determined to carry on his deadly legacy.

Islamic State of Iraq is declared

Zarqawi was dead but he had already made important structural changes to his organization to ensure its survival by trying to incorporate other jihadi groups. This would involve another name change and one that would further dilute the influence of al-Qaeda. On 15 January 2006, Zarqawi had announced the formation of the Mujahidin Shura Council (MSC); effectively this was a merger between his al-Qaeda in Iraq (AQI) organization and five other small groups of jihadi militants. In his audio message Zarqawi said the merger was important for those Sunnis who 'have chosen the path of jihad and war against the infidels of all different kinds to unite for the sake of the victory of Allah'.[24]

The name change and merger gave a strong indication that the Jordanian wanted to subjugate other insurgency groups to his will. Ominously one of the more obscure groups was called Jaish Ahlu al-Sunnah wa al-Jama'ah, or Army of the Sunni People.[25] Abu Bakr al-Baghdadi, the future 'caliph' of Islamic State, was the 'emir' of the Army of the Sunni People. As would emerge later, Baghdadi and Zarqawi were probably already long-time friends as well as jihadi associates. Three other groups refused to join the MSC because they opposed Zarqawi's total war on the Shia and the way it was harming 'the image of the jihad'.[26]

One jihadi group, the Islamic Army in Iraq (Jaysh al-Islam), spoke out against Zarqawi's brutal tactics and the endless slaughter of innocent bystanders. A spokesman for the group stated, 'We work against the US occupation without hurting innocents…If al-Qaeda [AQI] is against the ideology behind the insurgency, it's time to force them out of our country. We will kill the militants to show how far we will go to save the lives of innocent people.'[27] In October 2005, a bloody battle had been waged between Zarqawi and the Islamic Army in Iraq in the al-Taji district of northern Baghdad.[28]

In death, Zarqawi had bequeathed Iraq a ruinous civil war and a dark and dangerous future. There would be no 'Zarqawiism' to speak of and little to remember him by other than the grim dispatches from the interior ministry or the morgues, and a few hate-filled tracts promising more death and misery for the Shia and other *kuffar*. However, he had established the ground rules for his murderous organization for years to come. Zarqawi's 'methods' could best be summed up in the words of a Chinese colonel, Qiao Lang: 'the first rule of unrestricted warfare is that there are no rules with nothing forbidden'.[29] The Jordanian's successors believed that nothing, no height of cruelty or depth of depravity, should be excluded in pursuit of the caliphate.

Four days after Zarqawi's death, the MSC announced it was still very much in business by posting an Internet video showing the beheading of three Shia men – allegedly death squad members. There was also a message from the man who would replace Zarqawi, one Abu Omar al-Baghdadi, not to be confused – as so many people have done and still do – with 'Caliph' Abu Bakr al-Baghdadi.

In his first speech in the usual grandiloquent 'jihadese' language beloved of Zarqawi, Abu Omar, his successor, said, 'As for you the slaves of the Cross [coalition forces], the grandsons of bin al-Alqami [Shia] and every infidel of the Sunnis, we can't wait to sever your necks with our swords.'[30]

Abu Omar al-Baghdadi would be in charge for the next four

years, but he remains a hazy and mysterious figure, despite all the massacres committed in his name. That includes his chemical warfare, using women with Down's syndrome as suicide bombers, and the second-bloodiest terrorist attack in history after 9/11 – his bombing of the Yazidi minority in August 2007. Despite his murderous campaign, he still remained an enigma at best. Abu Omar was so obscure that the Iraqis falsely claimed to have arrested him three times in the course of one week in early March 2007.[31] Two months later, the Iraqis claimed to have killed Abu Omar during fighting in the town of Dhuluiya north of Baghdad.[32] In April 2009, the Iraqis said they had captured him for the fourth time, but yet again this proved to be false.[33] Yet to Islamic State and its caliph, Abu Omar is revered as a 'mountainous man' and latterly the 'founder of our state'.[34]

Naturally, Abu Omar al-Baghdadi was yet another *nom de guerre*, so who was he really? The answer came in May 2008 from the police chief of Haditha, a farming town in the huge western province of Anbar. Colonel Fareq al-Je'eify identified Abu Omar as one Hamid Dawood Muhammad Khalil al-Zawi, or Hamid al-Zawi for short. Zawi was a former security officer with the General Security Directorate (the Amn al-Aameh) under Saddam. The colonel based this on confessions he had obtained from a number of Abu Omar's fighters he had arrested in Haditha.

In an interview with the Arab TV station Al Arabiya, Colonel al-Je'eify said of Zawi/Abu Omar, 'He was an officer in the security services and was dismissed from the army because of his extremism.'[35] Following his dismissal, Abu Omar worked as an oil heater repairman in Haqlaniyah, an Anbari town on the river Euphrates. He also worked as a taxi driver in Baghdad.[36] The police colonel's important discovery received little publicity at the time, and appears not to have been taken seriously by the US military. Presumably this was because in July 2007, an American brigadier general called Kevin Bergner had confidently assured the world's media that Abu Omar al-Baghdadi was in fact a fictitious character played by an actor called Abu Abdullah al-Naima.[37] In fact, Abu Omar would often be referred to as 'the fictitious leader' even as he continued to release audiotapes of his various speeches and pronouncements.[38]

Peter Mansoor, a senior counter-insurgency strategist for the US military at this time, said, 'Baghdadi was somebody that we were after for a long time and at one point we thought we had killed him. At another point, we had a detainee tell us "It's basically a fiction, a fictional character that serves as a fictional figurehead". And we believed that for a period of time.'

We can be sure that Abu Omar really was Hamed al-Zawi because Colonel Je'eify also supplied a photo of him to Al Arabiya. It shows a balding round-faced man aged in his forties (he was believed to have been born in 1959 or perhaps even earlier) with a moustache and short beard. It is a complete match with the face in the photos taken and displayed in 2010 by the Iraqi government of Abu Omar's corpse following his violent death. The colonel's revelation about the dismissal of Abu Omar begs the question as to whether he fell foul of the de-Ba'athification purge. We may never know. Certainly his dismissal brought about a drastic change to his circumstances. Abu Omar's wife Jassem revealed later that theirs had been an arranged marriage and not perhaps a contented one. In an interview for the *Guardian*'s correspondent Martin Chulov she later said, 'Since I got married I have had a very hard life. All my life has been evasion and hardship.' As for Abu Omar, 'he did not listen to anyone including his own wife,' Jassem said. 'He did his own thing. All I did was raise children and prepare food.'[39] Jassem was being too modest. She was later found guilty of controlling the group's cash and suicide vests and sentenced to life in prison.[40]

Islamic State considers Abu Omar al-Baghdadi to be a key 'founding father' because, on 15 October 2006, there was yet another name change for the group. In a move that stunned and alarmed many jihadis, Abu Omar announced the establishment of the Islamic State of Iraq (ISI). Furthermore the former oil heater repairman was introduced as the *Amir al-Mu'minin*, meaning 'Prince of the Faithful' or even 'Commander of the Faithful'. He was no longer just plain Abu Omar al-Baghdadi; he was now Abu Omar *al-Husseini al-Qurayshi* al-Baghdadi.

Abu Omar's demand to be known by the title 'Prince of the Faithful' was probably the most alarming and astonishing declaration because for all intents and purposes it meant he was declaring himself caliph of his new Islamic State of Iraq. According to Bernard Lewis, one of the world's leading experts on the language of Islam, 'the title *Amir al-Mu'minin*, is said to have been introduced by the Caliph Umar [second caliph, 634–44 CE]. It soon became the standard and most common title of the Caliphs, and the one which for the longest period remained an exclusive caliphal prerogative, long after most other titles had been adopted by all kinds of lesser rulers.'[41]

In addition, by adding the name al-Qurayshi, Abu Omar was claiming to be descended from Muhammad's tribe, the Quraysh, which much of Islamic tradition demands as an essential requirement to be caliph. Islamic State's 'caliph' Abu Bakr al-Baghdadi has also claimed both the title of *Amir al-Mu'minin* and Qurayshi roots.

This extraordinary announcement was not lost on many of 'the faithful' including prolific jihadi writer Attiyet Allah, who suggested that Abu Omar had surely gone too far. Allah wrote:

It probably would have been better to call him 'Emir' without adding 'of the Faithful' so that the evident reference would be to 'Emir' of this 'State', because the term 'Commander of the Faithful' gives the illusion that he is the Grand Imam, and gives the impression that our brothers may consider him so! And it has been accepted as a tradition among Muslims…that the title is synonymous with the 'Grand Imam' who is also the Caliph.

And if it were to be added to that that he – may Allah preserve and aid him – is a Qurayshite…then the illusion is strengthened.[42]

Illusion perhaps, but it was the illusion that would-be caliph Abu Omar was desperate to maintain as he claimed leadership of the world's 1.6 billion Muslims, the *Ummah*.

'My beloved *Ummah*,' declared Abu Omar in his inaugural address on 22 December 2006, 'your men are determined to establish for Islam its state, where they will adjudicate according to its law, and follow its authority and gather its soldiers, and they have shed their blood for that after sacrificing their wealth, they are divorced from every desire, they have suffered much in yearning for that death that will bring either victory or martyrdom.'

Eventually, there would be an Islamic state stretching from China to Spain, he confirmed, as he then issued his extraordinary 'your Islamic State needs you' type of appeal: 'Initially we call upon officers of the former Iraqi army and that is from the rank of lieutenant to major to join the army of the Islamic State on condition that the applicant must know, at a minimum, three sections of the Holy Koran by rote and must pass an ideological examination by a clerical commission that exists in every region to make sure he is not beholden to the idolatry of the Ba'ath.'[43] This appeal to Saddam's former officers would reap long-term rewards; they would join ISI and help turn it into a more effective military machine. The group already knew their worth. Many former soldiers and security officials had already joined it either before or during their incarceration along with many of the jihadis in US prison camps. Their expertise would become more evident in 2014 when the group demonstrated real military professionalism during its conquest of huge swathes of Syria and Iraq.

Abu Omar also ordered the US military to depart Iraq immediately and leave all its valuable equipment behind: 'The withdrawal must be via troop transport trucks and passenger planes whereby each soldier is allowed to carry his own weapon only.' He added, 'They must not withdraw any of the heavy military equipment and the military bases must be handed over to the Mujahidin of the Islamic State and the duration of the withdrawal may not exceed a month.'[44]

For those who delved deeper, the announcement by Abu Omar was not just the outpouring of a deranged killer with ludicrous ideas above his station. There was a clear triumphalist tone. The declaration of an Islamic State of Iraq exposed a raw and terrifying reality for the Americans. Just a few months after the killing of Abu Musab al-Zarqawi, the US had realized it was losing the war and ISI had realized it was winning it. While the Shia militia continued with their horrifying counter-offensive of murder, torture and ethnic cleansing, the jihadis of ISI had all but cowed into submission the largely Sunni population of Iraq's vast western Anbar province, a mainly desert area making up a third of the country's land mass and with a population of around 1.25 million people. This was the reason for Abu Omar's vainglorious decree of an Islamic State of Iraq, a fact that was dramatically recognized by the US military itself, which now realized it was on the brink of defeat.

Just a few weeks previously in late November 2006, not long before Abu Omar's valedictory decrees and announcements, this spectre of humiliating defeat was starkly revealed to the US and the world in a secret report that had been written by a US Marine Corps intelligence officer called Colonel Peter Devlin. Devlin's report, dated 21 August 2006,[45] exposed the extent of the nascent caliphate established by ISI in Anbar. Devlin, the US military intelligence chief for Anbar,[46] concluded that the strength of Abu Omar al-Baghdadi and ISI had become so dominant in western Iraq that US and Iraqi troops were 'no longer capable of defeating the insurgency in Anbar' and that 'nearly all government institutions from the village to provincial level have disintegrated or have been thoroughly corrupted and infiltrated' by ISI. ISI was growing rich thanks to the millions of dollars provided by its illicit trade in oil. ISI had brought about 'the near complete collapse of social order' and had consequently become 'an integral part of the social fabric of western Iraq'.[47] For ISI, conflict was always about seizing territory and holding it for its caliphate.

Aside from being ninety-five percent Sunni, Anbar was also very important strategically. This vast territory encompasses much of Iraq's western territory and stretches out from Baghdad to the borders of Syria, Jordan and Saudi Arabia. Cities include Fallujah and Ramadi. Overwhelmingly the population is made up of Sunni tribespeople. Control of this territory was always critical for the group from the days of Zarqawi and Abu Omar up to 2014 when it provided a launch pad and base for Abu Bakr al-Baghdadi's blitzkrieg.

In his speech, Abu Omar announced his new cabinet for ISI. There would be ten ministries to govern the Anbar towns and territories, just the beginning of a new caliphate – including one for public relations, naturally. With no hint of irony, a Professor Abu Abdel-Jabbar al-Janabi would be 'minister of public security' while the 'ministry of martyrs' and prisoners' affairs' went to a minor tribal sheikh whose main income came from smuggling.[48]

There were other ministries for oil and agriculture and fish resources.

The all-important new 'minister for war' was 'Sheikh' Abu al-Muhajir, mainly known as 'Abu Ayyub al-Masri'. 'Masri' had acted as temporary leader following the death of Zarqawi. He was known to have one wife, Hasna Ali Yeyhe Hussein, and they would have three children.[49] Hussein's involvement in the activities of ISI would send her to the gallows later.[50] Masri was skinny with a gaunt face, almost ferrety features, and in one of the few photos we have of him he is wearing the traditional Arab *dishdasha* head-dress and robe.

Back in the US, the Pentagon considered Masri to be the real leader of ISI, particularly as Abu Omar was believed not to exist![51] The US believed Masri had met Zarqawi in Afghanistan and US intelligence experts described him as an expert in explosives, specializing in 'vehicle-borne improvised explosive devices' (VBIEDs) or car bombs for short. US officials said Masri worked the 'rat line' down the river Euphrates, supplying suicide bombers via Syria probably from his base in Fallujah.[52] Like Zarqawi, Masri was another foreigner, this time from Egypt. The jihadis believed that an Iraqi should be the face of ISI. That is why Abu Omar would be the ideal emir of the group, leaving military strategy to Masri.

In his declaration of himself as Muhammad's heir, Abu Omar al-Baghdadi had referred to Osama bin Laden by the much lesser title of sheikh. Zarqawi's death had cancelled the oath of allegiance or *bay'ah* that the Jordanian had made to al-Qaeda in 2004 and it was not renewed by his successor. Abu Omar instead demanded *bay'ah* from others.[53] The al-Qaeda–Zarqawi 'alliance' had long been a grisly and troubled marriage of convenience thanks to Zarqawi's extremism and extraordinary violence. 'Al-Qaeda Central' had made its feelings clear that the slaughtering of the Shia and beheading of hostages was doing untold harm to the jihad and ultimately the caliphate, as bin Laden's deputy, Ayman Zawahiri, had explained in 2005 in his highly critical letter to Zarqawi.[54]

Osama bin Laden had never claimed to be Leader of the Faithful or *Amir al-Mu'minin*. Abu Omar al-Baghdadi, a jihadist non-entity by comparison, had put himself level with the spiritual Leader of the Faithful of both al-Qaeda and the Taliban, Mullah Omar, as well as placing his organization at the head of jihad. Abu Omar's claim to Qurayshi lineage also ensured he trumped Mullah Omar who had never claimed it for himself.

Naturally, the 'decision' appears to have been made without consulting bin Laden or anyone else at 'al-Qaeda Central'[55] and should be seen as the real break between the two groups. In his July 2005 letter, Ayman al-Zawahiri of al-Qaeda had urged Zarqawi to establish an 'emirate' in territory he could hold and only after the US had been expelled. But there were still thousands of American troops in Iraq. Many jihadis, both outside and within the group, considered the ISI declaration premature and unwise. ISI would still be strongly identified as 'al-Qaeda in Iraq' but the truth is that the group would be a source of angst and embarrassment for bin Laden for years to come, as letters from his home in Pakistan would later reveal.[56]

For example, not long after Abu Omar's speech, an unnamed leading al-Qaeda member of Egyptian origin wrote a letter to a legal scholar called Hafiz Sultan. The writer clearly knew both Abu Omar al-Baghdadi and his 'minister of war' Masri and was desperately worried about the 'political mistakes' the ISI pair were making as they went about the jihad. 'They are extremists,' he wrote, adding that Abu Omar's speech was 'repulsive and lacks wisdom'.[57] Abu Omar's declaration also upset other jihadi rebel groups in Iraq which had already grown tired of ISI excesses and believed the announcement of ISI a step too far.

Towards the end of 2006, an authoritative survey published by the *Lancet*, the prestigious UK-based medical journal, estimated that more than 600,000 people had been killed in Iraq since the start of the 2003 US-led invasion, a staggering number way in excess of official figures that were already shocking. Based on an actual survey of households in Iraq, the *Lancet* estimated that more than a half of victims, around 336,000 people, had been shot dead and around 78,000 had been killed by car bombs, a particular speciality of Zarqawi's.[58] The report helped foster the widespread suspicion in Iraq that has persisted for years that there has been a consistent underreporting of casualty figures. By the time the *Lancet* report came out, in October 2006, the killing had reached unprecedented levels. Nearly three thousand were killed that month, almost two and half times the numbers killed in the previous October.[59] The killing would persist at this level for months to come.

Sensing that savagery was achieving the necessary conditions for the caliphate, ISI launched a series of devastating attacks from the beginning of 2007. Again the Shia were the main targets. An ISI suicide bomber detonated his huge lorry bomb in the crowded outdoor market in the mainly Shia area of Sadriyah in central Baghdad. At least 135 people died.[60] In March, ISI suicide bombers killed more than a hundred Shia pilgrims in Karbala.

In the last years of Saddam's rule, the Sunni tribes of Anbar had been increasingly granted enormous privileges and powers. Sheikhs received judicial and internal security powers as well as the right to collect tax on behalf of the central government. However, many sheikhs abused their powers by seeking extra revenues through smuggling, corruption and bribes.[61] After Saddam's fall the tribes of Anbar, like most Sunnis, also felt marginalized; the occupation resulted in a huge loss of status for them and so initially some sheikhs were willing to work with Zarqawi and Abu Omar and allowed their men to live among them. The sheikhs of Anbar swiftly realized they had made a cataclysmic mistake by making an accommodation with ISI.

In his inaugural speech to a bemused world in December 2006, Abu Omar al-Baghdadi claimed support for his Islamic State from seventy percent of Anbar tribes, who he stated had made an 'alliance' with the jihadis. This was, according to Abu Omar, 'the surest fruit and the greatest harvest', and he proclaimed, 'The Shari'ah is beginning to be implemented in most of the areas of that blessed state and by demand of our people themselves. We have appointed jurists to arbitrate disputes and settle feuds...we have also appointed workers to gather *zakat* [taxes] and alms in most areas of the Islamic State.'[62]

As ever, the jihadis liked to portray their regime as a model of Islamic rule guided by Sharia and beloved by the people they ruled, and as ever the reality was horribly different. In fact, it was the usual highly sinister and dysfunctional tyranny where they were allowed to plunder and butcher whoever they wanted. Abu Omar exerted a terrifying authority over the tribes and dealt viciously with any opposition. Increasingly, the tribes found the jihadis, often foreign fighters, intolerant and cruel, as well as being bad for business.

David Kilcullen was chief strategic adviser on counter-insurgency to the US state department at this time and would later work with the Anbari tribes in the fight against ISI. He told me, 'There were many, many examples of al-Qaeda [ISI] basically enforcing this incredibly brutal set of requirements on the community. It was also business, because they were also muscling in on a bunch of the illicit smuggling deals that the tribes were doing and that was putting the tribes out of business.'[63]

It was in Anbar, the Sunni heartlands at the supposed heart of the promised caliphate, where Zarqawi and Abu Omar committed some of their most atrocious crimes as they began to build their bloody empire. It was in Anbar where at last people would rise up against the jihadis and help drive them to the edge of extinction.

7
Wake-up call

2006–2010

Abu Musab al-Zarqawi and Abu Omar al-Baghdadi imposed their will on the Sunni tribes of Anbar through a combination of forced marriages, targeted assassination and acts of unspeakable barbarism. Four times the tribes rose up against them and four times they were crushed. It would take a fifth revolt in tandem with a determined military campaign by US troops to virtually eradicate Islamic State of Iraq.

Before terrorizing the population of Anbar, Zarqawi and Abu Omar had deliberately destroyed what little law and order remained there by attacking and eliminating the police in the areas under their control. Policemen were threatened with death unless they resigned and joined them. Those who refused were hunted down and killed. During its campaign to subjugate Anbar, ISI detonated a petrol tanker outside a police station, killing or burning everybody inside. The jihadis heard that one man who had survived with severe burns was being treated at home because his family were too afraid to take him to the local hospital, which the jihadis controlled. Abu Omar's men came for the man, tied rocks to his legs and threw him in the river Euphrates.[1]

Abu Omar's fighters forced families to provide them with food and shelter and imposed their extremely restricted version of Islam on their hosts. People were banned from smoking or drinking and in some areas, according to one report, the jihadis prohibited the sale of cucumbers and tomatoes together in a single purchase in case the combination resembled a man's sexual organs.[2]

They also robbed banks and before long they brought economic and social disaster as well as terror to Anbar. In the provincial capital, Ramadi, ISI issued fatwas closing factories, schools and universities. The government was no longer paying salaries; even employees of those banks that had not been robbed were not getting paid.[3]

It was all very similar to the regime imposed in Iraqi Kurdistan by Zarqawi and the Ansar al-Islam group back in 2002[4] and that imposed more than a decade later by Islamic State within its caliphate. The Sunni tribes quickly grew to hate Zarqawi and his fighters. Finally, in the spring of 2005, all-out fighting broke out around the Anbari city of Qaim on the Syrian border. The Albu Mahal tribe, based around Qaim, deeply resented the jihadis' attempt to take over their lucrative smuggling trade[5] and the terror they used to subjugate people in those territories. 'It was a disaster when al-Qaeda entered our country, killing and executing Iraqis,' the Albu Mahal's principal, Sheikh Sabah al-Aziz, said later. 'Whatever the Tatars did against humanity, al-Qaeda did it worse, worse than anyone that you can think of.'[6] In one incident, ISI publicly beheaded four members of the Salman tribe from Qaim but would not let the families collect the corpses. Finally, after ten days, the jihadis relented but not before sabotaging the bodies with TNT. When the relatives arrived at dawn to collect the badly decomposing bodies, ISI detonated the explosives, killing another eight people and injuring many others.[7]

Serious trouble for Zarqawi and his successors began in Anbar when he tried to assert control over the tribal sheikhs by insisting their daughters marry jihadis. In one case a sheikh refused to marry off his daughters to them and so he was killed. The sheikh's people rose up against Zarqawi and this time he reacted in a spectacularly gruesome way: his men abducted the young son of a prominent sheikh, butchered him, cooked the body and served it to his father.

Dr David Kilcullen heard the story when he was in Iraq as the chief strategist on counter-insurgency for the US state department. He told me:

> One of the stories circulating about this particular incident was that basically they had invited him [the sheikh] to a meal; they took his twelve- or thirteen-year-old son away and brought him baked him in a pot and then fed the dead child to the father...It may sound far fetched but it doesn't mean they didn't do it. They crucified kids in Raqqa; there's plenty of good photographic evidence of that.[8]

The child-cooking story may sound implausible, almost like an urban myth, even though Zarqawi and his successors have killed many thousands of children since 2003 and have often actively targeted them. As Kilcullen said, there is overwhelming evidence that Islamic State crucified and even beheaded children in the territories under its control.[9] Kilcullen's story is not without precedent, however. Weeks after he told it to me, the *Sun*, the UK tabloid newspaper, reported claims by a British man called Yasir Abdulla who took part in the fight against Islamic State. He claimed to have met a Kurdish woman whose son was captured by the jihadis in Mosul in northern Iraq, and subsequently murdered and chopped up. They served up the victim's remains with rice to the unsuspecting mother and she apparently consumed some of it unknowingly.[10]

I also tracked down evidence in two contemporaneous reports

of another horrendous episode during ISI's terrifying assault on Christian neighbourhoods in Baghdad, which reached the height of its ferocity during 2006, including the bombing of twelve churches and the murder of dozens of priests and children.[11] In October 2006, a toddler was abducted and a ransom demanded. The parents, Assyrian Christians, could not and would not pay the ransom. Eventually, the child was returned to them, beheaded, roasted and served on a mound of rice.[12]

David Kilcullen said, 'I also heard about the practices of killing children and then dropping the bodies off in front of the parents and doing it in a way that was extraordinarily gruesome. One of the things they would do was to cut the top off the kid's skull and put an electric drill into the brain. It was very clear from some of the injuries you saw that people had been tortured very horribly before they were killed.'[13]

Following the gruesome child murder, the Albu Mahal tribe formed the Hamza Battalion to fight the jihadis. They were supported by the Albu Nimr tribe but even with the backing of US marines, the Hamza Battalion failed to defeat Zarqawi. Furthermore the predominantly Shia government was hostile to the Hamza forces of the Abu Mahal tribe, declaring that such vigilantes had no place in Iraq. By September 2005, the Hamza brigade was overwhelmed but a further military assault by the US managed to push Zarqawi's forces off. US marines and Iraqi army personnel stayed behind to provide security, but three other uprisings against the jihadis elsewhere were brutally crushed.

Zarqawi and co. noticed that the sheikhs were beginning to cooperate with the US and therefore began to assassinate them, or as an internal AQI note revealed at the time, 'to cut the heads of Sheikhs of infidelity'.[14] With money from its extortion rackets and the revenue from its smuggling operations, AQI also had the financial resources it needed to control the sheikhs and Anbar.

It took an illiterate and charismatic sheikh to start the fightback in earnest. Sheikh Sattar al-Rishawi of the small Albu Risha tribe was an unabashed smuggler and highway robber, and he began fighting with AQI when it killed his father and two of his brothers[15] and moved in on his own illicit businesses. Rishawi lacked the strength to see off the jihadis so he formed an alliance with other tribes including the Albu Nimr to form the Anbar Salvation Council. This would become known as 'the Awakening'.

David Kilcullen, who played a key role in rewriting the US military textbook on counter-insurgency, thought the tribes had concluded they had to act against ISI before it was too late. He said:

> The tribes were brave but they were also desperate. It was the bravery of desperation. They realized that they didn't have a lot of other choices and that they were going to be slaughtered otherwise. Al-Qaeda [ISI] made themselves more of an enemy to northern Anbar than the coalition. That was their greatest strategic failure – that people saw them as more threatening and were willing to turn against them.[16]

The beginning of the Awakening coincided with the Americans' increasing desperation over the situation in Iraq. The stark intelligence assessment in 2006 by Marine Colonel Peter Devlin had revealed the extent of ISI's dominance of large areas of Anbar.[17] 'If anything the consequences of defeat in Iraq would be worse than in Vietnam,' President George W. Bush wrote about this time in office. 'We would leave al-Qaeda with a safe haven in a country with vast oil reserves.'[18] By the end of 2006, the war had cost the US $400 billion, and rising, as well as the lives of 2,900 Americans. A final bill of $2 trillion looked probable.[19]

The Americans had been agonizing for months during 2006

about how to deal with the bloody quagmire that was Iraq. In the wake of the Samarra bombing, the US Congress asked two former public officials, James Baker and Lee Hamilton, to head an inquiry into the chaos and come up with a plan to resolve it; the inquiry known as the Iraq Study Group reported back in December 2006. The main conundrum that needed solving was troop numbers. The group's report described Iraq's situation as 'grave and deteriorating' and concluded there were not enough US soldiers to stop the violence.[20] However, it recommended that no additional troops should be sent and urged the Bush administration to start withdrawing combat troops by early 2008.[21] In presenting the report, Hamilton, one of its principal authors, said, 'No course of action is guaranteed to stop a slide into chaos.'[22]

In January 2007, President George W. Bush rejected the report's recommendation on troop numbers and instead decided on an opposite strategy, a 'surge' of 21,000 additional troops that would take the war to ISI in Anbar and anywhere else it considered was part of its caliphate in Iraq. 'A struggle that will determine the direction of the global war on terror' is how Bush put it at the time.[23]

Kilcullen said it was Bush's realization that he faced a humiliating defeat at the hands of ISI that changed everything, followed quickly by the replacement of his controversial defense secretary, Donald Rumsfeld. He said, 'We were struggling to find our way; Bush was disengaged. It was when he fired Rumsfeld and took the management of the war into his own hands, and issued the plan for the Surge and gave that speech on 10 January 2007 when he laid out the plan – that's when things started to turn around.'[24]

Awake and surge

The Americans had started to support the Awakening revolt against ISI before the arrival of the extra Surge troops. Eventually, there would be nearly 29,000 extra troops – some five brigades in all. They provided security for the Awakening sheikhs' meetings and provided military support for the first battle with ISI in November 2006.

It would not take long before Abu Omar and his jihadists provoked the Awakening to begin in earnest. On 25 November 2006, ISI sent fighters to kill a particularly uncooperative sheikh – Jassim Suwaydawi of the Albu Soda tribe – in the Sufiyah district of the Anbari provincial capital, Ramadi. Accompanied by sixteen members of his family and the US infantry, the sheikh managed to fight off ISI and kill sixty-three terrorists. Furious, ISI turned against the local community, killing men, women and children. The US responded with artillery and support and eventually a defeated ISI retired hurt. Afterwards, for good measure, ISI abducted two of the victorious sheikh's sisters, tethered them to the back of a car and dragged them to their deaths.[25] Within two months every tribe in eastern Ramadi had risen up against ISI and Abu Omar al-Baghdadi,[26] and the uprising spread to other parts of Anbar through the first half of 2007.

I interviewed Peter R. Mansoor, one of the architects of the Surge. A historian and a soldier, Mansoor had originally opposed the war but had nevertheless served with distinction as brigade tank commander in Iraq for two years following the invasion. A colonel, he would return to Iraq in 2007 as the right-hand man, the executive officer, to the brilliant four-star general David Petraeus, who would lead the Surge. Mansoor also played a key role in the strategy to beat Abu Omar and ISI.

In late 2006, Mansoor had been a leading player in a specially convened conclave of senior colonels that had been tasked by the US joint chiefs of staff with finding a way to beat ISI. The so-called 'council of colonels' concluded that more troops were needed and that more Sunnis had to be brought into the political process and, crucially, into the security forces.[27] Mansoor argued that the Awakening was struggling and was going nowhere without the support of extra US troops promised in the Surge, adding:

> The Awakening really began in late summer of 2006 but it was really confined to Ramadi and it hadn't even taken over all of Ramadi when the Surge began.
>
> I scratch my head at the folks who say, 'Well the Surge didn't do anything because the Awakening did everything.' They don't see how the two intertwined. Without the support of General Petraeus the Awakening stays in Ramadi. He put his full weight behind the Awakening and that's when commanders reached out and tried to find sheikhs they could make deals with and the Awakening then had legs to grow and expand dramatically. The two were synergetic in their effects.[28]

General Petraeus sensed something extraordinary was happening and he was determined to take advantage and back it to the hilt with military support and money. He soon created reconciliation teams to seek out tribal leaders and recruit their tribesmen into armed neighbourhood watch organizations eventually called Sons of Iraq.[29] Petraeus's plan was to eventually incorporate the Sunni volunteers into the Iraqi police force. He would pay them from the US military's cash fund.[30] As a senior adviser to Petraeus in Iraq, David Kilcullen too had strongly advocated the strategy of working with the Awakening:

These sheikhs in Anbar weren't Jeffersonian democrats; a lot of these guys were basically gangsters who were used to things being a certain way and were not used to coming under state authority and to them it was actually quite a big deal to work with any government. So they saw their own community being systematically destroyed and decided the only thing to do to save the community was to ally with us, who they hated; they even hated us during the Awakening, but they saw us as the lesser of two evils.[31]

By the end of 2007, there were 73,000 Sons of Iraq on the payroll, a source of angst for senior Shia politicians running the government, who began to fear the emergence of this Sunni army.[32] The vetting process included taking fingerprints, biometric scans and photographs.[33] Tragically, as would become apparent, Shia prime minister Nouri al-Maliki, always deeply suspicious and fearful of the Awakening and the Sons of Iraq, would obtain this information later and use it against recruits to destroy the Awakening movement.

By March 2007, ISI had launched chemical warfare on the Sunni cities and towns it once terrorized at will. On 16 March, ISI suicide bombers detonated three truck bombs containing chlorine gas in Ramadi, Fallujah and Amiriyah. Surprisingly only two people died, both policemen – but around 350 people suffered from the effects of chlorine poisoning.[34] Eventually, ISI overcame the initial technical difficulties involved with chemical warfare and demonstrated its deadly new prowess with a chlorine attack on a market in the village of Abu Sayda, north of Baghdad, in which thirty-two people died.[35]

The gas attacks deeply worried the perpetrators of 9/11 and sundry other massacres back at al-Qaeda Central, as was revealed by a letter later discovered at the home of Osama bin Laden by the US. On 28 March 2007, an Egyptian, whose identity is not known, wrote a letter to a senior scholar respected by al-Qaeda, known as Brother Adnan Hafiz Sultan, expressing deep anxiety about the use of chlorine by ISI in its chemical war. At this stage, ISI was lying to bin Laden about its use. The Egyptian said further in his letter to 'Brother Adnan' that he had warned Abu Omar al-Baghdadi against the use of chlorine, saying, 'The gas could be difficult to control and might harm some people, which could tarnish our image, alienate people from us and so on.' He added with undeserved relief, 'Like we say, "it's not our business," or "we have enough problems," God help us. They [ISI] have put it on hold for now, but the best thing could be [for] you, brother "Adnan" to examine this issue with your experts.'[36]

ISI launched a ferocious chlorine attack on the very day the Egyptian wrote his letter of reassurance to the al-Qaeda leadership. This time the suicide attack was on the government centre at the heart of Fallujah. No deaths were reported but numerous Iraqi soldiers and policemen suffered from poisoning. Chlorine gas would be used repeatedly by the group. In September 2014, it was confirmed that Islamic State had gassed to death three hundred soldiers using chlorine at Saqlawiyah, north of Fallujah.[37]

A cache of ISI documents dating from this time was discovered in the northern Iraqi town of Sinjar and revealed much not only about how the group operated but also a great deal about the foreign fighters who were coming across into Iraq from neighbouring Syria. Of the 576 fighters that listed their nationality, 41% were from Saudi Arabia, with Libya as the next most represented country. Syria, Yemen and Algeria made up 19.2%.[38] The vast majority of recruits were in their twenties with some as young as sixteen.[39] ISI asked the recruits to bring money and fill in forms detailing the tasks they would undertake in Iraq. Of the 376 fighters who wanted at that stage to stipulate those tasks, some 56.4% – 212 young men – volunteered to be suicide bombers.[40] The organization's suicide battalion was known as al-Barra bin Malik, and was led by one Abu Dajana al-Ansari. The foreign Arab volunteers made up the majority of its high-turnover membership but by 2006, the real influx of Iraqi volunteers had begun.[41]

In early 2007, experts based in the US state department estimated ISI strength at around 1,000 fighters,[42] a very small number when compared to the 50,000–70,000 that Abu Bakr al-Baghdadi and Islamic State were said to command by late 2015. Despite this relatively small number of jihadis, ISI was still able to project enormous violence and terror and almost bring the US superpower to the brink of apparent defeat.

The big idea behind the Surge was for US troops to 'live among the people' to provide security and services instead of being outside the population in their big secure military bases.[43] This meant setting up more than a hundred small outposts and joint security stations, three quarters of them in the most crucial sectors of Baghdad. The capital had suffered much of the worst violence, including a five-car bomb attack in November 2006 in the huge predominantly Shia slum Sadr City that had left more than 160 dead.[44] By June 2007, the US had established sixty-eight small forts across the capital[45] and was systematically targeting areas where the violence was worst. Once a neighbourhood was secure, essential services would then be provided to the local people there. This often led to fierce fighting with ISI as well as some Shia militia determined not to cede territory to the Americans. In a raid on an ISI safe house, the Americans found important computer files and crucially a hand-drawn sketch by Abu Ayyub al-Masri, the group's military leader.[46] It revealed how he had broken Baghdad down into ISI's own specified sectors with each area under the control of a different leader. The drawing also revealed the organization's so-called support 'belts' around the Iraqi capital, providing the terrorists with sanctuary and places to make car bombs.[47]

As General Petraeus's right-hand man and executive officer, Peter Mansoor also helped to devise the strategy to take on the ISI car bombers. He said, 'The best way is to find the car bomb factories and to shut them down. As the Surge progressed, we had pretty good intelligence especially in the Baghdad belts where these cars were being produced and then injected into Baghdad. And inside Baghdad itself we would find the machine shops and so on.'[48]

Effectively expelled from Ramadi, Fallujah and most of Anbar by the spring of 2007, ISI moved the capital of its crumbling caliphate to Amiriyah,[49] the run-down, predominantly Sunni city west of Baghdad where it was already firmly entrenched. Mansoor said, 'We knew all along that the jihadists wanted a caliphate; I knew that as early as 2003 when I was there as a brigade commander. So they kept moving their capital of the caliphate around as we kept destroying their control over various areas. At one point it was Fallujah, then Ramadi and then it was Baqubah.'[50]

The Sunnis of Amiriyah were terrified of the Shia militia but many had come to despise ISI. They were sickened by the sight of elderly Christians being dragged off to their deaths and the ISI habit of dumping the booby-trapped corpses of their victims in the rubbish. Dogs were left to eat the body of a ten-year-old boy, who had been beheaded, because people were too afraid to collect him.[51]

Even Amiriyah would eventually enjoy relative calm under the protection of US troops and local recruits because by the summer of 2007 ISI was also being chased out of Baghdad and surrounding areas. The Americans took credit for this although some leading commentators would later pin the reduction in violence on the brutal campaign of ethnic cleansing of Sunni or mixed neighbourhoods by the Shia militias.[52]

Through the spring and summer of 2007, two major US Surge offensives were well under way against ISI. Operation Phantom Thunder was the largest coordinated military operation since the 2003 invasion. Led by Lieutenant General Ray Odierno, the operation took the fight to ISI in Abu Omar al-Baghdadi's so-called 'belts' around Baghdad and throughout central Iraq. The overarching objective was to prevent Abu Omar's terrorists in the provinces feeding the violence in the Iraqi capital.[53] A separate mission, Operation Arrowhead Ripper, formed part of the offensive. More than ten thousand US and Iraqi troops inflicted a decisive defeat on ISI in the group's stronghold of Baqubah in the Diyala province north of Baghdad. The troops then destroyed ISI positions north-east of Baqubah along the Diyala River valley.[54] A letter found at Osama bin Laden's house in 2011 revealed the concern of some leading jihadis about the scale of the assault on ISI. Written by an unknown Egyptian jihadi to a scholar respected by bin Laden, the note said 'the fighting against them is very fierce in every respect.' The letter addressed to 'Dear Brother Adnan', added that 'We ask God to give them strength and to deliver them and make them victorious over the ungodly and unjust.'[55]

In June 2007, Abu Omar tried to fan the sectarian flames of hatred by launching another successful bombing attack on the wrecked shrine in Samarra, this time destroying the remaining minarets. A unit of provincial policemen from the Salahadin emergency response unit, charged with guarding the shrine, were promptly arrested on suspicion of carrying out the bombing, and the US imposed a curfew to limit opportunities for further violence.[56]

The Surge also took the war to the ISI media cells to kill 'the message' as well as the men. The main job of the cells was to film attacks on coalition forces and Iraqi troops and then post the grisly scenes as propaganda on the web. The US went out of its way to smash as many of these units as possible.[57] Peter Mansoor said:

> We focused intently on destroying their capacity to produce propaganda. We targeted and killed most of their media cells, for the lack of a better term; there were about half a dozen of them. That was one of the priorities for our intelligence – to figure out who were the people who were distributing the propaganda and then deciding 'Let's go and get them'.
>
> There was also an information war fought in all the various means of distribution, including the Internet. I just can't go any further into it than that but let's just say we paid attention to all the various ways propaganda can be distributed and people can be recruited. There was a holistic campaign to win the information war.[58]

As a result, ISI's propaganda output was significantly affected. Its media arm, al-Furqan, released 111 videos in 2007; between January and September 2008, only 34 videos were released,[59] and, as became apparent, some of those were fake.

By 13 August 2007, 6,702 suspects had been detained and 1,196 terrorists had been killed. Some 382 'high value targets' had also been killed or captured.[60] ISI had been engulfed in a perfect storm of its own making. Further military offensives over the next year would almost eliminate the threat of ISI but despite this crisis, the group was still able to pull off some terror spectaculars.

On the morning of 14 August 2007, ISI suicide bombers attacked the villages of Qataniya and Adnaniya in Kurd-controlled north-western Iraq on the Syrian border. Four ISI suicide bombers used three cars and a petrol tanker packed with a total of around two tons of explosives. At least 500 people were killed and another 375 injured in the blasts, which levelled whole swathes of the two villages, leaving entire families buried under the rubble.[61] The final toll cannot be stated with certainty but it has been estimated at around 800. As of 2015, it was the second-deadliest terrorist attack in history, after 9/11.

The people in the villages were the ultimate *kuffar* as far as ISI was concerned; they were mainly Yazidis, one of the region's oldest peoples both ethnically and religiously. ISI considered Yazidis 'devil worshippers' because they believe that God has placed the world principally under the care of the 'Peacock Angel', Melek Taus, an archangel identified by ISI as 'Shaitan' or Satan because he refused to bow down to Adam. Along with the Shia and the Christians, the Yazidis were another target of the genocidal bloodlust of ISI and would remain so for 'Caliph' Abu Bakr al-Baghdadi during his murderous onslaught against them in August 2014. Abu Omar's man in the area, one Abu Muhammad al-Afri, the ISI 'emir' in the northern city of Mosul, had planned the atrocity. Within three weeks of the attack on 3 September 2007, Afri was reportedly killed in a US air strike,[62] apparent testimony to General Petraeus's growing military confidence.

ISI also stepped up its assassination campaign against the tribal leaders of the Awakening who had driven them from Anbar, the caliphate's heart. On 25 June 2007, an ISI suicide bomber managed to launch a deadly attack on the Melia Hotel located on the west bank of the river Tigris in the Baghdad district of al-Mansour where the tribal sheikhs of the Anbar Salvation Council were meeting. Twelve people died including four important Sunni sheikhs.[63] Within three months, in mid-September, ISI scored a pyrrhic victory by killing the man who started the uprising, Sheikh Abdul Sattar al-Rishawi.[64] After eleven attempts on his life, ISI finally killed Rishawi along with three of his guards on 13 September 2007 with an improvised explosive device planted near his home.[65] He was succeeded by his brother Sheikh Ahmad al-Rishawi, who said later of ISI, 'The organization concentrated on my brother, peace be upon him. They conducted twelve suicide attacks against him. The twelfth operation finally hit him exactly a year after the inception conference.'[66] The Awakening continued.

From January 2008, the US launched Operation Phantom Phoenix, aimed at destroying what was left of ISI in Iraq. Another 900 terrorists were killed and 2,500 more captured.[67] Increasingly ISI seeped northwards into Iraq's second city, Mosul, and managed to survive the onslaught over the following years. The success of both the Surge and the Awakening told in the diminishing civilian death tolls. In the first half of 2007, around 2,500 to 3,000 were being killed each month in Iraq; by 2010, the numbers were around a tenth of that.[68] Although encouraging, the figures showed ISI was still killing; it had not quite been finished off.

On 1 February 2008, ISI sent two women with Down's syndrome they had abducted earlier into Baghdad's popular al-Ghazl pet market, strapped into suicide vests filled with dynamite and ball bearings. At 10.20 a.m., as the market filled with families looking for a cat or a dog, or hoping to buy birdseed, ISI used a mobile phone to remotely detonate the vest worn by the first woman, killing approximately forty-six people.[69] She had been well known by the predominantly Shia people living in this part of south-east Baghdad as 'the crazy lady' who used to sell ice cream in the market.[70] Twenty minutes later, ISI detonated the second bomb strapped to the other woman with Down's syndrome. A total of ninety-one people were killed in the twin bombings and hundreds were injured. It was three years to the day since Amar Ahmed Mohammed, the nineteen-year-old with Down's syndrome, had died after Zarqawi's men had turned him into a human bomb to attack a polling station. Other children had also been used by ISI for attacks. One boy captured by Iraq police in September 2007 told how he had been forced to murder people and even how he was told to assist in the beheadings of victims by grabbing tight hold of their feet. He revealed how he had been brainwashed and repeatedly sodomized by the terrorists.[71]

The Surge had made people feel increasingly confident but the awful truth about the pet market bombing was that it reminded everyone that ISI was prepared to stoop to any tactic to inflict as much damage and kill as many people as possible, as long as it possessed the capability. It would always pose a threat, unless it was completely eradicated. The Surge and the Awakening helped to improve security dramatically in Iraq and both initiatives in tandem came tantalizingly close to destroying ISI.

The pet market bombing and the use of two defenceless women with Down's syndrome to carry it out was also a sign of how desperate the group had become. The Surge had dramatically reduced the number of foreign fighters getting into Iraq, from an estimated 80–110 each month from February to June 2007 to only 12–15 each month between January and August 2008.[72]

In September 2008, strong documentary evidence emerged of the impending demise of Islamic State of Iraq.[73] Coalition forces intercepted a series of communications between Ayman al-Zawahiri, deputy leader of al-Qaeda Central, and 'Caliph' Abu Omar al-Baghdadi and ISI military leader Abu Ayyub al-Masri. The letters were discovered on the corpse of a senior ISI leader called Abu Nizar (real name Ali Hamid Ardeny al-Essawi). Nizar died after pulling a gun at an Iraqi military checkpoint, never the wisest of moves. The letters tell a story of dismay and disarray within ISI as it became overwhelmed by both the Surge and the Awakening.

It is clear the blame game for the disaster had already begun within ISI. In the most revealing letter, there is particular criticism of Masri by an ISI Sharia 'Judge' Abu Suleiman al-Otaibi, a Saudi national and the former 'head of the legal system' of ISI. In late 2007, an embittered and disheartened Otaibi had travelled to Pakistan and Afghanistan to complain in person to the leaders of al-Qaeda Central about the parlous state of ISI and what he saw as mismanagement of the group as well as the poor and paranoid 'military' leadership of Masri. At this stage, Otaibi appears to have been using al-Qaeda as a kind of father confessor rather than an organization with any real say in the affairs of ISI. Afterwards, a letter from al-Qaeda Central dated 25 January 2008, probably written by Zawahiri and certainly with his knowledge,[74] was sent to Abu Omar and Masri detailing Otaibi's serious criticisms of incompetence, mismanagement and dishonesty at ISI.

Otaibi had made the sensational accusation that the group's dishonesty extended to the declaration of the Islamic State of Iraq itself because Masri and Abu Omar had grossly exaggerated the support they had from the Sunni tribes: 'He [Otaibi] considers the declaration of the [Islamic] State, in the manner with which it was declared and informed, to have been a mistake, and that there was exaggeration (to a degree which could be called lying) in what was said in terms of the presence and support for it among the heads of the tribes.'[75] Otaibi clearly recognized the damage the declaration had done to ISI's already deteriorating relationship with the Sunni tribes and how far it had gone in sparking the Awakening. Osama bin Laden and Zawahiri must have interpreted the declaration of ISI in October 2006 as a hugely significant slight on their authority and a usurpation of their role at the head of the global jihad. Perhaps they relished Otaibi's criticisms of the upstart organization and saw them as a rare opportunity to exert some control at long last over a deeply demoralized and errant ISI.

Masri is criticized for being 'too weak to handle this great responsibility, and…occasionally display[ing] a weakness when facing certain decisions'. Furthermore, he was 'almost absent from the details of what goes on in the battlefield' and 'totally isolated, barely seeing or seen by anyone, except a very select few'. ISI was also fraudulently using for propaganda purposes old archival fighting footage from the days of the Tawid al-Jihad, Zarqawi's first group, and passing it off as 'though it was new operations'. Otaibi said that this was 'fraud and a concealment of the truth'.[76]

The letters convinced many people that ISI had been defeated, and was in a state of 'irreparable deterioration'. An ISI operative captured in August 2008 had revealed that the group was in severe financial difficulties and that its biggest concern was 'where to sleep at night without being arrested'.[77] However, General Petraeus was not convinced ISI had been totally defeated, telling the influential Long War Journal blog in September 2008, 'No one here is doing victory dances in the end zone. [ISI] remains lethal and dangerous.'

So why didn't the US finish off ISI when it was so clearly on its last legs? According to James Franklin Jeffrey, the US Ambassador to Iraq for almost two years from August 2010, it was down to a lack of resources and commitment from Washington. Jeffrey, also a former senior White House security official between two diplomatic tours of Iraq, told me, 'In 2010 and 2011 we were doing everything we could do to finish off al-Qaeda [ISI]. That was our priority. But they were dug in around West Mosul and it was very difficult. They were using suicide bombers against us and they ran all kinds of criminal gangs there to raise funds and keep going. That was the citadel of their movement and we never had the operational freedom to take them on there.' Jeffrey, a critic of the Obama White House's long term anti-IS strategy added, 'We had plans to go after them but in the end the plans didn't materialize because we didn't keep our troops on and secondly, through misadventure as much with the US government as with the Iraqi government, the complex decisions, actions and budgets that would have allowed us to continue the counter terrorism action inside Iraq didn't happen.'[78]

Architects of the Surge also believe the job was never finished. ISI had been pushed to the edge of oblivion but not into it. Peter Mansoor, who left the army shortly after the Surge, said, 'If you don't get rid of all the cancer cells and if the environment is such that it is conducive to the cells then multiplying, in other words you stop the chemotherapy, then the cancer can come back, and that is an excellent parallel to what's happened with ISIS.'[79]

8
Savagery under new management – the rise of Abu Bakr al-Baghdadi

1971–2010

The Iraqi prime minister, Nouri al-Maliki, finally put an end to the increasingly tiresome speculation over the existence of Abu Omar al-Baghdadi by producing a photograph of his bloodied corpse at a press conference on 18 April 2010. For good measure Maliki produced a similar photograph of Islamic State of Iraq's 'military commander', Abu Ayyub al-Masri.

As with Zarqawi back in 2006, the pair had been betrayed from within. On 11 March 2010, acting on a tip from the US, Iraqi troops at a checkpoint arrested Manaf al-Rahim al-Rawi, the ISI 'emir' for Baghdad. Rawi was wanted for the assassination of an Iraqi MP as well as the coordinated bombings of the ministries of foreign affairs and finance and several Baghdad hotels during August 2009. The attacks killed more than a hundred people and injured another 565.[1] Rawi was one of the few to enjoy direct access to Abu Omar. The arrest was not announced so as to avoid alerting ISI to the capture of a potentially dangerous informant, and Rawi evidently cooperated in his interrogation.[2] He would later hang for his crimes.

Acting on Rawi's information, Iraqi intelligence managed to get a listening device and GPS location tracker delivered to Abu Omar's safe house in a flower box.[3]

The gadgets proved that Abu Omar and Masri were together in the safe house, which was located in the Tharthar area of Iraq around six miles south-west of Saddam Hussein's home town of Tikrit and seventy or so miles north of Baghdad. On 18 April 2010, Iraqi and US commandos surrounded the house and then advanced on it from all sides. A huge blast suddenly reverberated throughout the whole house. Trapped and realizing that all was lost, both Abu Omar and Masri detonated their suicide belts without even saying goodbye to their families.[4] Their wrecked corpses were photographed and their widows and children were captured and jailed. Both widows were convicted of participation in their husband's crimes. As detailed in Chapter 6, Jassem, Abu Omar's wife, was jailed for life[5] while Masri's, Hussein, was hanged.[6]

The death of the two ISI leaders was a significant coup in its own right but it also meant that most of the organization's remaining leadership could now be rolled up. Over the following days, based on intelligence from Rawi and computer files and documents seized from the safe house, other key ISI members were killed or captured. Ahmad al-Ubaydi, a senior ISI commander for three northern Iraqi provinces, was killed on 20 April. Two other leaders were killed during a raid in Mosul and the ISI military leader for Anbar, Mahmoud Suleiman, was arrested.[7]

A confidential US security assessment on 29 June 2010 said:

Over the last 90 days, Iraqi and US forces have eliminated more than 80 percent of the Islamic State of Iraq's (ISI's) top leadership…these personnel losses are compounded by the fact that that the al-Qaeda-inspired jihadist group has been struggling financially and is reportedly having problems getting foreign fighters into the country.

These setbacks will invariably complicate the ISI's efforts to continue its campaign. While it is unlikely that the ISI's propensity for violent attacks will wane, the group's diminished leadership, operational capacity and logistics infrastructure make the militant organization's future seem bleak.[8]

The US had become increasingly contemptuous of the threat posed by the ISI leadership, as the state department demonstrated by reducing the initial \$5 million bounty offered for Masri first to \$1 million and then to a mere \$100,000.[9] Back in June 2008, the US military said dismissively of Masri, 'The current assessment, based on a number of factors, shows that he is not as an effective leader of al-Qaeda in Iraq as he was last year.'[10]

David Kilcullen, the former US state department chief strategist on counter-insurgency, believes that the US and Iraqi military became dangerously complacent about their apparent victory over ISI. He said:

By 2010, we had gotten Islamic State of Iraq down to about five percent of their strength and only two or three percent of their activity, and we had a workable truce going with the Sunni and we had a pretty decent set of technically capable people in the police and the military and we were starting with a more effective administration but it was nowhere close to done.

Like his former colleague Peter Mansoor, Kilcullen has a mixed metaphor for what this meant: 'I liken it to that we took the first few days of our antibiotics and then we stopped taking them. You know what happens if you do that, you get the drug-resistant bacteria that come bouncing back. That's kind of what ISIS is; it's the drug resistant strain of al-Qaeda in Iraq [Islamic State of Iraq] that survived the Surge and was then allowed to reboot.'[11]

It is hard to think of a better description for the resilience of the ferocious almost demonic figure who would take the helm of the shattered Islamic State of Iraq following the liquidation of most of its leadership. On 16 May 2010, ISI announced that its new leader would be Abu Bakr al-Qurayshi al-Husseini al-Baghdadi. The new 'military leader' was announced as Nasser al-Din Allah Abu Suleiman. US security experts were initially baffled by the announcement of the new leadership. 'Any idea who any of these guys are?' asked a baffled analyst with the private intelligence company Stratfor. 'They are likely *nom de guerres* [*sic*] but are they associated with anyone we know?'[12]

Back at his hideout in the Pakistani town of Abbottabad, Osama bin Laden was just as curious about the new appointments, over which he clearly had no influence. In a letter later recovered by US Navy SEALS from his house, bin Laden wrote:

It would be good for you to provide us with detailed information about our brother Abu Bakr al-Baghdadi, who has been appointed as a replacement for our brother Abu 'Umar al-Baghdadi, Allah have mercy on his soul.

It would be better for you to ask among several sources among our brothers there, whom you trust, about them so the matter becomes clear to us.[13]

Within a year, the Iraqis claimed to have killed Suleiman [14] in the town of Hit west of Baghdad. Certainly very little has been heard of him since, although in November 2014 he was rumoured to be still alive and occupying a senior position within Islamic State. Suleiman seems to have embraced obscurity if he still lives. Baghdadi, on the other hand, would not possess the undoubted charisma of Osama bin Laden but he would far surpass the al-Qaeda leader both in power and number of innocent victims. The new ISI 'emir' would take his group from the point of extinction to becoming one of the deadliest terrorist organizations of the early twenty-first century. Through mass murder and genocide, he would turn the old jihadi dream of a caliphate into reality. Others who had to fight ISI and recognized the name of Abu Bakr al-Baghdadi, such as Awakening leader Sheikh Jassim al-Dulaimi, knew immediately 'the post of caliph' had been given to 'the most brutal individual and the most aggressive on the issuing of fatwas; he doesn't refrain from doing anything'.[15]

The quiet man of Tobchi

Investigating an enigma like Abu Bakr al-Baghdadi is rather like grappling with fog. At the beginning of 2015, again it was not clear even if the 'caliph' of Islamic State was still alive or dead. In November 2014, Baghdadi was 'confirmed' injured in a US-led coalition air strike,[16] but this was never confirmed and was almost certainly inaccurate. In April 2015, it was again reported that Baghdadi had been badly injured and possibly crippled for life in a separate air strike, possibly carried out on 18 March.[17] This report by the *Guardian* newspaper felt substantially more credible, not least because news leaked out that Islamic State had appointed an 'acting emir', Abu Alaa al-Afri, to fulfil many of the 'caliph's' duties.[18] So alive or dead, Baghdadi is, or was, a mystery.

Professor Fawaz Gerges, a leading Middle East scholar based at the London School of Economics, told me, 'There is a great deal that we don't know about Abu Bakr al-Baghdadi; we need to tell people is that what we do not know is more important than what we know.'[19] Baghdadi had been proclaimed 'caliph' of an Islamic empire that he hoped would control much of the earth's surface and yet he had not submitted so much as a curriculum vitae for the inspection of his billions of potential subjects. For some time, it was said he even wore a mask while addressing his commanders, earning him the title 'the Invisible Sheikh'.[20] That is what helped make his sudden appearance in Mosul in July 2014 at the first Friday prayer service of Ramadan so dramatic. However, neither before nor since his speech has he made any effort to help the outside world understand him or his motives. He seemed content to allow people to judge him by his conquests and many murders.

Gradually, pieces of the Abu Bakr al-Baghdadi jigsaw are falling into place. More information is emerging from a variety of sources, including one intriguing source, apparently close to the leadership of IS, or close enough to observe its machinations: the source known only as 'Wikibaghdady'. US intelligence officials believe Wikibaghdady to be a senior Islamic State leader, possibly even a member of its governing *shura* council – such is the credibility of his information.[21]

Baghdadi's *nom de guerre* already gave a few clues about the man. 'Abu Bakr' was the name of the first Sunni caliph to succeed the Prophet Muhammad back in 632. *Abu* is Arabic for 'father', so he presumably had children. In fact, he was known to have six by two wives. Probably most important, Baghdadi also claimed to be 'al-Qurayshi', claiming descent from the Prophet's tribe, as did Abu Omar before him.[22] Many Islamic scholars consider this an essential requirement to become caliph and it is clear that Baghdadi and ISI believed the qualification to be equally important at the time. Abu Bakr's first military leader, Abu Suleiman, also claimed to be 'al-Qurayshi', presumably meaning that the organization would still have a caliph in waiting should one or the other of them be killed or captured. The *nom de guerre* 'al-Baghdadi' suggests that Abu Bakr was from Baghdad, but he was not.

Abu Bakr's real name and its variations also tell us much about him. His first identity card, unearthed later by German journalists, revealed his real name to be Ibrahim Awad Ibrahim al-Badri, showing that he is from the Albu Badri tribe, which he later claimed to be descended from the Qurayshi and therefore the Prophet Muhammad.[23] He would also later add 'al-Samarrai', showing he was also from the city of Samarra, home to the famous shrine attacked first by Zarqawi in 2006 and then for good measure by Abu Omar al-Baghdadi the following year. He would also be known as 'Abu Dua'. The ID card, number 234250, showed he was born on 1 July 1971 in Samarra. He was the third of four sons.

What appears to be a short semi-authorized biography of Baghdadi, apparently written by a Bahraini ideologue called Abid Humam al-Athari,[24] asserts that his father was a Sheikh Awad, a religious man, as was his grandfather, Haj Ibrahim Ali al-Badri, 'a man known of his persistence on congregational prayer'.[25] They were said to be farmers. Haj apparently lived to the age of almost ninety-five and long enough to witness the US-led occupation. The family's creed is described as 'Salafiya', meaning Baghdadi comes from a line of Salafis, which would also make sense, given that his *takfir-ism* certainly mutated from his Salafi belief. Abu Bakr attended the Ahmad bin Hanbal mosque in Samarra,[26] and may have even preached there.[27] The brief Athari hagiography said of Baghdadi, 'He is a man from a religious family. His brothers and uncles include preachers and teachers in Arabic, eloquence and logic.' Abu Bakr's mother, who is not named, is described as one of the 'notables' of the al-Badri tribe, someone who 'loves religion' and 'one of the supporters of promoting virtue and prohibiting vice'.[28]

Official education records from Samarra high school, attended by the future self-proclaimed 'caliph', have also recently revealed that Baghdadi had to retake his high-school certificate in 1991 and that he scored 481 out of 600 possible points. He scored additional points as a 'brother of a martyr' meaning that one of his brothers had probably fought and died for Saddam in either the Iraq–Iran War (1980–8) or the First Gulf War over Kuwait from late 1990 to early 1991.[29] The man whose jihadist army would later conquer huge swathes of the Middle East in just a few months was, apparently, deemed unfit for military service in the Iraqi military because he was short-sighted.[30] A photograph taken by the US military of Baghdadi in glasses emerged in 2015.

According to an investigation by Al Monitor, Baghdadi's three brothers are called Shamsi, Jomaa and Ahmad. Of the three, Jomaa is said to have been the closest to Baghdadi and is rumoured to have acted as one of his bodyguards. Shamsi and Baghdadi were said to have argued frequently about Baghdadi's decision to join the jihad. Shamsi is now said to be in an Iraqi intelligence facility.[31] Little is known of the third brother Ahmad other than that he had money problems, something people could never say of his famous brother and his wealthy terror organization.

Baghdadi's high-school grades were not apparently good enough to study any of his first three choices of law, languages and educational science at Baghdad University. There is a common misconception that Baghdadi earned bachelor's and master's degrees at Baghdad University, but it seems he attended another less prestigious institution in Baghdad called the Islamic University,[32] now known as the Iraqi University, where he studied Islamic law (Sharia), and reportedly, later, the Koran.[33] He would put his Islamic knowledge to deadly effect.

By almost common consent, Baghdadi is described as quiet and unassuming. In Baghdad I met up with someone who knew him when he was a student. Dr Hisham al-Hashimi is now a writer and security analyst, as well as one of the world's leading experts on Islamic State. I asked Hashimi what Baghdadi was like as a young man. He said:

> I met him in Baghdad at an Islamic studies course. There was a bunch of us, around thirty or forty students. He was someone from a village who had come to Baghdad. He struck me as nothing special; he was shy and quiet at the same time, and he was also poor. He was just very normal, nothing special.
>
> He was religious because he was from a very religious family. His father was an imam in a mosque. He was religious but he wasn't extremist at the time.[34]

At the time, Baghdadi lived in a room adjoining the Zagal mosque in the ramshackle district of Tobchi in northern Baghdad, where both Sunni and Shia live side by side. Hashimi said he and Baghdadi studied under an imam who, like Baghdadi, came from Samarra. The imam died in 2012 but it is possible that local connections in his hometown had secured Baghdadi's berth at the Zagal mosque. This is where he was known to play regular football, for the mosque.[35] Sometimes in Tobchi, people would hear Baghdadi calling them to prayer from the mosque when he was asked to act as the muezzin.[36]

In early adulthood, Abu Bakr al-Baghdadi was a member of the Iraqi branch of the Muslim Brotherhood, the mainstream transnational Islamist organization that also wants to bring about a caliphate. The future caliph disagreed with the Brotherhood's strategy for how to bring about an Islamic empire stretching from Spain to Indonesia. Fawaz Gerges, a leading Middle East scholar based in London, said, 'On the whole, the Muslim Brotherhood basically renounced the use of force and violence in the late 1960s and early 1970s. We know that he [Baghdadi] became disgruntled. He didn't like the Muslim Brotherhood, because the Muslim Brotherhood no longer believed in the use of violence in the service of politics.'[37] Baghdadi's membership of the Muslim Brotherhood was confirmed by its highly influential spiritual leader Sheikh Yusuf al-Qaradawi, an Egyptian cleric residing in Qatar. In a TV interview in October 2014, Qaradawi, then aged eighty-eight, confirmed Baghdadi's membership, referring to the future IS leader rather grandly as 'this youngster'.[38] Qaradawi said Baghdadi had referred to himself as 'Ikhwan', the name of a Wahhabi religious militia that first appeared in Saudi Arabia in the early twentieth century.

For many people, Baghdadi's life was something of a mystery until he came to the US authorities' attention in 2004 as a terrorist suspect. The almost universally accepted narrative has Baghdadi becoming radicalized in 2004 by jihadi inmates during his incarceration in the US prison in southern Iraq, Camp Bucca. If that were the case, it would mean that he would have gone from being an angry former prison camp inmate to the head of a dangerous jihadi terrorist organization in a little more than half a decade. This theory seems unlikely and would later strike some of Baghdadi's former prison guards as absurd. It would also mean Baghdadi started his terror career at the relatively grand old age of 33, which is positively ancient in jihadi terms. Surely, he would have needed more of a track record in fighting for the jihad? There is also hardening evidence that, like so many others including Zarqawi and Bin Laden before him, Baghdadi may have started his career as a jihadist fighter in Afghanistan and may even have known Zarqawi there.

Recently, Afghan security officials have asserted confidently that Baghdadi lived with Zarqawi in the Wazir Akbar Khan district of the Afghan capital, Kabul, between 1996 and 2000.[39] This would mean Baghdadi would have been in his mid-twenties before leaving for Afghanistan, a respectable age for a jihadi starting out, but still a little on the old side. The city was then under the rule of the Taliban, and Afghan security officials have also said that Baghdadi was involved with a group of fanatically anti-Shia *takfiri* extremists called the Ishaq Group, also known as Lashkar-e-Jhangvi, or LeJ. Headed by Maulvi Ishaq, the group was active in Bagram, a small town in the north-east of Afghanistan. Founded in 1996, Lashkar-e-Jhangvi took its name from a Sunni terrorist called Haq Nawaz Jhangvi, who was killed by Shia militants in 1990. The aim of LeJ was to transform Pakistan into a Sunni state, primarily through violence.[40]

Zarqawi also appears to have had a long-standing relationship with LeJ leaders and members stretching back to his first stint in Afghanistan between 1989 and 1993.[41] He is thought to have run a training camp in Afghanistan near the Pakistani border that was hosted by the group. It is also believed that Zarqawi helped train the Pakistani jihadis carry out attacks on Shia Muslims in Punjab.[42]

People have also claimed that they saw Baghdadi playing football in Afghanistan and remembered him often playing at the Amani high school, which indeed does have its own sports field. Baghdadi is known to have enjoyed playing football in Iraq and was said to have been a good player; a former associate who played with him in Baghdad once described him as 'the Messi of our team'.[43] The Amani high school was under the control of the Afghan ministry of education, then run by Hamdullah Nomani, the Taliban education minister. He was also said to have been a friend of Baghdadi.[44]

An unnamed Taliban commander confirmed to the Afghan reporter Zeerak Fahim that he had met Baghdadi and Zarqawi together after they had been the victims of a Taliban cash sting. The Taliban leader was reported as saying:

> I met Abu Musab al-Zarqawi, Abu Bakr al-Baghdadi and their friends who came to me in connection of a problem.
>
> They gave $400 to a low-level Taliban official to buy weapons. But the Taliban neither purchased the arms nor returned their money. I told the late Zarqawi to forget about the money and [that] the Taliban official had extorted money from a number of people.[45]

What is puzzling about Baghdadi is that after the invasion he did not join up formally with Zarqawi and would not do so until early 2006. If they had been such good friends, as the Afghan sources claim, why did Baghdadi go it alone with his own group before joining forces with the Jordanian? According to his official-looking 'biography' by Abid Humam al-Athari, Baghdadi set up a smaller group of jihadis called the Jaish Ahlu al-Sunnah Wa al-Jama'ah, or Army of the Sunni People.[46] This operated in Baghdad and in and around Samarra and was described back in 2006 as a 'small and relatively unknown Islamist terror group'.[47]

Baghdadi was arrested on 4 February 2004 in Fallujah[48] at the home of Nessayif Numan Nessayif, an old student friend from his days at the Islamic University.[49] His detainee card gives his profession as 'administrative work (secretary)'. He was released a little more than ten months later on 8 December 2004. I spoke to Lieutenant Colonel Myles B. Caggins III, who is the main spokesman for detainee policy at the US department of defense. He told me:

> A lot of guys were being picked up at the time. He wasn't ever charged with anything; he was arrested in a kind of a round-up. There was no evidence, it was just a case of 'We're think you're bad, you're associating with bad people so come to us.' But there was nothing to hold him on. At the time we did not collect evidence in any kind of mature way like we do now.[50]

Baghdadi was jailed at Camp Bucca, the huge detention facility run by the US military in southern Iraq. The US defence department told me he was placed in Compound 6, which was characterized as a 'medium security Sunni compound'.[51] It was here he would meet many of the Ba'athist army officers who would help him build his Islamic State. At least nine Islamic State leaders, including Baghdadi, are known to have been in Bucca at various times during the camp's five-year existence. The list of Bucca alumni includes Abu Qasim (aka Abdullah Ahmad al-Meshadani), in charge of foreign fighters and suicide bombers; Abu Muslim al-Turkmani (aka Fadil Ahmad Abdallah Hayyali), onetime deputy to Baghdadi; Islamic State 'media sheikh' Abu Mohammed al-Adnani; and Haji Bakr (aka Samir Abd Muhammad al-Khlifawi), Baghdadi's ruthless one-time military leader and chief adviser.[52] Many people such as Hisham al-Hashimi believe that it was this experience that transformed Baghdadi into the ruthless terrorist he became. Hashimi told me, 'When he was captured in Fallujah, he was innocent; the Americans were looking for someone else. When they captured him, they humiliated him and they treated him badly. This made him full of hate for the

Americans.'[53] There are few people more knowledgeable than Hashimi when it comes to Islamic State but again, perhaps this may be a case of filling in the gaps in the absence of hard facts and real knowledge. Baghdadi may well have been humiliated in Bucca but by then he had also set up his own jihadi insurgency in the shape of the Army of the Sunni People, as well as, it is alleged, spending four years in Afghanistan in the company of Abu Musab al-Zarqawi.

Camp Bucca processed 100,000 suspected Sunni insurgents in the five years of its operation and became known as a 'terrorist' university,[54] and at one time by the US officers running the Surge as 'the most decisive place on the battleground'.[55] The US military realized it was not just housing detainees but, thanks to 24/7 brainwashing of inmates by the well-established insurgency in the camp, it was 'creating the next terrorist class'. Peter Mansoor, the senior colonel who acted as executive officer to General David Petraeus during the Surge, told me, 'We had always treated Bucca as a minimum security facility and it really enabled the extreme among them to proselytize to the not-so-extreme, and it turned it into a jihadist university. Through the Surge we tried to change that but by then a lot of the damage had already been done.'[56]

I also spoke to James Skylar Gerrond, who spent two years as a former reserve military police captain at Bucca. He described the detainees at Bucca:

> They were prisoners in the sense that the vast majority of them had not gone through any kind of trial process, so they were being held but they weren't being held because there was a judicial mechanism in place that had pronounced them guilty.
>
> The detainees themselves were largely Sunni, I would say as many as eighty to eighty-five percent. Within that group, there

was a gradation of ideological belief and different levels of radicalization.

Gerrond said the prison held a mixed bag of jihadis and ex-Ba'athist insurgents who now had the opportunity to get to know each other and plot what to do on their release. He believes inmates were radicalized in Bucca, saying:

> We [were] very mindful of the fact that a lot of these guys were motivated out of practicality. Some of the insurgent groups were well funded. They got paid to be an insurgent; this was a job for some of them. Our mechanism for capturing detainees and bringing them to Bucca was not perfect either.
>
> Some detainees were dead to rights and we knew exactly who they were. But in other cases, say if a convoy had been ambushed from a particular location maybe multiple times, then they [the US military] would go back and gather up all the military-age males and some of them were absolutely innocent. In theory these guys would have got out as they were processed through the system but the legal process was so slow.
>
> Our concern about the radicalization was primarily with regards to bringing people in who may have literally been our allies beforehand, people who supported the Americans and the invasion and our mission of bringing democracy to Iraq. Then what we do is round them up and put them in a detention facility. Our biggest concern was that we were locking up people who were not ideologically motivated before they came but would become that way thanks to some of the more radical elements inside.

Gerrond doesn't believe that to be the case with Baghdadi, adding:

The masters of savagery: Abu Musab al-Zarqawi appears in a video message, circa 2005 (above) and Abu Bakr al-Baghdadi, Islamic State's 'Caliph', addresses Muslims in Mosul, 2014 (below).

The devastation left behind by a car bombing on al-Mutanabbi Street which killed thirty-eight people, 5 March 2007. Baghdad's booksellers' district had been a place where all groups of Iraqi society were welcome.

IS gunmen massacre more than 1,500 unarmed men, most of them Shia military cadets – Tikrit, June 2014.

Shia militia recruits train to use guns in the fight against IS… even though they don't have any – Najaf, July 2014.

When they took Mosul in the summer of 2014, IS destroyed six important Shia mosques across the Nineveh province.

In a museum in Mosul, IS men destroy precious artefacts from Iraq's ancient history.

An ambulance man returns from the scene of an IS suicide bombing in Baghdad, late 2014. Around ten people died when an IS bomber attacked a Shia mosque during morning prayers.

The wheelchair salesmen of al-Sadoun Street, Baghdad, do a good trade thanks to bombings but have to import their wheelchairs through Basra because of IS.

Jordanian pilot Moaz al-Kasasbeh, moments before he was burned to death by IS in early 2015.

A boy watches the video of al-Kasasbeh being burned alive as it plays on giant screens erected by IS in Raqqa, Syria.

IS instil fear – a Christian is crucified, a gay man is thrown from a rooftop, a woman is led to where she will be stoned to death, a 'lion cub' appears to execute two Russian spies.

Two Christian boys at a refugee camp in Erbil, Iraqi Kurdistan, March 2015. Since the American-led invasion of 2003, violence has displaced over three million people in Iraq.

An Anbar sheikh at the same refugee camp in Iraqi Kurdistan, March 2015. He says even five-year-olds can fight IS.

The idea that he went into Bucca as some kind of innocent 'wrong place at the wrong time' kind of guy and then he had this complete personality change to the extent that he would be the leader of a multinational Islamic insurgency/caliphate – that is beyond belief. It is more believable to me that he came in as some kind of younger middle management kind of insurgent leader, or a local insurgent leader, who then through a series of events over the last eight to ten years rose up through the ranks and is now leading ISIS. To say we had him and let him slip through our fingers when we could not have known what he would become is just silly.[57]

After Bucca

Eventually, in December 2004, Baghdadi was released after a panel of US military officers called a combined review and release board reviewed his case. 'They looked at his record and there was nothing to hold him for,' said Lieutenant Colonel Caggins. Hisham al-Hashimi claimed that on his release from Bucca, Baghdadi lived in Syria for two years, until around 2006, working for Zarqawi, but again details about exactly what he was doing in Syria are vague. Apparently, according to US intelligence, Baghdadi was active in the Anbari town of Qaim, which is on the Syrian border, and was allegedly involved in the torture and public execution of local civilians.[58] This also sounds likely. After all, Qaim was where the Sunni sheikhs first rose up against Zarqawi in 2005 and the subsequent brutal suppression by the jihadis involved both torture and public executions, and worse.[59] Who better to put down a rebellion than the ruthless and cruel administration assistant and PhD student? Hashimi thought Baghdadi was involved in the group's propaganda during his stay in Syria. That again would make sense when you take into account the huge priority given to propaganda by Islamic State later.

It is known that Baghdadi had started his doctorate in Baghdad at some stage before his imprisonment and that he had returned to it by 2007, again it is thought at the Islamic University. Baghdadi's PhD in Islamic studies would help his advance through the ranks of his fellow jihadis. But he did not impress one of his tutors at the time, who spoke of Baghdadi following his 2014 military offensive, possibly with the benefit of hindsight. Jaysh al-Mujahideen, a Sharia expert, said of the Islamic State leader: 'He was of limited intelligence, slow to understand, pale in intuitive grasp and I had got to know him very well.'[60]

Nevertheless, in March 2007, Baghdadi submitted his doctoral thesis; it received eighty-two points out of a hundred and was marked 'very good', but the thesis itself has gone missing.[61] At the end of January 2006, Baghdadi joined his Army of the Sunni People to Zarqawi's Mujahidin Shura Council (MSC). Zarqawi had appealed grandiosely 'to all armies and brigades of Ahlu Al-Sunnah Wa Al-Jama'ah, I appeal to all of you, I appeal to all of you, I appeal to all of you, my people! Answer Allah's call for unity, consolidation of efforts, and straitening of the array.'[62]

By all accounts, Baghdadi rose quickly through the MSC, becoming a member of the organization's Majilis al-Shura Council, its main political and decision-making body. Following the declaration of the Islamic State of Iraq in October 2006, he also became 'General Supervisor of the Shari'ah Committees, putting to test his knowledge of Islamic law'.[63] He also grew close to Abu Omar al-Baghdadi, as one of only three men the ISI leader trusted as his personal couriers, and often drafted his most important messages.[64]

Baghdadi is thought to have at least two wives, Iraa Rajab al-Qaisi,[65] and Asma Fawzi Mohammed al-Kubeisi.[66] The biography penned by Abu Humam al-Athari claims that Baghdadi combined 'the calmness and leisureliness of Abu Omar al-Baghdadi and his high security sense, and took much of the cleverness and courage of Abu Ayyub al-Masri'.[67] He would easily outdo these ferocious men in the management of savagery.

In 2010, Hashimi was stunned to hear that his fellow student had risen to the top of what was left of ISI. 'I had heard he was a religious leader within the organization,' he said, 'but I was shocked to hear that he had become the leader of the organization.'[68]

The source known as 'Wikibaghdady' asserts that the former Ba'athist intelligence brigadier Haji Bakr acted as kingmaker for Baghdadi in the days following the deaths of Masri and Abu Omar. Haji Bakr quickly became Baghdadi's right-hand man and probably his most important strategist.[69] According to Wikibaghdady, 'a lot of people considered Haji Bakr to be arrogant next to Abu Bakr al-Baghdadi, who many considered to be a quiet personality.'[70] Hashimi described Haji Bakr as 'highly intelligent, firm and an excellent logistician'.[71] When the US dissolved Iraq's army and security institutions, Bakr was left 'bitter and unemployed' like so many others.[72] Bakr joined forces with Zarqawi and was eventually held in Bucca for approximately two years, from 2006 to 2008.[73] Many other Ba'athist officers would form Baghdadi's inner circle.

Wikibaghdady also claimed, 'Every person in al-Baghdadi's inner circle is 100 percent Iraqi and he doesn't accept any other nationality because he does not trust anyone.' Haji Bakr and Baghdadi drew up a hit list of rivals and other enemies to be killed, starting with twenty people; soon the list lengthened to a hundred. The pair charged another ex-officer, Abu Omar's cousin[72] and future 'security chief'[75] Abu Safwan Rifaii, with the task of carrying out the assassinations. It seems an extraordinary strategy for a group whose leadership had been all but wiped out by the US and Iraqi military, but it demonstrates the relentlessness and ruthlessness employed by ISI leaders even against their own. Baghdadi and Haji Bakr also consolidated their power by loading the ISI's governing *shura* council with their own men.

The next three years would be relatively lean killing years for the Baghdadi organization; the annual civilian death toll in Iraq fell to around 4,300, almost seven times less than in the bloody years of 2006 and 2007 and a third of the figure in the three years following the invasion of 2003.[76] However, Baghdadi would soon prove to the world how lethal he could be, and in 2011 he took the critical decision that would lead ultimately to the caliphate in 2014 – to enter the Syrian civil war. He also rebuilt ISI finances thanks to a number of extortion rackets. The fundraising included placing checkpoints on the roads and forcing lorry and truck drivers to hand over $200 a time, as well as terrifying minorities such as the Christians into handing over money. Any company boss awarded a government contract would be targeted and threatened with death unless a payment was made. The fundraising would also include one of the group's tried and tested rackets – selling oil on the black market.[77]

By October 2011, the US had recognized the danger posed by Baghdadi, and the state department posted up a $10 million reward for information leading to his whereabouts.[78] By US standards, this was a huge amount of money and clearly indicated America's growing concern about a possible resurgence by ISI. James Jeffrey, the US Ambassador to Iraq at the time, said America knew that Baghdadi was a more serious threat compared to his predecessors.[79] 'We knew all about him from 2010,' said Jeffrey. 'We knew his background that he was a Sunni and had been in Bucca. But we just couldn't find him. This guy had much better operational security [than Masri and Abu Omar al-Baghdadi]. He had learned from what had happened to his predecessors.'

Baghdad's Christians were the first victims of Baghdadi's first high profile act of terror. On 31 October 2010, Baghdadi sent about six suicide bombers to attack the heavily fortified Assyrian Chaldean Catholic church of Our Lady of Salvation, in the Karrada district of Baghdad, in yet another lethal ISI assault on Iraq's Christian minority. They struck at evening Mass and started killing worshippers immediately; one jihadi screamed, 'We will go to paradise if we kill you and you will go to hell.'[80] When Iraqi commandos stormed the church, the jihadis exploded their suicide vests. A total of fifty-eight people died, including priests and policemen.[81]

In Baghdad I went with Michael, a Christian friend, to the Our Lady of Salvation church, which is enclosed behind concrete blast walls and swirls of barbed wire. 'The sister of a friend of mine survived the attack because she was small enough to hide inside the piano,' Michael said. 'Another of my friends lost her sister-in-law and all their kids. It was [a] very big tragedy for us Christians.' Michael said the attack caused an exodus of Christians from Iraq. 'People were grabbing any chance of getting out of this country,' he said. 'Since the attack I know personally of at least seven or eight families who have left.

'We used to live in peaceful coexistence. We used to have midnight Masses and to go to parties during our festivals; now it's different. All that became impossible.'[82]

The attack even disgusted leading members of al-Qaeda. A letter written shortly afterwards, probably in January 2011, was found at Osama bin Laden's house referring to the attack. Thought to have been written by the US al-Qaeda spokesman Adam Ghadan,[83] who had been preparing to write to Christians inviting them to 'join Islam', the letter demanded that al-Qaeda should 'declare its disapproval of these and other actions that the organization so-called the Islamic State of Iraq is carrying [out].' Ghadan added revealingly:

I believe sooner or later – hopefully sooner – it is necessary that al-Qaeda publicly announces that it severs its organizational ties with the Islamic State of Iraq, and to make it known that the relationship between its leadership and that of the State [ISI] have [sic] not existed for several years, and that the decision to declare a state was taken without consultation with the leadership and this innovation led to divisions among jihadis and their supporters inside and outside Iraq.[84]

Not long afterwards, on 2 May 2011, the letter would be among the treasure trove of documents seized by US Navy SEALS at Abbottabad after they had killed bin Laden. In a statement issued a week after the Abbottabad mission, Baghdadi warned there would be revenge attacks for bin Laden's death. 'I swear by God, blood for blood and destruction for destruction,' he said.[85] In August 2011, Baghdadi issued a further statement promising a hundred terror attacks in retaliation for the deaths of bin Laden, Abu Omar al-Baghdadi and Masri. 'It will be diversified,' he promised, 'between storming and martyrdom operations, in addition to devices, silencers, and snipers in all the cities, villages and provinces.'[86] Ten days later a suicide bomber hid his bomb in a fake splint and entered the Umm al-Qura mosque in western Baghdad. The explosion killed twenty-eight people including the important Sunni politician Khalid al-Fahdawi.[87] At least sixty-nine Iraqis died in a string of bomb attacks in Baghdad on 22 December 2011.[88]

Increasingly, these ISI spectaculars were finding it harder to lead the news bulletins. During 2011, the world had been focused on the tumult of the Arab Spring. Many people had long tired of hearing about the endless violence in Iraq. Baghdadi would also turn his deadly attention to the Arab Spring and the tragedy unfolding across the border in Syria. In mid-2011, almost on a hunch, the ISI leader decided to send a tiny group of jihadis, eight in total,[89] across the border to fight in the increasingly ferocious civil war. The decision would have huge ramifications for the future of the region and the world. It led to the rebirth of ISI, a war with al-Qaeda and ultimately to the creation of the caliphate.

9
Shia folly
2006–2012

Driving anywhere in Baghdad is mind-numbingly slow and fraught with danger. There is the ever-present risk of kidnapping or being caught up in a bombing. As a Westerner, you need to take security men with you wherever you go and you often have to travel in armoured vehicles for even the simplest of trips outside. There are so many neighbourhoods you cannot go to because of the security risk, and from 2014 onwards, there was always the chance of running into Islamic State militants if you did manage to get out of the capital. The traffic often turns into a turgid metallic sludge at the city's many checkpoints, made even worse by the heat and pollution and the realization that if IS bombers decided to strike your particular military post, you would not stand a chance.

At the checkpoints you will often see bored-looking soldiers and police using bomb detectors, walking up and down the side of your car holding this curious black gadget like a gun; but instead of a muzzle, it has some kind of weird wand-like antenna waggling from side to side. As the policemen walk alongside you they point the thing towards the ground and read the meter on the back of the device. Sadly, though, the gadgets are utterly useless; the real purpose of the detectors was not to save lives but to make money – and lots of it – for the crooks who sold them and the crooks who bought them.

It has been established beyond any doubt that all the bomb detectors are fake and that they were sold to Iraq by unscrupulous fraudsters who have been convicted and jailed for their part in a crime of astounding greed and breathtaking cynicism. Incredibly, though, the Iraqi interior ministry still insisted on using them for years afterwards. On a trip to Baghdad in late 2014, I raised the issue with Brigadier General Saad Maan, the ministry's main spokesman and the same man who assured the world a few months earlier that it was 'indisputably not' Abu Bakr al-Baghdadi at the mosque in Mosul when it was.[1] The interview took on a somewhat surreal quality.

Andrew Hosken: Why are you still using this fraudulent piece of kit?

Brigadier General Saad Maan: Actually we do not depend on this ADE [Advanced Detection Equipment] detector 100 per cent; we have dogs and hand searches, as well as X-ray vehicles, and in the coming weeks we have some contracts with some companies which specialize in this technology. By the end of the year we will have this new equipment, which will work on the street. Then we will replace these detectors.

AH: Why are you using the detectors at all if they don't work?

SM: Really, frankly, it works let's say thirty to forty percent because—

AH: But there's nothing in them. There is no technology within them.

SM: No, really, I'm talking practically. If you take the recent attack on al Kadhimiya [Baghdad], all of the attacks were on the first security filters at al-Kadhimiya. All the time the victims are the people who are using the detectors...This process will force the suicide bomber to detonate his car on the first filter [of security] and this means logically that this filter is working. And we capture so many vehicles by the using of this detector. I'm not saying it's ideal and yes, there has been some kind of corruption involved with this at least, but we are practical and we have this instrument right now; we must use it for at least for this while. When we can replace it with a new instrument – we will.[2]

General Maan is widely considered to be an intelligent and decent guy with an impossible job to do in the circumstances but I wondered how on earth he could possibly believe that the fake detectors worked because the very sight of them forced the suicide bomber to panic and detonate his device, obliterating the first line of defence but hopefully no one else. Did he seriously believe that the news of the fake detectors had yet to reach Baghdadi and his suicide bombers?

As a senior official of Iraq's troubled interior ministry General Maan knows better than most that the detectors, although useless at detecting bombs, have at least exposed some dark corners of Iraqi public life and government. Corruption combined with sectarianism, Shia versus Sunni, helped create the perfect conditions for Abu Bakr al-Baghdadi; this toxic mix proved to be the decisive factor in his success of 2014 and, in particular, his shocking capture of Iraq's second-biggest city, Mosul, in June of that year. Corruption and sectarianism together have proven to be the foundation stones of his caliphate.

Caroline Hawley, the former BBC Baghdad correspondent, and her producer colleague Meirion Jones, helped expose the scandal. Hawley had long concluded that Iraq was riddled with corruption. She said:

At one point we were on the tarmac at Baghdad airport for a last security check; you had to check your bags on the tarmac before they went into the hold and even then we had to pay a bribe to someone to get our bags onto the plane. I just thought the corruption is absolutely everywhere and at every level. I remember thinking, 'How could people believe in a national project?' It was so corrosive and it definitely played a part in why the Iraqi army ended up in the state it was.[3]

Hawley and Jones focused on the so-called 'Advanced Detection Equipment', the 'ADE-651 detector' produced by a British conman called James McCormick, based in Somerset. Incredibly, this former police officer, with no experience in either electronics or electrical engineering, managed to sell more than six thousand of his useless fake gadgets[4] for up to an eye-watering $40,000 apiece to the Iraqi government, a total of $85 million.[5] Hawley added:

The idea came from the so-called 'Amazing Golf Ball Finder'. You can look it up on Amazon and it doesn't even get a good review as a golf ball finder! But for his first ones, McCormick just got hold of these things and put his own labels on them. The ADE-651 was supposed to be the top-of-the-range model with all the bells and whistles, with the card reader, and that was the one he sold in such quantities. Somehow we got hold of someone in one of the companies who gave us the card that you slot into the ADE-651 and that will magically track your substance or explosive material. We had it taken apart by experts and there was nothing in it except for a cheap anti-theft tag that would have cost a couple of pence.

When it went to trial McCormick kept claiming that we had prejudiced the jury by claiming that this thing had cost lives. He could never have done what he did had Iraq not been so astonishingly corrupt.[6]

Following Hawley's reports, the UK government swiftly banned the export of the gadgets and McCormick was arrested. At his criminal trial in London, it was revealed that McCormick had indeed based the gadgets on novelty golf ball detectors from the US, which he had bought for less than $20 each. No one will ever know how many Iraqi lives were destroyed by McCormick as a result of what the trial judge Mr Justice Hone had described as a 'callous confidence trick' that had 'promoted a false sense of security and in all probability materially contributed to causing death and injury to innocent individuals'. McCormick was jailed for ten years.[7]

The Iraqi general who bought the batch of ADE-651s was the unfortunately named Jihad al-Jabiri, a senior official with the Iraqi interior ministry, which controls the police. Jabiri was arrested in February 2011,[8] and the following year was jailed for four and a half years. He was far from being an exception. In 2005, for example, in an unrelated matter, Iraq issued arrest warrants for the then defence minister, Hazim al-Shaalan, and twenty-six other government officials on charges of embezzling a total of $1 billion.[9] Investigators described the corruption in the ministry of defence as 'staggering'.[10] In one case they discovered that the ministry had been billed around $1 million for military uniforms that had actually been a gift from a donor country.[11] Shaalan denied the allegations but took the precaution of leaving Iraq and was convicted in 2007 in absentia.

Iraq is one of the most corrupt nations on earth; in fact, according to the experts at the anti-corruption organization Transparency International, only five countries suffer more from the scourge of bribery, fraud and wholesale plundering of the public sector.[12] Corruption seeps into every aspect of Iraqi public life but most obviously and most dangerously into the army and police. Over the years, it has hollowed out Iraq, destroyed its army and left it horribly vulnerable to Abu Bakr al-Baghdadi and his jihadis. It has also had a deadly effect on the deeply troubled relations between the Sunni minority and Shia majority.

Corruption in the army went hand in hand with sectarian cronyism that saw predominantly Shia senior politicians hand out important military jobs to fellow Shias regardless of merit. Iraq has been a country where military positions have been for sale. A highly critical report by respected US-based experts in December 2013 complained that the army and police suffered from 'political interference in command positions, the sale of other positions at every level and other forms of corruption'.[13] A further report stated that corruption was endemic 'throughout much of the Iraq military and police with appointments and promotions being openly sold or awarded on the basis of nepotism, ethnic and sectarian ties, and political influence'.[14] Meanwhile, according to the United Nations, twenty percent of Iraqis were unemployed and twenty-three percent lived in 'absolute poverty'.[15]

Bribes of $5,000 were demanded for a place at the Officer Training Academy; the price of a promotion to general was $30,000.[16] At one point in 2008, the government's overwhelmed anti-corruption unit was dealing with 736 cases of corruption just involving the interior ministry.[17] The Iraqi government would later concede that it was paying the salaries of 50,000 soldiers who did not exist; the money was going straight into the bank accounts of the army's many corrupt officers.[18] Was it any wonder that Islamic State managed to conquer huge swathes of Iraq in 2014?

I spoke to Leah Wawro and Tobias Bock at Transparency International about their own investigations into the corruption in the Iraqi army. Wawro said:

> In a really wide range of places we keep on seeing this connection between corruption and instability: you see it in Ukraine and Nigeria. Again in Central America the links between organized crime and instability there are just enormous. The Iraqi government has been perceived by the people of Iraq to be corrupt. It doesn't do well on service delivery and the average member of the public feels so disenfranchised, and that creates a certain environment that an organization like Islamic State can thrive in.[19]

Bock said the corruption in the Iraqi army was so deep that officers were thieving off their own men and would often invent them altogether so they could harvest the salaries paid to what are often referred to as 'ghost soldiers' and 'phantom battalions'. This was one of the biggest factors in the army's defeat in Mosul in 2014. Bock continued:

> This has also been a big problem in places like Afghanistan where the soldiers' wages are paid to the senior officers instead of directly into the soldiers' bank accounts.
>
> In Iraq, the commanders were responsible for paying their own soldiers and in many cases they would either just keep the money or lie about the numbers, or even pretend the money had never reached the bank accounts of the recipients who might be from some remote part of the country. If the men actually do exist they are told by their officers 'Really sorry, but the money never came from the ministry.'[20]

The paranoia of Nouri al-Maliki

Corruption helped foment the view for many people that the state was both weak and even illegitimate. For millions of Sunnis, the feeling they were discriminated against and marginalized exacerbated this deepening resentment. This would eventually lead to protests by Sunnis that would play into the hands of Baghdadi as he prepared to build his caliphate. The one man who would ultimately be blamed for presiding over the mess was Iraq's two-term Shia prime minister Nouri al-Maliki.

Ali Khedery, the important Iraqi-American US adviser, described the events leading up to the appointment of Nouri al-Maliki as prime minister. By 2005 the Americans had tired of Prime Minister Ibrahim al-Jaafari. There had been too many mistakes and, furthermore, the terrible interior ministry scandal, in which hundreds of young Sunni men were abused and tortured, had happened on his watch.[21] Khedery said:

Ibrahim al-Jaafari was a catastrophic prime minister; he was feckless, he was indecisive, he was a poor leader. He just liked to give long incoherent speeches and sermons. The only thing he had ever done before was give religious sermons. Under Jaafari's reign we had the bunker scandal where hundreds of Sunnis were sodomized and tortured; you had the Samarra mosque incident and all the ethnic killing afterwards because Jaafari had refused to declare a curfew. I can go on. From President Bush on downwards, it was decided that Jaafari could not return as prime minister after the election in 2005.

Other leading Shia contenders for the job had been ruled out or had effectively ruled themselves out, mainly because of their extremely close links to Iran, remembered Khedery. The strong perception had grown among Sunnis that, for all intents and purposes, Iran controlled senior Shia politicians and the Shia militias, even that Iranians had been involved in the running of death squads. Khedery added:

> So basically what we were left with was Maliki and only a handful of us knew who he was. At one point I was the only one who would take his phone calls at the American embassy. I remember he used to call me early on in 2006 asking for Green Zone badges and US government-issue cell phones and other such things. Maliki struck me as an Arab nationalist type; he also struck me as less prone to formal Iranian connections and that he was decisive. Sure enough, frankly, in his first term he demonstrated that he was decisive and that he was capable of leading and that he was willing to tackle alike both Sunni and Shia entities like al-Qaeda [ISI] and Jaysh al-Mahdi [the so-called Mahdi Army, under the controversial Shia cleric Muqtada al-Sadr].[22]

Maliki had been a senior Shia opponent of Saddam and spent twenty-four years in exile dodging the Iraqi dictator's assassins before returning to Iraq following the US invasion like so many of his fellow Shia politicians. He was a senior member of the Shia Dawa party, which together with the other main Shia party, the Supreme Council for Islamic Revolution in Iraq, SCIRI, won both of the national elections held in 2005. Dawa had a violent past and was known to have carried out bombings and assassinations before the fall of Saddam. To many, Maliki's big round face expressed 'utter joylessness'. An associate of Maliki's once said, 'He never smiles, he never says thank you and I've never seen him say "I'm sorry".'[23]

As the years went by, it became clear that Maliki had been scarred by his years in exile, hunted as he had been by Saddam and the Ba'athists. The US military soon formed a low opinion of him. 'We thought that primarily Maliki was out for himself,' said Peter Mansoor, who often got to meet Maliki in the company of his own boss, General David Petraeus.

> Maliki was highly paranoid and suspicious and above all he craved power. We didn't know whether he was highly sectarian or not but we knew the people around him definitely were. So he was being advised by people who were definitely in bed with the Iranians. That was something we kept a close eye on. We had to battle all the time against policies and even individual actions that were sectarian in nature.[24]

Ali Khedery and other influential voices in the US–Iraqi power structure had supported Maliki to become prime minister. With US support, Jaafari was pushed out and in May 2006, Maliki replaced him just as the civil war was getting under way. Within weeks of taking over, Maliki would face a huge scandal which would have enormous repercussions for him and Iraq years later. On 30 May 2006, a US–Iraqi inspection team discovered 1,400 predominantly Sunni male detainees, including children, being held in 'squalid, cramped conditions' in two secret detention centres in Baghdad that were actually run by the Iraqi ministry of the interior (MOI) with the full knowledge and connivance of senior officers within the MOI. Yet again it involved the Ministry of Interior over which Maliki would exercise personal control. A secret cable written by the then US ambassador, Zalmay Khalilzad, revealed the shocking extent of the abuse of the Sunnis in the facility known as 'Site 4'.

'It would be difficult if not impossible for senior MOI...

leadership responsible for Site 4 to be unaware of the prevalence of detainee abuse at the facility,' wrote Ambassador Khalilzad. 'This is suggested by the large number of detainees with serious physical injuries at Site 4, the obvious and illegal presence of 37 juvenile individuals and the fact that hooks and pulleys used to hang detainees from the ceiling were kept in plain sight.'[25] He added, 'Detainees in most cells have insufficient space to lie down and must sit entwined, knee-to-knee. Air circulation is poor, and the cellblocks are fetid…many detainees, who are allowed little or no access to fresh air, suffer from lice, scabies and infections.'

The report describes Maliki's 'appalled' reaction to the news when Americans briefed him on 5 June, nearly a week after their discovery of Site 4. The US was worried about the impact that Site 4 could have on the ferocious conflict between Shia and Sunni that had already threatened to unravel the country along sectarian lines and they demanded action taken against the MOI officials responsible for the fiasco. It was a particularly sensitive issue for the Americans. Back in 2003–4, the US was embroiled in an enormous scandal over its own appalling and illegal mistreatment of inmates at Abu Ghraib prison.[26] Rogue US military personnel had subjected men and women prisoners to 'abuse, rape and torture'.[27] The victims included suspected Sunni insurgents and the affair did enormous damage to the reputation of the US in the eyes of both the Iraqis and the international community. The Americans were deeply anxious that there should be no cover-up or any sectarian-motivated excuses to prevent any culpable MOI officials from being prosecuted.

When it came to Site 4, the Americans wanted action taken in particular against a senior MOI police commander, one Lieutenant General Mahdi Gharawi, who was in overall charge of the facility. In a later cable, officials at the US embassy believed that Gharawi had committed 'gross human rights violations and extra-judicial killings' at Site 4.[28]

In the spring of 2007, Khalilzad was succeeded by Ambassador Ryan Crocker, who also demanded that Gharawi be arrested. According to a secret cable written in May 2007 by Crocker, Gharawi was very close to his fellow Shia Nouri al-Maliki; the Iraqi prime minister had appointed him as a member of his own select team at the MOI.[29]

The Americans went repeatedly to Maliki and demanded Gharawi's arrest but the prime minister refused. According to Ambassador Crocker, 'Mehdi [Mahdi Gharawi] has proven valuable enough to Maliki, however, and he [Maliki] rebuffed our request that he execute an Iraqi warrant for Mehdi's arrest'.[30] Even General David Petraeus intervened with Maliki. 'General Petraeus pressed the PM very hard on the Mahdi case,' another secret report disclosed.[31] An Iraqi court eventually charged Gharawi in 2008, but the MOI, then under Maliki's personal influence, got the charges dropped under an Iraqi law designed to prevent the unfair sectarian targeting of – presumably – innocent people.[32] A few years later, Maliki would make another serious error of judgement by appointing Gharawi as military commander for the province of Nineveh, based in the provincial capital of Mosul. Gharawi would be responsible for the defence of Mosul against a determined assault by ISIS in 2014 and would be blamed for the catastrophic fall of the city.

Maliki was also accused repeatedly of not doing enough to tackle the Shia militias that were engaged in ethnic cleansing and slaughtering Sunnis they suspected of being jihadists. Another secret report by Ambassador Ryan Crocker in July 2007 revealed the terrifying extent of the ethnic cleansing in Baghdad by both sides of the sectarian divide. 'Sectarian violence has caused significant demographic shifts in Baghdad,' wrote Ambassador Crocker, who went on to describe the flight of the Christians from the capital and how entire neighbourhoods were being cleansed of either Sunni or Shia.[33] Maliki also faced accusations of increasing personal interference with the army and the security forces. In early 2007, he established a new department for himself, the 'office of commander in chief', which gave him direct control over the armed forces and even over the appointments of generals and other senior officers. US security officials feared that such a concentration of power in the hands of a Shia politician would result in 'worsening the country's sectarian divide'.[34] One unnamed US intelligence source complained that Maliki's 'office of commander in chief' was 'ensuring the emplacement of commanders it favours and can control, regardless of what the ministries want'.

The Americans grew increasingly alarmed as Maliki tightened his personal grip on the army and bypassed traditional chains of military command. The US had spent billions on building and training a new army for Iraq following the abolition of the old one and was desperate for it to be made anew along non-sectarian lines. The portentously named office of commander in chief started to give direct orders to individual Iraqi commanders, bypassing the chain of command, allegedly to get rid of certain Sunni commanders.[35] Individual Iraqi commanders, many considered good and non-sectarian by the Americans, were forced out or removed by Maliki.[36] A secret cable written by Ambassador Crocker on 15 May 2007 stated, 'Prime Minister Nouri al Maliki's efforts to reshape the Iraqi national security architecture seem to be producing increasing centralization of power in the hands of an inner circle of Shia Islamists at the expense of the formal chain of command.' Senior Iraqi defence officials were warning that 'Maliki's methods are similar to Saddam's approach to controlling the military'.[37] Later US Ambassadors to Iraq were appalled at the cronyism Maliki had introduced to the army. James Jeffrey, the Ambassador from 2010 to 2012, told me,

'Maliki micro managed the army. While it was not a great military, Maliki destroyed whatever professionalism it had.'[38]

Elsewhere the secret US memo refers to 'Maliki's paranoid perspective', adding, 'Maliki has repeatedly expressed fears of coups and conspiracies against him and his government...Maliki's twin bêtes noires are Ba'athist resurgence and military coup.' Ambassador Crocker revealed that of the twenty-four generals making up the staff of Maliki's office of commander in chief, twenty were Shia and just four were Sunnis, an astonishing reversal of fortunes in the once Sunni-dominated army.[39]

In March 2008, Maliki demonstrated his control of the Iraqi army by personally leading military assaults against a Shia militia that opposed him. Operation Charge of the Knights was launched mainly against the troublesome Mahdi Army of Muqtada al-Sadr, first in Iraq's southern city of Basra and then in the huge mainly Shia neighbourhood of Sadr City, where Maliki was witnessed directing Iraqi divisions over his mobile phone.[40] However, the main future targets of his personal military power would be the country's Sunni minority. Maliki stands accused of effectively destroying the Awakening movement, which had played such a vital role in the defeat of Abu Omar al-Baghdadi and Islamic State of Iraq by 2009. This is a particularly serious allegation because the Awakening tribesmen and the so-called 'Sons of Iraq' Sunni militias could have helped to prevent ISIS from re-establishing its deadly hold over Anbar in 2014.

Maliki had always been wary of the Sons of Iraq, part of the Awakening movement; he thought them a fifth column that had the potential to form an army and act independently of the state. The Iraqi prime minister repeatedly reminded the Americans that members of the Sons had themselves been insurgents in the past. 'These guys used to point their guns at us and you,' Maliki is reported to have told General Petraeus during one of their stand-offs, arguing that the US could not risk backing dangerous former Sunni insurgents. 'Now they are pointing their guns at AQI [al-Qaeda in Iraq, or ISI]. Do you want them to point their guns back at us and kill our soldiers and yours?'[41]

The Awakening is put to sleep

By 2009, there were an estimated 70,000 to 90,000 Sons of Iraq but Maliki was clearly reluctant to have them ingested into the police, seeing the volunteers as thugs or Sunni terrorists, 'a hidden army'.[42] 'Nobody cares about the Awakening groups,' one high-ranking Iraqi officer told US researchers. 'The population hates them, and from the government's point of view, they only carry light weapons. The army has enough men, means and discipline to crush them militarily on any given day!'[43]

Maliki's greatest weapon in killing off the Awakening movement proved to be the biometric data collected by the US when signing up recruits. The data had been taken to screen out dangerous criminals and certain irredeemable insurgents but this material was clearly handed over to the Iraqis later, as a report revealed: 'US military officers also believe Iraqi security forces can deal with recidivist insurgents, having good biometric and other personal data on each Sons of Iraq participant.'[44] How could the Iraqis do that without getting the data gathered by the US? In 2009, the Iraqi government arrested around forty Awakening leaders and sentenced one to death for terrorist activity. The movement was disbanded the same year.[45] The Sunni recruits were between a rock and a hard place, targeted by the government and also by ISI jihadis.[46] These arrests continued as the US continued to withdraw its troops from Iraq and its influence gradually waned.

Only around thirty percent of Sons of Iraq were absorbed into the police or low-paid office security jobs. Those who were fired lost their $350 a month pay packet and faced the possibility of arrest. There would be no Sons of Iraq to defend Anbar against the ISIS invasion of late 2013. In fact Abu Bakr al-Baghdadi would not have succeeded without the support of some of the Sunni tribes that had taken part in the Awakening against his predecessors. Human rights activist and former Sunni MP Nada al-Jabouri told me that the Shia militias killed many former members of the Awakening, also known as al-Sahwa. She said:

Many of them in my area, Adhamiya [near central Baghdad], have been killed and yet without the Awakening and the American army, we could not have lived there. The security forces were not able to keep them secure.

The government cut their payments. I have a driver with me in Adhamiya and I asked him why he left the Awakening, the Sahwa, and he told me, 'Because there is no future and I will be killed.' Many Sunnis said to me, 'Why should we fight? For whom? Why should we fight for a sectarian government and for Iran?'[47]

The national parliamentary election of 2010 presented the ideal opportunity to be rid of Maliki. A non-religious coalition of both Shia and Sunni politicians called the Iraqiya List won ninety-one seats and effectively defeated Maliki's bloc of Shia parties, the so-called State of Law coalition, which managed to win just eighty-nine. A significant majority of Sunnis in Anbar and Nineveh, the two provinces later successfully invaded by ISIS in 2014, voted for Iraqiya.

Ali Khedery had long concluded that Maliki should go. He told me, 'By 2010, I had changed my position on Maliki, because

Iraq had gotten through the civil war; violence was down by ninety percent from pre-Surge high. What we needed was an economically minded prime minister, a unifier, to unite the country, not a divisive, sectarian, increasingly Iranian-allied individual like Maliki.'[48] Iraqiya did not enjoy an overwhelming majority but it did have the largest number of seats in the new parliament and it was certainly in pole position.

However, in talks over the forming of the government, Iraqiya's secular leader, Ayad Allawi, a Shia ex-Ba'athist, insisted on being prime minister. Other Shia parties that had not been part of Maliki's coalition feared the return of Ba'athists under Allawi and supported Maliki.[49] Joining forces with him, they managed to form the largest power bloc. Critically, Maliki won the support of both the US and neighbouring Iran, the two countries with the most influence on Iraq. Shia Iran had and still enjoys the most profound hold on the country and is known to fund and support Shia politicians and militias.

Khedery was in despair. He said:

> Maliki continually did not fulfil the promises he made to us privately, and these were literally made in my presence. That included not suspending the so-called office of the commander in chief, which was his sort of Saddam-like organizational structure where all divisional commanders reported to him; he did not suspend his secret torture and intelligence authorities, which we knew about and confronted him about; he did not pass a general amnesty to free the vast majority of Sunni detainees. He betrayed the promises he made to the Kurds and us. He also betrayed his power-sharing promises generally to his political partners to include [the] Sunni. In other words he did exactly what some of us predicted, which was that he continued to consolidate power.

Khedery believes the 2010 election, effectively lost by Maliki, was a golden opportunity for Iraq that was tragically passed up.

> The reality was that the Surge had succeeded tremendously, much more than any of our wildest expectations, as evidenced by the fact that for the first time since 2003 a vast majority of the Kurds and Sunnis and Shia all participated in the elections and that a secular, moderate, Western-leaning, cross-sectarian alliance, Iraqiya, won the election. That was the biggest gift granted to the United States of America and our coalition allies in decades. This is exactly the list we dreamed that would win one day. Instead what happened was that we betrayed our promises to these folks, to our national allies, the Kurds and the secular Sunnis and Shia, and we ended up backing Maliki for a second term despite the fact that he had lost the election. As a result we tacitly got into bed with the Iranians and fomented a theocracy, a sectarian government, a corrupt government and a dictatorial government which led us to exactly where we are today.[50]

By December 2010, Maliki was still prime minister and still in direct control of the interior and defence ministries.[51] Iraqiya was marginalized and leading members accepted comparatively minor ministries in the new government. Increasingly the Sunnis they represented began to feel even more ignored. Maliki was now accused of forging a dictatorship. The accusation was made explicitly in 2011 by Saleh al-Mutlaq, a Sunni deputy prime minister, who said, 'Maliki is heading toward a system run by one party and one man, with the Dawa Party replacing the Ba'ath Party and Maliki taking the place of Saddam Hussein.'[52] Maliki ordered hundreds of arrests mainly of suspected 'Ba'athists'. In one case, in September 2011, 145 university employees were arrested in Tikrit and accused of being Ba'athists.[53] The US Ambassador at the time, James Jeffrey, believed that Maliki had initially wanted to do more to integrate the Sunni, but that he had been essentially captured by his many of his fellow Shia politicians and the ever present Iranians. 'They could have encouraged him to integrate,' said Jeffrey, 'but instead they supported the most egregious anti-Sunni efforts made by Maliki.'[54]

In late 2011, Maliki would try to arrest top Iraqiya Sunni leaders. Strategically this proved a disastrous move and played a significant part in the resurgence of Abu Bakr al-Baghdadi and his jihadis. Ironically, Maliki attempted the arrests on the day another of his greatest long-term strategic errors was being played out. On 15 December 2011, a ceremony marked the final withdrawal of all US troops from Iraq. Around 80,000 had pulled out since Barack Obama had become president in January 2009. Eventually, Maliki insisted on a complete withdrawal[55] although Saddam's former deputy prime minister Tariq Aziz, languishing in his jail cell, accused the US of 'leaving Iraq to the wolves'.[56] President Obama had wanted to keep a residual force in Iraq of 5,000 troops but he could not get the necessary legal protection for them from the Iraqis. 'We insisted on strict inviolability for our troops,' said James Jeffrey, former US Ambassador to Iraq, 'but the Iraqi political system couldn't swallow that and Obama didn't fight hard enough for it and neither did anyone else.' Lieutenant General Babaker Zebari, the Iraqi army's chief of staff, said the US army should have stayed because the Iraqi army would not be ready until 2020.[57] Peter Mansoor, the former military aide to General Petraeus, thought the withdrawal of all troops had been a grave mistake by the US, not only in terms of Iraq's security, but also because it removed an important weapon of leverage on Maliki and Iraq. He said:

Withdrawing US forces took away that leverage of having a four-star general and an ambassador constantly acting as a check and balance against the sectarian nature of the government in Baghdad. When our troops left we had no more reason to go to Maliki and say 'You shouldn't be doing this, or doing that.'

I primarily viewed any residual military force as diplomatic leverage. As long as you had those troops there, you had a reason to meet with Maliki every week. When we had 160,000 troops in Iraq, I called them 160,000 points of leverage.[58]

On the very day that the last US soldiers left, Maliki sent troops and tanks to surround the homes of three senior Sunni politicians from Iraqiya, Tariq al-Hashimi, the country's vice-president, Rafi al-Issawi, the finance minister, and the deputy prime minister, Saleh al-Mutlaq. Maliki's own son and head of security, Ahmed, had personally led the troops in the operation and placed the trio of Sunni politicians under house arrest. Maliki was accusing two of the politicians, Issawi and Hashimi, of running a death squad called Hamas of Iraq. Hashimi flew north to Iraqi Kurdistan to avoid being charged with murder. The following year, he was sentenced to death in absentia.[59]

As must be patently obvious, Iraq is a very long way from being a normal functioning democracy. Despite holding elections, both Sunni and Shia politicians have been accused of having links with militias and death squads, as well as being involved with torture and the ordering of assassinations. However, Hashimi always insisted on his 'absolute innocence'.[60] Many Sunnis saw the arrests of their most senior leaders as an attack on their community, although a close adviser of Maliki, Saad al-Muttalibi, told me there were good grounds for Hashimi's arrest. 'Hashimi was convicted of four murders,' said Muttalibi. 'The evidence was very clear. There was physical evidence of Hashimi's direct involvement in providing orders for the assassination of a lawyer, indeed of another lawyer, of sending booby-trapped cars into the Karrada area of Baghdad using one of his staff members. So there was complete evidence of his involvement, and I was told that by the judge, who was a friend of mine.'[61]

Issawi, who also maintained his innocence, was released along with Deputy Prime Minister Mutlaq the following day. However, a year later, in December 2012, Maliki went after his finance minister once more by yet again raiding Issawi's house in Fallujah and arresting ten of his bodyguards on suspicion of murder.[62] This time several thousand Sunnis took to the streets of Fallujah to protest, carrying posters reading 'resistance is still in our veins'. Muttalibi accused Issawi of stoking up the problem. Again Muttalibi insists that Maliki had just cause in taking on Issawi, claiming that twelve of Issawi's bodyguards had been involved in the murder of twenty men from Fallujah. 'I actually met those twenty families in Maliki's office,' said Muttalibi. 'The families claimed the executions were carried out by twelve of Mr Issawi's bodyguards so the order for the arrest of the twelve bodyguards was issued. The moment they arrested those bodyguards, Mr Issawi went and started this campaign and started the protest camp. And then it took another form. At that time there was no request to arrest him. Then the investigation happened into the ministry of finance and of course he was the minister of finance at the time, and there were financial irregularities and illegal distribution of land in Iraq.'

Sunni leaders were now warning they might withdraw from the government and accused Maliki of abusing his power to target election opponents.[63] All the pent-up fury and angst felt by Sunnis over discrimination, de-Ba'athification, corruption and the destruction of the Awakening began to spill over and protests spread across the country. On 28 December 2012, there was a mass protest called the 'Friday of Honour' with tens of thousands of Sunnis taking part, particularly in the Sunni heartlands of Anbar and to the north in Nineveh.

Widespread Sunni protests took place throughout the winter of 2012–13 and into the spring. Maliki became convinced that Baghdadi and ISI were also involved in the growing mayhem and were heavily involved in organizing some of the protests. The sectarian strife was helping to create the right conditions for the resurrection of ISI, and the jihadis were attracting new recruits to their cause. This time, their management of savagery would be impeccable. After years of humiliation and defeat, ISI would soon metastasize remorselessly across huge areas of Syria and Iraq. 2013 was the comeback year, the year they would start to build their caliphate.

10
Scourge of Syria
2011–2014

In January 2013, the Sunni MP Dr Alaa Makki was in Washington DC and paid a visit to his friends in the US state department. Makki, a member of the Iraqi Islamic Party, the biggest Sunni party in Iraq, had two disturbing warnings for the Americans. He said, 'I went to the state department and they became angry. I told them, "You've spent billions, like $20 billion at that time, on the Iraqi army but there is no military doctrine in the Iraqi army at all," and they became angry at that time, but it was the truth.'[1] With the resurgence of sectarian violence and killing by Abu Bakr al-Baghdadi, all that stood between Iraq and disaster was its corrupted and highly dysfunctional police and army.

Makki's second warning concerned Islamic State of Iraq and was even more chilling. He said:

It was at the time of the beginning of the Sunni demonstrations and the reappearance of the Anbar tribes. I read the situation and I warned the United States about the danger posed by Da'esh,[2] as we call ISIS [ISI]. I told the US, 'The Sunnis are now losing

160

everything, and there's no promising future for them, and this could mean a return for Da'esh.'

Also I could see the danger from the civil war in Syria. I could guess, both as an Iraqi and a Sunni, that there could be a transfer of this danger to Iraq. And that is what happened later on.[3]

By April 2013, as Iraq threatened to descend into chaos, Baghdadi had turned his attention again to Syria. After all, the Syrian dictator, Bashar al-Assad, and most of his ruling elite were from a sect of the hated Shia known as Alawites. However, Baghdadi was no more interested in the Syrians' fight for freedom than he was in the Iraqi Sunnis' desire for equality and fairness. Baghdadi would exploit both these natural aspirations for human dignity in his hunger for power and territory. In fact he would soon enslave Iraqis and Syrians by the millions and kill them by the many thousands. As ever, Baghdadi was obsessed about how these two conflagrations either side of the border could flame together and burn out the first territories for his new Islamic empire.

In mid-2011, as Syria descended rapidly from public protests – violently suppressed – into all-out civil war, Baghdadi dispatched a tiny team of jihadis across the border with the instruction that they should secrete themselves at first discreetly among the myriad opposition groups opposing Assad.[4] Heading the team was a young Syrian jihadi with the *nom de guerre* of Abu Muhammad al-Jawlani, or 'Golani' – apparently taking his name from the Golan Heights, an area of the Syrian border mostly occupied by Israel since the Six Day War of 1967. Jawlani established a group of fighters called Jabhat al-Nusra ash-Sham, or Nusra for short. The full name means 'the Support Front for the People of the Levant'; for jihadists the Levant comprises Syria, Lebanon and Palestine, including Israel, as well as Jordan and even Egypt. Understandably in the heat of battle, the jihadi comrades of Nusra quickly felt they had become an independent fighting force, separate from ISI and Baghdadi, and that's the way it wanted to keep things. The ensuing conflict between Baghdadi and Nusra would have huge consequences.

Nusra first came to prominence in the civil war in Syria with a series of devastating suicide bombings. The first attack was a lethal suicide bombing in the Syrian capital, Damascus, on 27 April 2012, which killed eleven people and injured another twenty-eight. Following the bombing, Nusra issued a rather strange statement entitled 'A Martyrdom-seeking Operation against a Gathering of Security Elements in the Midan Neighbourhood' and added rather perfunctorily, '[The] martyrdom seeking operation was carried out by the hero Abu Omar al-Shami.'[5]

With his experience of fighting with ISI in Iraq, Jawlani moulded his Nusra in Syria and he quickly rose to prominence among the hundreds of militia leaders then battling Assad. Nusra enjoyed a regular supply of arms, funding and fighters from foreign donors and ISI. Nusra was ferocious in its assaults on Assad's army and allies, but in the territories it controlled the group largely tried to avoid the brutal executions and atrocities that made ISI feared and hated wherever it set up camp.[6] In some ways, outside observers thought Nusra 'more subtle and insidious'.[7] Unlike ISI, and the Iraqis, Nusra had been partially successful in portraying a humanitarian face to many Syrian people, carrying out polio vaccination programmes, for example, in territories under its control, and dealing with corruption or arbitrating in disputes between other parties.

A Syrian security analyst based in Washington spoke to me on condition of anonymity. He wanted to protect his family and friends still in Syria. He said:

> For the most part, at least so far, civilian casualties do mean something to Nusra. It doesn't want to be hated…It doesn't necessarily

want to rule [territory] in spite of the Syrian people as much as ISIS did. ISIS was obvious – they said 'This is what we're doing; anyone who stands in our way, whether they are Muslim or non-Muslim, we are going to exterminate them', and that has been very clear. It has not distinguished between Muslim and non-Muslim. In fact the number of Muslims ISIS have attacked has far exceeded the number of non-Muslims.[8]

Among the estimated 1,600 rebel groups in Syria,[9] Nusra was most effective at carrying out high-profile and high-casualty attacks. The group boasted that it carried out most of the suicide bombings in Syria,[10] but it also did something that Baghdadi and ISIS craved – it took territory. Finally, in March 2013, after more than a year of hard fighting and dying, Nusra took part in the dramatic conquest of the first city to fall to the rebels, Raqqa, and occupied it soon afterwards.[11] Raqqa was the key to control of much of northern Syria and the city would become the capital of Baghdadi's caliphate the following year. Jawlani was not just taking the fight to the enemy in Syria; he was taking cities too.

On hearing of the fall of Raqqa, Abu Bakr al-Baghdadi decided to travel to Syria and bring Jawlani and Nusra back under his personal control. To do this, he planned to dissolve both Nusra and Islamic State of Iraq, merge the two groups and declare a new Islamic State of Iraq and Syria or ISIS, confusingly also known as the Islamic State of Iraq and the Levant (ISIL – the Levant can also include Lebanon, Jordan, Palestine and even Egypt). So much for the best-laid plans of men and jihadis! It seems clear that Baghdadi was becoming paranoid about the success of the brutal and charismatic Jawlani. There is strong evidence to believe in Abu Bakr's paranoia thanks to the source 'Wikibaghdady', who US intelligence believes is close to the IS leadership.[12] Wikibaghdady revealed that Baghdadi travelled to Syria in mid-March 2013, just days after the fall of Raqqa, to announce the new Islamic State of Iraq and Syria. Haji Bakr, Baghdadi's master strategist, had already taken up residence in a house in the town of Tal Rifaat. It was here that the 'Lord of the Shadows', as Haji Bakr became known, started to sketch out the structure of the future Islamic State security apparatus, according to documents later discovered at the house and given to *Der Spiegel* magazine.[13]

Wikibaghdady revealed how Baghdadi was becoming concerned about Jawlani's success, adding, 'Al-Nusra started growing with the leadership of Abu Mohammed Jawlani and he became even more popular. Fighters from the Gulf, Tunisia, Libya, Morocco, Algeria, and Europe began joining al-Nusra Front. This scared Abu Bakr al-Baghdadi because members of al-Nusra Front didn't have any loyalty towards him.'[14]

Baghdadi was in charge of the 'big picture', which meant creating a caliphate with as large an army as he could muster under his own banner and through effective management of savagery. On 9 April 2013, Baghdadi announced the abolition of both ISI and Nusra and the creation of ISIS, without even consulting Jawlani or Nusra beforehand. Apparently Jawlani had declined invitations to attend any meetings convened by Baghdadi to discuss the merger because he was concerned, justifiably, about being assassinated.[15]

On 10 April, the day after Baghdadi's announcement of the merger, Jawlani issued a furious statement to reject the proclamation, claiming to have learned of Baghdadi's speech only through the media. Jawlani complained about not being 'consulted' and said, 'The banner of the [Nusra] Front will remain as it is without any change despite our appreciation for the banner of the State [Baghdadi's Islamic State of Iraq] and who carries it and who sacrificed his blood from our brothers under its banner.' Furthermore, Jawlani pledged his allegiance not to Baghdadi but to Ayman al-Zawahiri, the man who had succeeded the slain Osama bin Laden to the leadership of al-Qaeda.[16]

Before turning deadly, the dispute quickly became a public fiasco with Zawahiri then issuing a haughty rebuke to both Jawlani and Baghdadi, saying 'the proponents of Jihad' were all 'dismayed by the dispute that occurred on the media between our beloved brothers'.[17] However, it was clear that Zawahiri sided with Jawlani by declaring the abolition of Abu Bakr's shiny new ISIS. In his own words the al-Qaeda boss decreed, 'the Islamic State in Iraq and the Levant is to be dissolved' and ordered that Nusra and ISI carry on as before, separately and presumably without trying to kill each other. To add insult to injury Zawahiri pompously announced that Baghdadi's position as 'emir' of ISI should be reviewed a year hence.[18] All Zawahiri did was to make clear his own impotence when it came to the jihad. As far as ISIS was concerned, its fighters had been in the field for a decade in Iraq and now Syria while the old warhorses of al-Qaeda Central had been cowering in safe houses and bunkers boasting of past glories.

A few days after Zawahiri's announcement, Baghdadi publicly repudiated the al-Qaeda leader in a statement asserting that 'the Islamic State of Iraq and the Levant will remain as long as we have a vein pumping or an eye blinking. It remains and we will not compromise nor give it up.'[19] Baghdadi refused to dissolve ISIS or leave Syria. His decision would lead to war with Nusra and other rebel groups.

According to Wikibaghdady, Baghdadi then issued an ultimatum to Jawlani and his Nusra commanders saying 'they could either change their loyalty or they were going to be killed'. Baghdadi and his military commander, the former brigadier Haji Bakr, quickly assembled a security team to seize control of the warehouses containing Nusra's weapons and 'create[d] an assassination team to kill all the leaders of al-Nusra Front, starting with

Jawlani and then the rest. The plan was to find out all their movements and then murder them using car bombs.'[20] Those plans
came to nothing; Jawlani was too smart and kept one step ahead
of Baghdadi. ISIS would remain in Syria and before long the two
groups would be at war with each other.

An early glimpse into the character of Baghdadi in Syria comes
again from Wikibaghdady, who recalled an order from the head of
ISIS to 'execute everyone in the prisons in Aleppo and not leave
any single person alive'.[21] Disturbingly for Baghdadi, he was now
shedding fighters who were leaving him to join Nusra. He asked
how many fighters he had at that time and was told only 1,757,
mostly from Tunisia, Saudi Arabia, Libya and Algeria. Wikibaghdady
adds, 'He also found out that most fighters who left him would go
to al-Nusra Front.' Baghdadi was determined not only to staunch
the exodus of men to Nusra but to increase his own fighting
strength and so he began to improve his propaganda to attract
more jihadis to his black flag.[22]

Clearly Baghdadi felt threatened by Nusra on all fronts and yet,
at this apparent nadir in his fortunes, he was only a year away from
standing in the Great Mosque of Mosul declaring himself head of
a caliphate stretching more than four hundred miles from west to
east. Before that, rivers of blood would flow, many enemies would
be slaughtered and towns and cities won and lost in a day during
the course of a multi-front war on both sides of the Iraqi–Syrian
border. Over the next year, Baghdadi and the professional ex-army
officers who surrounded him would orchestrate this confusing,
sprawling, hideous conflict relentlessly, through a combination of
ex-Ba'athist security enforcers, underground terror cells and their
fanatical, well-trained jihadi battalions.

Some believe Baghdadi's successes in Syria were also the result
of western policy towards the regime of Bashar al-Assad, particularly the tough sanctions aimed at the Syrian military. Peter Ford

was the UK Ambassador to Damascus between 2003 and 2006 and has maintained a close interest in events there. He told me, 'We should have expected this [ISIS success in Syria] when we hamstrung the Syrian army at every opportunity. This was the only force capable of defeating ISIS. But we hamstrung it in several ways through sanctions basically on supplies to Syria, by restricting things like the flow of jet fuel and by generally weakening the Syrian economy.'

'I think by all the actions we took that were designed to weaken the government militarily in response to the uprising, we paved the way for ISIS to supersede the weaker opposition groups. We continued to back these weaker groups even when we suspected that arms we were supplying them were being passed on to ISIS or were simply being grabbed by ISIS.'[23]

Baghdadi's determination to seize territory in the war-torn lands of Syria soon brought him into conflict with a plethora of other opposition groups. The view taken by other groups, including Nusra, was that questions of permanent state building and governance should wait until Assad's defeat.[24] Baghdadi wanted to destroy the main jihadi competition before launching his military campaign to seize territory for the caliphate. In a deliberate campaign, he embarked on a series of assassinations of other rebel leaders. Many rebel groups would soon look on ISIS and Assad as the common enemy. Haji Bakr provided Baghdadi with the intelligence and the lethal organization he needed to kill his jihadi competitors and seize territory in Syria.

ISIS murdered senior commanders with the Western-backed rebels, the Free Syrian Army (FSA), including Kamal Hamami, a member of the FSA's supreme military council, and Brigadier General Ahmed Moshai'el.[25] Hamami was considered particularly important because of his authority and Western links, both critical factors at a time when the FSA was desperate for arms from the

West.[26] Other rebel commanders were assassinated, including the entire leadership of the moderate Ghurabaa al-Sham Brigade near the city of Idlib, all forced to kneel on the ground and dispatched by ISIS assassins with a shot in the back of the head. ISIS also targeted the important Ahrar al-Sham militia, torturing and murdering one of its most senior commanders, a physician called Dr Hussein al-Suleiman. His mutilated corpse was discovered with an ear cut off and teeth knocked out.[27]

One of the more bizarre ISIS executions was its 'accidental' beheading late in 2013 of a commander of Ahrar al-Sham. ISIS put out a press statement asking for 'understanding and forgiveness' for decapitating the commander, one Muhammad Fares, and then holding up his head to a crowd in Aleppo. Rather implausibly, ISIS claimed it wrongly mistook this important leader of the Sunni Ahrar al-Sham for a Shia militiaman fighting for Assad. The ISIS spokesman at that time, a Mr Omar al-Qahtani, said 'the appropriate judicial authorities' would investigate the 'incident'.[28] It is peculiar perhaps that a few months later ISIS failed to apologize when it assassinated the actual leader of the very same Ahrar al-Sham group or when, a few months after that, it murdered the leader who succeeded him along with most of his senior commanders.[29]

Tales of classic ISIS savagery and tyranny emerged everywhere throughout Syria following the declaration of ISIS. In an initially bloodless move in early autumn 2013, Baghdadi occupied the city of Raqqa after Nusra fighters left the place and travelled thirty-four miles west to the town of al-Tabqa. Soon ISIS subjected Raqqa to a predictable reign of terror, the same cracked template of a caliphate as that inflicted on the people of Kurdistan in the early 2000s and on the people of Anbar a few years later. As in other places in Syria, ISIS planted itself in Raqqa by first opening a 'Dawah' office, *dawah* meaning 'invitation' or 'summons'. It often refers to the preaching and spreading of Islam, but for ISIS the Dawah office was the headquarters for its fighters and the start of its insidious takeover of Raqqa.[30] Working from lists drawn up apparently by Haji Bakr, ISIS began to eliminate any potential opposition, starting with the kidnapping of the human rights activist and director of the city council, Abdullah al-Khalil, in May 2013.[31] Khalil was never seen again. Many others followed him. At first, many people spoke out against the cruelty and extremism of ISIS but they were dealt with in the customary way. Activists and city council officials were targeted for abduction and torture.

Thanks to its ruthlessness and growing wealth, ISIS managed gradually to exert total control over Raqqa and its population of around 220,000. It took control of vital public services and transportation, as well as the production and distribution of bread. It added to its funds by demanding *zakat*, or taxes, from people.[32] As well as running protection rackets to extort money from businesses in the city, it imposed strict dress codes on women, and segregated girls from boys in Raqqa's schools and colleges. Christians were routinely persecuted.

On 17 October 2013, the group was confident enough to hold a public meeting in Raqqa. Two well-respected local men spoke up and accused the group of committing crimes; naturally they were murdered within days and in public places.[33] Raqqa was the first proper ISIS foothold in Syria and provided a crucial base for the group and later its capital as it established its caliphate.

Azad Heyder, a Syrian Kurd, once headed the Syrian rebels' organization in Sweden and feels his fellow countrymen have only themselves to blame. He told me he despaired once he heard that ISIS had joined the rebels.

The thing is it is not just ISIS; we brought ISIS inside Syria. We brought in ISIS, we the Syrian opposition, which was based in

Qatar, Saudi [Arabia] and Turkey. We brought them in and helped them. The Muslim Brotherhood helped them. They got money from Qatar to Saudi. ISIS is like a cancer, when it comes to your body, you can't control it. They thought they would control ISIS, get rid of Assad and take the power.

I told someone from the Muslim Brotherhood in Sweden, 'This will be suicide for you and for all Syria and for me.' They said, 'After six months, when we've got rid of Assad, we will take them out of Syria.'[34]

Hawija

Across the border in Iraq, the Sunni protests, particularly in the heartlands of Anbar, were also escalating. Demonstrators and police had started to die. Nouri al-Maliki was becoming increasingly alarmed at some of the protest camps set up by Sunnis and was convinced that terrorists, particularly Baghdadi, were behind them.

One Sunni protest camp had been established at Hawija, a town to the south-west of Kirkuk in northern Iraq. It proved to be the powder keg that would intensify the demonstrations and help lead to thousands more deaths in resurgent ISIS bombings and shootings during 2013. On 19 April 2013, a police officer was killed when Sunni protestors advanced on one of the town's checkpoints; they then refused to hand over the culprits. The government suspected the involvement of Sunni insurgents, the so-called Naqshbandi Order[35] headed by Saddam's former deputy president, Izzat Ibrahim al-Douri, who was then still at large.[36] The camp was placed under siege and as the situation continued to worsen, it was clear an armed assault by the Iraq military was imminent.

In the early hours of Tuesday 23 April 2013, the day of the

anticipated attack, the human rights activist and former Sunni MP Dr Nada al-Jabouri became increasingly disturbed not only about the potential bloodshed but also about the long-term consequences of any armed assault. She was desperate to get the attack called off or at least postponed to allow for further talks. At around 2 a.m., she went to the Baghdad home of the country's acting defence minister, Saadoun al-Dulaimi. Jabouri told me, 'I said to al-Dulaimi's guards, "I'm not going to leave if you don't wake him. I have to talk to him." They woke the minister and I asked him not to shoot. But it was no use. Within three hours they started shooting the people in Hawija.'[37]

The assault started at 5 a.m. when security forces supported by four helicopters stormed the Hawija camp. The raid left at least fifty-three dead and dozens more injured, and sparked off more violence across the country.[38] Jabouri said, 'Al-Dulaimi said he didn't give the order and Nouri al-Maliki said he was sleeping [at the time]. Everyone came up with a different story. But we knew then that it was a disaster and the real trouble would start.'[39] Following the assault, two Sunni government ministers resigned in protest and the main Anbari cities of Fallujah and Ramadi witnessed huge demonstrations.[40] Within three days of Hawija, approximately 170 people had been killed and Nouri al-Maliki was warning of a return to a 'sectarian civil war'.[41] By then his failure to integrate Sunni Arabs into a political system that they felt genuinely represented them was all too clear.

By the summer of 2013, Baghdadi was strong enough to orchestrate a mass breakout of an estimated five hundred of his jihadis from two jails near Baghdad, including the notorious Abu Ghraib. Most of the escapees, well trained in the dark arts of savagery, had been sentenced to death and after their escape they were put to immediate use.[42]

In October and November 2013 it was clear that Baghdadi's

cells of assassins and bombers were making a strong comeback, particularly in the Iraqi capital, where they were intensifying their attacks against the Shia. In 2012, more than 4,600 civilians had reportedly died violently in Iraq, a figure too horrendous to comprehend for people who live in peaceful democracies but still very low by Iraq's abysmal post-invasion standards.[43] By the end of 2013, the official death toll would more than double to over 9,700.[44]

By the beginning of 2014, ISIS had grown in numbers, cash and confidence, so much so that on 31 March it decided to publish a second glossy annual report itemizing its many shootings and bombings with ghoulish obsessiveness. By this time, ISIS had grown certain of military success in Syria and Iraq. In his report, called *Al-Naba* ('The Report'), Baghdadi boasted of conducting 1,083 assassinations in 2013, double the number of targeted killings of 2012. Whereas he had conducted only 330 car bombings during 2012, his cells detonated 537 so-called 'vehicle-borne improvised explosive devices' (VBIEDs) during 2013. Oddly, knife murders were way down from a total of forty-eight in 2012 to precisely zero in 2013;[45] clearly the 'accidental' beheading by knife of the unfortunate Muhammad Fares in Aleppo in November 2013 did not count.

It was also clear to everyone in Baghdad towards the end of 2013 that ISIS was gaining strength in Anbar and that huge parts of the province had become no-go areas for reporters like me, along with the vast majority of humanity who were considered *kuffar*. Even then, few people I spoke to in Baghdad during those weeks predicted the calamity ahead, or appreciated the deep rot in the Iraqi military that would help bring it about. However, as the bombs went off all around us in Baghdad there was growing concern at the coming together of the two conflicts, which, after all, were separated only by a line in the sand, that most vulnerable of delineations.[46] Events would continue to play out to the advantage of ISIS.

On 21 December 2013, ISIS assassinated the commander of the Iraqi army's 7th division, Major General Muhammad al-Karawi,[47] the brigade commander who had led the highly controversial raid on the Sunni protest camp at Hawija earlier that year.[48] It was an astonishing coup for ISIS that impressed many Sunnis. Nouri al-Maliki was furious about the death of a loyal commander and decided to liquidate another long-standing Sunni protest camp at Ramadi, the city where the Awakening against ISI had first succeeded in late 2006. Maliki was convinced that Baghdadi was involved in the year-long protest at Ramadi, and that as many as thirty-six ISIS leaders were quartered there.[49] He described the camp as 'an al-Qaeda headquarters'.[50] As Saad al-Muttalibi, the prime minister's close adviser, told me:

> It's important to remember and stress that these demonstrations were broken up by the local police – not the Iraqi army. Secondly it is clear that these demonstrations became the breeding ground for ISIS. We have the actual videos of people at these demonstrations shouting out 'We are al-Qaeda and we cut heads, and we do this and we do that.' There's no way any country which respects its citizens would allow ISIS to shout out its accomplishments in front of the cameras. There were protests which used ISIS as a tool against the federal government.

However, I spoke to senior Sunni spokesmen and MPs who insist the protests were mostly genuine and heartfelt against a deeply sectarian and divisive government.

Maliki ordered a raid on the Ramadi camp to arrest the protest organizer, the Sunni MP Ahmed al-Alwani, another prominent member of the Iraqiya cross-party and non-sectarian alliance, on 'terrorism charges'; as a result Alwani's brother and sister as well as five of his guards were killed.[51] There were allegations that Alwani was tortured. He was later sentenced to death for his alleged murder of two soldiers.[52]

The raid was followed by more violence and demonstrations; more than forty Iraqi Sunni MPs submitted their resignations in protest.[53] To help placate the angry Sunni clans, Iraqi troops were ordered to withdraw from Anbar cities. ISIS gunmen moved in immediately after the soldiers had departed.[54]

Coming of the caliphate

By January 2014, ISIS was fighting Nusra and Ahrar al-Sham in Raqqa as well as battling against the Iraqi army in Anbar. Its ferocity was thanks mainly to the expertise of the ex-military officers fighting for it as well as alongside, particularly in the shape of the Naqshbandi Order under the command of Saddam's former vice-president, Izzat Ibrahim al-Douri. Baghdadi's recruiting drive for more fighters had been successful. In November 2013, a group of mainly Russian-speaking Chechen jihadis called Jaish al-Muhajireen wa Ansar ('the Army of Emigrants and Helpers') swore an oath of allegiance to Baghdadi.[55] A grateful Baghdadi rewarded the group's leader, Omar al-Chechen, also known as Omar al-Shishani, by making him a *wali* or ISIS governor for a swathe of Syria including the Aleppo, Idlib and Latakia areas.[56]

In addition to the foreign fighters, ISIS was also strengthened enormously by some Syrian tribes pledging allegiance to Baghdadi, particularly in the north, in areas such as Aleppo and Raqqa.[57] Possibly through coercion, the Afadila tribe was one that swore allegiance to ISIS, helping to cement its control over these strategically important Syrian territories.

Over the next five months of fierce fighting, Baghdadi would conquer a strip of territory stretching approximately 280 miles eastwards from Raqqa, first seizing the strategically vital border town of al-Qaim and the surrounding land, almost the whole way to Iraq's second-biggest city, Mosul, before making his astonishing assault on the city itself.

On 14 January 2014, ISIS raised its black flag over government buildings in Fallujah, just fifty miles or so west of Baghdad, and declared an 'Islamic State'.[58] It also took effective control over parts of the Anbari capital of Ramadi,[59] before withdrawing. By mid-January, ISIS managed to defeat Nusra and Ahrar al-Sham and then consolidate its hold on its capital, Raqqa. Control of two important cities provided ISIS with a powerful recruiting sergeant as well as a strategically vital base in both Syria and Iraq. But for some keen Iraq watchers back in Washington, it was the fall of Fallujah that caused the most alarm. James Jeffrey, the former US Ambassador to Iraq and a critic of Obama's Middle East strategy, said, 'I was surprised about Fallujah. That to me was the warning sign and I was talking to people in the [Obama] administration about how we were going to respond to this. From what I heard, the administration did nothing except hold a few meetings. I knew what this smelled like. It smelled like what bureaucracy does when it has no leadership or when the leader says one thing and it's clear he wants something else.'[60]

In late February 2014 came the final break with al-Qaeda's central command. Al-Qaeda leader Ayman al-Zawahiri had named as his official Syria intermediary Abu Khali al-Suri (real name Muhammad Bahaiah), a senior leader of Ahrar al-Sham, the jihadi group often targeted by Baghdadi, and one-time confidant of Osama bin Laden. On 22 February 2014,[61] two ISIS suicide bombers killed Suri in Aleppo.[62] Zawahiri had looked to Suri to mediate between the warring jihadist factions and his killing demonstrated Zawahiri's weakness in the face of ISIS as well as his total eclipse as leader of the jihad.

By now Zawahiri had given up on ISIS and 'expelled' it, but from what? That is not entirely certain. ISIS's loose affiliation with al-Qaeda was over long before. Zawahiri impotently declared something that had been regarded as a reality in jihadi circles for years – that al-Qaeda 'has no links to the ISIS group. We were not informed about its creation, nor consulted.' He added, 'Nor is al-Qaeda responsible for its actions and behaviours.'[63] Pointedly Zawahiri referred to some sort of jihadi 'code of honour' 'that we don't hasten to create states/emirates without consulting scholars, leaders, mujahidin and then enforcing it on people', and he added for good measure that true jihadis should always distance themselves from 'any behaviour that will result in oppressing a mujahid or a Muslim OR a non-Muslim'. The war started by ISIS on fellow jihadis had been 'a catastrophe' for the jihad in Syria, stressed Zawahiri.[64]

By February 2014, ISIS had an estimated fighting force of ten thousand,[65] and more recruits were joining by the day from among the disaffected Sunni youth and tribes or from abroad. By now the lethal effectiveness of the Jihadi-Ba'ath war machine was evident, with ISIS suicide bombers often providing the shock troops in many an assault and Saddam's ex-soldiers and spies providing the tactical and security expertise needed to capture and hold towns and territory. By mid-March 2014, the scale of the humanitarian disaster caused by the ISIS campaign was becoming clear. At least 300,000 people from Anbar were recognized as 'internally displaced', making a total of 2.1 million internally displaced persons or IDPs in Iraq,[66] many living in heartbreaking conditions in temporary camps around Baghdad.[67]

Worse was to come in June 2014, in Iraq's northern city of Mosul, where the rancid mix of Shia–Sunni sectarianism and rampant corruption in the army would bring about a calamity, shock the world and, at last, alert it to the menace posed by ISIS. Instead of protecting Mosul against a sinister and deadly threat, the officers and soldiers of the 2nd division of the Iraqi army simply evaporated.

As with much of the Iraqi army, the 2nd division had been already been hollowed out by embezzlement and greed long before ISIS turned up to threaten its men with extinction. Officers, who had often bought their commissions,[68] had been keeping hold of the money deducted from the pay of serving troops that was supposed to be spent on their food. Soldiers were becoming increasingly disgruntled about this obvious theft and having to buy their own food. Higher-ranking officers kept absent men on the payroll – so-called phantom soldiers – in return for a portion of the salaries they were paid.[69] Furthermore, Mosul had long been a stronghold for ISIS going back to the days of Zarqawi and Abu Omar; their suicide bombers and gunmen often targeted senior army officers and police in the city. The city had also provided the group with its last refuge when it faced annihilation during the Surge and the Awakening. ISIS spread rumours that the families of Sunni soldiers would be targeted if they fought, and the soldiers themselves were not confident of being protected by the army.[70] One former Iraqi officer in Mosul said later that his soldiers would often refuse to follow orders during fighting.[71]

There were also serious problems with the man appointed by Nouri al-Maliki as the overall military commander for Mosul – none other than Lieutenant General Mahdi Gharawi. Gharawi had of course been the man put in charge of the notorious Site 4 detention centre in Baghdad, where 1,400 mainly Sunni detainees had been subjected to terrible abuse and torture, some allegedly at the hands of Gharawi personally.

In 2011, Maliki had made what turned out to be the fateful appointment of Gharawi as military commander not only of

Mosul, but also for the whole of the surrounding northern province of Nineveh. This had not gone down well with the area's predominantly Sunni population, as it proved. Many residents considered the mainly Shia-run Iraqi army as an occupying force.[72] Gharawi's men were often accused of human rights abuses and occasionally extrajudicial killing.

In one incident, in June 2013, a year before Mosul fell, the respected Human Rights Watch organization reported that members of the 3rd police division, under Gharawi's overall command, 'executed' four men and a boy near the village of East Mustantiq, and demanded an inquiry.[73] After Mosul fell, Maliki would fire Gharawi and charge him with dereliction of duty. History may well have been different had Maliki not protected him from possible justice some seven or so years earlier.

The fall of Mosul took everyone by surprise, not least ISIS. Hoping only to take and hold a neighbourhood for a few hours, the jihadis found little resistance when they entered the city at dawn on 6 June 2014. On paper the first line of defence, the 6th brigade of the 3rd division, was 2,500 strong. In reality there were just 500 poorly armed troops, an investigation by the news agency Reuters later discovered.[74] Hardly surprisingly, few of the 'phantom soldiers' signed up for duty. There were supposed to be 25,000 soldiers and police guarding Mosul. At best there were just 10,000 disillusioned and scared troops up against determined jihadis. What followed next was a complete fiasco.

Sensing a crisis, both ISIS and the Naqshbandi Army of the red-headed old Saddam warhorse Izzat Ibrahim al-Douri mobilized swiftly and descended on the beleaguered and poorly defended city; around two thousand ISIS fighters swarmed into Mosul over the next few days. Hundreds more from ISIS terrorist cells already secreted in the city had been activated and apparently many people in Sunni neighbourhoods, who despised Gharawi's men, started supporting the group. On 8 June 2014, around four hundred ISIS troops made a determined and ultimately decisive assault on the centre of the city.

After Mosul fell to ISIS on 10 June 2014 there was much vitriol about who gave the final order to capitulate and go home, but Gharawi insisted that the collapse was brought about by the decision by two of his superiors to leave an important position on Mosul's west bank during the heat of battle in full view of Iraqi troops. Apparently, the troops assumed wrongly that both of these senior commanders, lieutenant generals Aboud Qanbar (deputy chief of staff) and Ali Ghaidan (commander of the ground forces), were in full flight and this sparked many desertions.[75] Even some local police joined ISIS and fought their old comrades.

The final straw, according to Gharawi later, came when Qanbar and Ghaidan stripped him of his men and fourteen vehicles and moved to a new HQ on the eastern edge of Mosul, before ordering him to evacuate himself and his staff and then abandoning the city altogether.[76] Again more soldiers thought their commanders had disappeared and deserted in ever greater droves. Asil Nujaifi, the Sunni provincial governor for the Nineveh province, of which Mosul is the capital, would later blame Nouri al-Maliki for the fall of the city, claiming the Iraqi prime minister 'never listened' to repeated warnings about ISIS.[77]

As for Maliki, he in turn blamed Governor Nujaifi for the loss of Mosul. Maliki's close adviser Saad al-Muttalibi said he had met with Maliki after the fall of Mosul and both men held a postmortem into the catastrophe. According to Muttalibi, Maliki said he had evidence in the form of telegrams and the minutes of a meeting held in Mosul that revealed that a decision had been taken by local officials in Mosul not to oppose ISIS when the group entered the city. Muttalibi said:

Mr Maliki had a copy of the minutes of a meeting held in Mosul by the governor of Mosul and Mr Asil Nujaifi very clearly said in the meeting, 'There will be changes; people are coming; we have ordered the local police not to get involved and advised the others not to be involved and we have a new plan.' So there seems to have been a local decision to allow ISIS to enter Mosul, using ISIS as a tool.[78]

According to Muttalibi, Maliki believed this was a plot hatched between Mosul and the Kurds, allowing the Kurds to occupy cities such as Kirkuk in northern Iraq in response to the ISIS threat. Kirkuk has long been described as 'disputed territory' because the Kurds believe it should be a part of Kurdistan, and not in the rest of Iraq.

Muttalibi also alleges that sixty percent of the troops were Kurds and the rest were mainly local people. 'They also claim they got orders to go home from their officers,' he said. 'It does indicate that something was planned in advance, and that is what Mr Maliki told me himself.' The Kurdish Peshmerga troops did occupy Kirkuk in response to the ISIS threat but the alleged plot may have been the product of an apparently paranoid prime minister known to suspect conspiracies everywhere.

Following the fall of Mosul, the jihadis committed a number of massacres. They stormed the city's Badush prison and separated out the Shia and Sunni prisoners. An estimated 480 Shia men were then lined up and shot. A few prisoners managed to survive by hiding underneath the bodies.[79] In the days that followed, IS slaughtered hundreds of the policemen and soldiers who had laid down their guns and refused to fight them.[80]

Abu Bakr al-Baghdadi could not have imagined in his wildest dreams that he would proclaim himself caliph from the *minbar* of the greatest mosque in Iraq's second biggest city on 4 July 2014.

The imam of the mosque, Muhammad al-Mansuri, had coura-geously refused to pledge allegiance to IS two days after the group had taken Mosul so al-Baghdadi had ordered his immediate 'exe-cution'.[81] The IS leader had been fortunate in his enemies. In just six months, he had carved out a caliphate stretching more than four-hundred miles from northern Syria to within sixty miles of the Iranian border and held an essentially captive population of more than six million people. His fighters were on the march. This was just the beginning.

I asked the Iraqi Sunni MP Dr Alaa Makki about what hap-pened in Mosul and the failure of the Iraqi troops. After all, he had warned the US about the state of the army earlier that year. He had a medical analogy: 'I am a consultant haematologist,' he said. 'People come to me and say they have gone down with a strong influenza virus. I tell them it is not the strength of the flu virus at all, it is the weak immunity that you have.'[82]

The disaster had many causes. The terrible ceaseless war in Syria was a canker that had rotted outwards across into Iraq as it had into other neighbouring countries like Jordan and Lebanon. It had given ISIS the kick-start it desperately needed. Baghdadi deserves credit too for his relentless campaign of conquest and mayhem. Many blamed Gharawi or Maliki; others blamed the US for withdrawing its troops too early and the West generally for losing interest in Iraq. However, for the previous decade, Iraq, its government, military and people had been engulfed by tides of corruption and sectarianism, aided and abetted by Zarqawi and the ruthless men who followed him, but these chronic blights were also of the Iraqis' own making. In the final analysis the fall of Mosul and the creation of the caliphate are defeats that Iraq also inflicted on itself.

11
The furnace of war
2014

It seems extraordinary now and it felt extraordinary then but Iraq, officially, had no government when Mosul fell in June 2014, even though parliamentary elections had been held at the end of April, more than five weeks earlier. No one seemed to be in too much of a hurry to form a new government, much less recall the Council of Representatives (the Iraqi parliament), despite the fact that Islamic State fighters were less than forty minutes' drive westwards down the road from the centre of Baghdad and threatening the country with destruction.

On 1 July 2014, the Council of Representatives met for the first time since the elections to form a government to save the country from ISIS, soon to become Islamic State. So it was with great anticipation that we reporters jumped in our cars and headed towards the bridge over the river Tigris that would take us into the Green Zone, the fortress city within a city that harbours the parliament. We were stopped at a security checkpoint to await final clearance and festered in the heavy traffic while temperatures outside began their ascent through the thirties and forties. The city felt jittery and on edge. It wasn't entirely clear what was causing the hold-up, possibly something about the paperwork not being in order or the understandably heightened security concerns. What better target could there be for the two hundred IS terror cells than the Iraqi parliament on the day it met to save the country from Baghdadi?

As things turned out, we need not have bothered; the parliamentary proceedings collapsed in scenes of farce. According to the post-election rules, the parliament had to first choose a new speaker, who must be a Sunni. The speaker then had fifteen days to select the prime minister, who must be a Shia. The prime minister had a further thirty days to select a president, who must be a Kurd. There were growing divisions among Shia MPs about whether Nouri al-Maliki, now widely seen as spoiled goods, should be replaced. A huge row had broken out over comments made by the Kurds' president, Masoud Barzani, to the BBC's Middle East correspondent Jim Muir promising an independence referendum for Iraqi Kurdistan within months.[1] It was the first real evidence that Iraq could break apart completely thanks to ISIS.

Baghdadi's onslaught was a threat in particular to the four ethnic groups in his path – the Shia, the Kurds, the Christians and the Yazidi people. ISIS had threatened all with annihilation. With a political impasse in Baghdad, we planned to travel south of Baghdad to Karbala and Najaf to talk to people there but first I decided to talk to the Christians about the disaster that had engulfed them, particularly in the north in Mosul and Nineveh province.

Before setting off for the Shia heartlands, I went to see the Reverend Canon Andrew White, one of the more remarkable people in Baghdad. He was the vicar of St George's Church, the sole Anglican church, not only in Baghdad but in the whole of Iraq. Known as the 'Vicar of Baghdad', Canon White was once a doctor as well as a Conservative councillor in the London borough of Wandsworth. For more than a decade, he was one of the few forces to stand between his congregation and destruction. A man of great warmth and wit, he spoke with a slight but compelling drawl, a sign of his multiple sclerosis. He could scarcely comprehend the catastrophe suffered by the ancient Christian community of Nineveh, of which Mosul is the capital, a community that had been augmented over the years by refugees fleeing the jihadis' pogroms in Baghdad.[2]

'At one stage I had a congregation of six and a half thousand; too much – I couldn't fit them all in,' he said. 'Now 1,272 of my congregation have been killed in the last ten years.[3] I don't how many have fled in the last four weeks but so many who had fled from here back to Mosul have now gone [from Mosul] as well – so we have lost hundreds.' I reminded Canon White, not that he needed reminding, that according to official figures two thirds of Iraq's Christians had already fled Iraq in the previous decade, from a pre-invasion 2003 population of 1.2 million down to 400,000. The exodus was certainly hastened by Abu Bakr al-Baghdadi's murderous suicide assault on the Chaldean Catholic Our Lady of Salvation Church in October 2010, in which more than fifty people were killed.[4] Abu Musab al-Zarqawi and Abu Omar al-Baghdadi had also persecuted and murdered Christians, not least during their terrorizing of the Assyrian Catholics in 2006 and 2007.[5]

'Yes, two thirds have gone,' he added. 'And a very large percentage of them were in the north and now they are increasingly in Kurdistan because the north of Iraq is no longer safe for them.' Canon White seemed haunted by the fate of Iraq's Jews, who once made up a third of Baghdad's population.[6] The pogroms and persecutions of Iraq's Jews intensified after the declaration of the state of Israel in 1948 to the extent that most left in the following years. Between 1950 and 1952, the Israeli operations Ezra and Nehemiah airlifted around 130,000 Jews to Israel.[7]

'I look after the Jewish community as well,' said Canon White. 'I'm not just a priest; I'm like a rabbi as well. Here we have the Passover Seder [the ritual feast marking the start of the Jewish holiday of Passover].' He added darkly, 'Do you know how many Jews there are remaining in Iraq? There are six Jews left and I know each of them individually.'

It was time for evening prayers and Canon White's congregation had arrived at the security barriers of the heavily fortified St George's. Even nuns were thoroughly checked by the security guards before being allowed into the church. Canon White briefed his congregation, packing out the pews of St George's, about his recent trip to the north and Nineveh to see the unfolding crisis for himself and then said, 'I will promise I will never leave you; don't you leave me. So many of our people have left but we are still here.'[8] But in late 2014, Canon White was indeed forced to leave Iraq after constant death threats from Islamic State militants.[9]

The Shia also had much to be worried about. 'Sheikh' Abu Mohammed al-Adnani, al-Baghdadi's media spokesman, had also issued the darkest of threats against Nouri al-Maliki and the Shia, as well as their holiest of shrines in Najaf and Karbala. 'What have you done with your people, little fool?' Adnani admonished the Iraqi prime minister.

> You have nothing to do with politics and military leadership. You wasted a historic chance for your people to control Iraq. The *Rafidah* [a derogatory term for the Shia] will continue to curse you as long as some of them exist. Truly, between us is a settling of debts. You spoke the truth although you are a liar. There will be a heavy and long account. However, the settling of debts will not be in Samarra and Baghdad, rather in Karbala *al-munajjash* [the defiled] and Najaf *al-ashrak* [the most polytheistic].[10]

To underscore its threat, Islamic State demolished six important Shia mosques and shrines across Nineveh province.[11]

However, even by early July 2014 there was a feeling that, in military terms, stalemate was setting in. Islamic State could not get closer to Baghdad, either from the north or from the west, whereas south of Baghdad the Shia of Karbala and Najaf were organizing their defences. At a Najaf football stadium, we saw thousands of enthusiastic young Shia men preparing for battle with Islamic State. Military trainers drilled them under the careful eye of one of the local ayatollahs. Increasingly the Shia militias were stepping into the apparent void left by the military to save Iraq. As we watched the young recruits being put through their paces the ayatollah told me, 'Our shrines are being destroyed in the north, but we are determined to protect our holy places here. Millions are volunteering to fight ISIS. We're not interested in getting into a sectarian conflict with other Iraqis. We wish to defend our country.'[12]

Then we travelled to Wadi al-Salaam, the Valley of Peace, the gargantuan cemetery of five million souls on the outskirts of Najaf. For the past 1,400 years, the Shia have regarded this as their final resting place. Every few minutes a minibus arrived with a coffin strapped to the roof. Then the bodies were taken to special washrooms to be prepared for burial. Many victims of Islamic State were among the dead. I spoke to two men who had respectively lost a brother and a nephew to IS suicide bombers. Already by early morning, the heat was oppressive and pitiful sounds of grief filled the air. One young man who had lost his father was so overcome that he passed out in front of us and started having a fit, and had to receive immediate medical treatment.

The fall of Mosul forced the rest of the world to go through its own 'awakening'. Many people outside Iraq had not heard much about Mosul or even comprehended its importance, but they soon realized that the capture by a genocidal organization like ISIS of such an important city with a population of two million people was something that could not be taken lightly. Suddenly the threat posed by ISIS to the world as a whole felt as real as that first posed to the people of Anbar in western Iraq by Zarqawi and the killers who followed him.

For years, many news organizations had simply coalesced with the sensibilities of their consumers, particularly in the West, in recoiling from Iraq, the endless insurgency and the steady drumbeat of apparently pointless sectarian violence. During the first half of 2014, Syria, Ukraine and Libya had monopolized the Twittersphere, the newspapers and the radio and television bulletins. News from and about Iraq had long slipstreamed behind the stories many felt should be important and instead had become a sort of spam narrative that could be safely dumped into a folder marked 'things that no longer need concern us'.

Few people even realized that ISIS was simply the latest reincarnation of an old menace that had refused to die. Zarqawi was forgotten; Abu Omar al-Baghdadi had scarcely even registered in the public attention and neither had his former courier and successor, Abu Bakr al-Baghdadi, who had now emerged as caliph. It was as if ISIS were aliens from another planet. Inevitably, the right questions emerged. Who or what had helped nurture this threat and who or what had fed and funded it? These questions have proved awkward not just for the West and the elites of Iraq but also for the country's glowering neighbours, principally Saudi Arabia, Turkey and particularly Iran. Iraq had never just been about Iraq. While the rest of the world struggled to keep up, Abu Bakr al-Baghdadi and his grim Ba'athist commanders seemed to intensify the swarming nature of their invasion.

Baghdadi had wasted no time luxuriating in his surprise capture of Mosul. Immediately, he realized that the prize of Baghdad, the city he had terrorized for years, lay in his grasp. As Mosul fell, Baghdadi sent his jihadis south towards the Iraqi capital down Route One to seize Saddam Hussein's home city of Tikrit. The city fell, but even worse was to follow.

Near Tikrit, the jihadis seized Camp Speicher, a one-time US forward operating base. There they captured more than a thousand unarmed Iraqi Air Force cadets, predominantly Shia. They were tied up, loaded onto trucks and taken to wasteland nearby. Many were laid face down on the ground and machine-gunned to death; some were beheaded and others were strangled. Later, Baghdadi's media machine boasted of killing 1,700 young soldiers.[13] Their bodies would be exhumed in April 2015 after the Iraqis recaptured Tikrit.[14] Meanwhile, Mosul itself witnessed an exodus of half a million people. Many were Christians who had sought refuge there from the Islamic State of Iraq pogrom of Baghdad in 2006.[15]

There seemed to be a real risk of Baghdadi's men advancing on Baghdad from Tikrit in the north and from Fallujah, just forty or so miles to the west, and taking the capital. There was more than a note of triumphalism in the message issued by Islamic State's media 'sheikh', Abu Mohammed al-Adnani: 'March to meet your Lord. Don't be distracted by victory. Don't be gentle with your enemy, after Allah has granted you their shoulders. Continue your advance, for the furnace of war has not yet been fully heated.'[16]

On paper, it seemed impossible that Baghdad could fall to Islamic State. After all, some thirty thousand jihadis could surely not be a match for more than four million Shia who lived in Baghdad alone? No man is an island and neither are nation states, even if they are islands. Iraq's tragedy had long been a cause of deep anxiety to its neighbours. The key question is: in their concern and cynicism and insecurity had Iraq's neighbours, both Shia and Sunni, contributed to the rise of ISIS and the calamity that had suddenly befallen their region? The answer is assuredly 'yes'.

Iraq had contributed to its own disaster, but it had been aided and abetted by the states on its borders.

Iranians to the rescue

At this moment of crisis, what was left of Iraq would be rescued not by an Iraqi government already consumed by recriminations over the fall of Mosul but by two Iranians. Both men, one a senior cleric and the other a ruthless general, may have had different motives and different masters but their interventions in June 2014 proved critical in fending off the advance of Baghdadi.

During Friday prayers on 13 June 2014, Iraq's most important Shia cleric, Grand Ayatollah Ali al-Sistani, issued a historic fatwa calling on all Iraqis to fight ISIS. The ayatollah insisted that this was not just a call to arms aimed at his Shia followers. 'ISIS are a threat to Sunnis, too,' he told an acquaintance at the time.[17]

In the years following the US-led invasion, Grand Ayatollah Sistani remained steadfastly one of the few repositories of decency and common sense among Iraq's leaders. Born in August 1930, he was already into his seventies by the start of the occupation. Sistani's base was a modest house in Najaf and from here he dispensed advice on a whole range of issues from politics to matters of sex, although he was widely condemned for an anti-gay fatwa which he was later forced to withdraw following the murder of a fourteen-year-old Iraqi boy accused of homosexuality.[18] Few issues fell outside the grand ayatollah's remit when considering his followers. Sistani advised people on what types of fish they were allowed to eat ('permissible sea animals' included fish with scales, and shrimps) and men on when they should shave off their beard (only permissible if they were at risk of death by not shaving or if they were forced to shave it for medical reasons).[19]

Sistani was widely admired because, although he was a Shia and an Iranian, he considered himself to be essentially non-sectarian and an Iraqi nationalist. He had called for democratic elections in the face of the growing violence from 2003 onwards and had called on the Shia not to retaliate against the Sunnis following the Samarra shrine bombing in February 2006.[20] He sent instructions to his followers forbidding attacks on Sunni mosques. Sistani was disobeyed but he had tried to rein in the worst of the excesses following the attack. On several occasions, journalists and commentators had even recommended Sistani for the Nobel Peace Prize. In 2005, the American journalist and author Thomas L. Friedman had written in the *New York Times* to say, 'Lady Luck has shined on us by keeping alive this seventy-five-year-old ayatollah who resides in a small house in a narrow alley in Najaf and almost never goes out the door. How someone with his instincts and wisdom could have emerged from the train wreck of Saddam Hussein's Iraq I will never know.'[21] Sistani had also issued a fatwa in late 2013 denouncing and condemning the growing sectarian violence directed against Sunnis.[22]

Sistani's fatwa of June 2014 was a remarkable proclamation because it was a call for one jihad against another, that of 'Caliph' Baghdadi. The cleric had brushed off repeated calls for a fatwa for jihad after the Samarra bombing, a decision that probably reduced the ferocity of the civil war that followed and certainly saved lives. In June 2014, Sistani's call was for a defensive jihad not just to save the holy cities of Najaf and Karbala, but also to rescue the Sunni cities Mosul and Tikrit.[23] He urged all 'able-bodied' volunteers to enlist in the army according to the law and he made it clear that the 'the number of volunteers does not need to exceed the sufficient force that can accomplish the objective of protecting Iraq, its people and its sacred places'.

Sistani would also play an important part in the eventual

downfall of Nouri al-Maliki. Around six weeks before the fall of Mosul, Sistani demonstrated his disfavour of Maliki by refusing to receive the prime minister in Najaf.[24] At the height of the political crisis following the loss of Mosul, Sistani took the unusual step of writing to Maliki, urging him to step down.[25] Maliki resigned not long after, to be replaced by the Shia deputy speaker of parliament, Haidar al-Abadi.[26]

The second Iranian to come to Iraq's aid had already mobilized his own forces to fend off the jihadi tsunami. On 11 June 2014, the day before Adnani's genocidal message against the Shia, one General Qassem Suleimani from neighbouring Shia-dominated Iran deployed two battalions of his elite Revolutionary Guards, known as the Quds Force, into Iraq to fight ISIS.[27] Quds is not just any old elite brigade of fighters; its commander, Suleimani, reported directly to the president of Iran. The force takes its name from Quds, the Persian name for Jerusalem, which its fighters have promised to 'liberate' from Israeli occupation.

Back in September 2013, General Suleimani was described as 'the single most powerful operative in the Middle East', the sharp and brutal end of Iran's covert foreign policy throughout the region from Lebanon to Iraq.[28] He rose through the ranks during the bloody quagmire of the 1980–8 Iran-Iraq War to become one of Iran's youngest and most capable divisional commanders. Suleimani's Quds Force has extremely close links to Hezbollah, which was largely created and developed under Iranian guidance. Essentially, Hezbollah is considered to be the Lebanese branch of Quds.[29] With Hezbollah, Suleimani coordinated the military strategy of Bashar al-Assad, Syria's Alawite Shia president, and he would do the same for Shia-dominated Iraq after the fall of Mosul.

However, Suleimani's interference in the affairs of Iraq in the years running up to the ISIS incursion was already well established, extremely pervasive and not a little controversial. Unlike

Sistani, a native Iranian who wanted the best for Iraq, the principal beneficiary of Suleimani's nefarious activities was always going to be Iran. Sunni Iraqi politicians believed Iran was protecting itself by fostering insecurity and political instability in Iraq. The theory went that America would be too busy dealing with chaos in Iraq even to think of using it as a base for targeting Iran. Iran's funding and support for Shia political parties gave it immense influence in the country.[30] Later, the priority in 2014 was to prevent Iraq being completely overrun by genocidal Sunni terrorists. After the fall of Mosul, highly placed US security sources were convinced that Iran would have intervened much more aggressively, possibly with a full-scale invasion, had ISIS looked likely to take Samarra or threaten other holy Shia cities like Najaf.[31]

From 1980 to 1988, Iran and Iraq had been locked in a terrible war that cost an estimated one million lives and brought financial ruin on both countries. It had begun shortly after the Iranian Revolution, which toppled the Shah and brought to power the hardline Shia cleric Ayatollah Ruhollah Khomeini. Khomeini had lived in Najaf until he was thrown out of Iraq by Saddam Hussein in 1978, a year before his takeover of Iran. The ayatollah repaid the compliment by calling on the Shia of Iraq to overthrow Saddam and the Ba'ath. Saddam launched an invasion of Iran not long afterwards. The Iran-Iraq War also exposed the sectarian divide between Sunni and Shia long before the US-led invasion of Iraq. Iran had enormous vested interests in its turbulent western neighbour.

Through Suleimani, Iran's influence and power extended into Iraq's Shia political parties and militias. The armed groups funded by Quds carried out attacks on coalition and Iraqi troops. For example in January 2007, Quds was accused of attacking a military compound in Karbala, resulting in the kidnapping and 'execution' of four US soldiers. A fifth American soldier also died in the operation. The Pentagon believed that the assault was in retaliation for the Americans' capture on 11 January 2007 of five Quds fighters in Erbil, the capital of north Iraqi Kurdistan.

The US also repeatedly accused Quds of financing, training and arming Shia terror groups operating in Iraq. Both Quds and Hezbollah allegedly ran training camps for the so-called 'special groups' within Iran before sending them across the border into Iraq to participate in sectarian violence or attacks on coalition forces. In one raid on the offices of a mainstream Shia political party in Erbil at the beginning of 2007, US forces arrested three Quds operatives, including two senior commanders,[32] and seized documents including organization charts, lists of weapons, papers relating to the shipments of weapons and explosive charges into Iraq.

During 2007, the Americans made two more important arrests within Iraq, capturing the senior Quds commander, Mahmud Farhadj, as well as Ali Musa Daqduq, a senior officer in Hezbollah.[33] Daqduq was supposedly tasked with 'special groups' within the Mahdi Army, the militia associated with the cleric Muqtada al-Sadr. When the Americans talked of 'Iranian-backed militias', they meant primarily those groups supported and financed by Iran through Quds and Hezbollah. These groups and militias may have helped to save Iraq in the weeks and months following the fall of Mosul but they had also been a source of long-term instability and sectarian violence in Iraq. The five main Shia militias have proved to be a double-edged sword for Iraq.[34] In 2014, under Iranian direction, they essentially prevented IS from capturing Baghdad and possibly conquering the entire country.

However, the militias always remained capable of plunging the country into sectarian violence as they had in 2006 after the Samarra bombing.[35] Following the fall of Mosul, some militias were accused of abducting and killing Sunni men in response to IS attacks and bombings. An investigation by Amnesty International in late 2014 revealed how 170 predominantly Sunni young men were abducted in their home town of Samarra. Dozens were later found dead. On one day, 6 June 2014, more than thirty Samarris were abducted near their homes and shot dead. Their bodies were dumped nearby. The militias murdered some victims even after their families had paid the ransoms demanded. In May 2014, two young men, a 31-year-old civil servant and father of three and a 30-year-old engineer, were abducted. Their families paid up the agreed ransom of around $90,000 and a day later the corpses of both hostages turned up, with hands handcuffed behind their backs and gunshot wounds to the back of the head.[36] In April 2015, after being instrumental in the recapture of Tikrit under the command of General Suleimani, the Shia militias were accused of going on the rampage, looting, killing captured IS fighters and burning down hundreds of houses.[37] The militia's protection of Iraq has come at a heavy price.

Iran's growing influence is an important factor in the acrimonious debate about which countries may have helped fuel the rise of ISIS with money and weapons and whether or not Iran's activities in Iraq helped fuel Sunni support for the jihadis not just inside Iraq but also it seems from within predominantly Sunni nations in the Middle East, turning Iraq into a toxic regional political football. In particular, Iraq has been a battlefield for the proxy cold war between Sunni Saudi Arabia and Shia Iran. Saudi Arabia and Qatar, also predominantly Sunni, have even been accused of supporting and even funding ISIS and Sunni jihadi groups to help counter the growing influence of Tehran.

General Suleimani is also believed to be the patron of one of the most widely feared Shia militias, known as Asa'ib Ahl al-Haq, the so-called 'League of the Righteous'. Among the militia's commanders was the notorious power drill-wielding killer of Sunni men and boys first mentioned in Chapter 5, Abu Dura, also known as the 'Shiite Zarqawi'.[38] Abu Dura, whose real name is Ismail Hafiz al-Lami, was allegedly given shelter for two years by Iran before being allowed to return to Baghdad in 2010 to continue his 'work' in protecting the Shia majority.[39] Quds was also integral to the formation of the Shia political party the Supreme Council for the Islamic Revolution in Iraq, or SCIRI. The SCIRI militia, the Badr Corps, renamed the Badr Organization,[40] operated essentially as a unit of Quds. The Badr Organization was also implicated in the torture and murder of predominantly Sunni young men in the interior ministry scandal of 2005.[41]

Many Shia also resented Iran's enormous influence in Iraq, and particularly its main political ally, SCIRI, later renamed the Islamic Supreme Council of Iraq, or ISCI. Muqtada al-Sadr was also suspicious of Iranian influence although he was content enough on occasion to receive training and funds from Tehran.[42] Aside from SCIRI/ISCI, Iran had formidably close links with the Islamic Dawa, another important Shia political party whose leading members included Nouri al-Maliki.[43] In the days of Saddam, the leaders of these groups were political refugees, and often the guests of Iran. At one time SCIRI went as far as to recognize Iran's Ayatollah Khomeini as its effective supreme leader and even supported it in its war against Iraq. Many of these Dawa refugees returned to rule Iraq after the invasion, but they were often accused of remaining beholden to Tehran.

In Baghdad, around eight months before the fall of Mosul, I visited Hanna Edward, a prominent Iraqi human rights activist, to discuss the influence of Iran and other issues. She said:

Facing pressure from America and the West, Iran used Iraq as a buffer zone to defend themselves, and this means supporting the militias. Sometimes we even heard Iran supported al-Qaeda. The unstable situation has given the Iranians the opportunity to work in their own interests. In such a situation they can really play a big role within the Shia political parties and the others too.[44]

At the same time I also went to see the senior Shia political adviser Saad al-Muttalibi. He was kind enough to receive me at his Baghdad home despite just having survived an assassination attempt. A Shia militia apparently carried out the attempt, which he happily survived without injury, although he did not seem too keen to discuss the issue. His bullet-riddled utility vehicle sat on the drive outside. Around his desks were several weapons, including an AK-47 Kalashnikov and handguns. There were also some swords available by the mantelpiece.

Muttalibi acknowledged the influence of Iran but countered by pointing out the extensive meddling of neighbouring predominantly Sunni countries. He accused the Sunni former Iraqi deputy president Tariq al-Hashimi, later convicted of murder in absentia,[45] of 'actually receiving orders from Turkey'. When I pointed out that Iran funded Shia political parties in Iraq, Muttalibi replied, 'And so does Qatar and Saudi Arabia. We get nowhere by throwing around these accusations. It's also a fact that Saudi Arabia, Jordan, Qatar, Turkey and Egypt support certain Sunni politicians.'

By late 2013, Muttalibi had long been convinced that the Wahhabis, the extreme Salafi sect from which the Saudi royal family derives its religious legitimacy, were to blame for the rise of ISIS. He told me:

There is an organized genocide against Shias in Iraq and it has been recognized as such by several international organizations. We believe there is a religious organization behind it. The Wahhabis are a cult with an extremist view on Islam; they believe in the political Islamization of things; they believe in jihad. They believe that anyone who disagrees with them deserves to die and should be killed. They emphasize the necessity of killing all men, women and children of Shias because they consider them more dangerous than the Jews. After they have exterminated the Shia, they will then kill all the Jews and the Sunnis who do not agree with them.

Wahhabism granted legitimacy to the throne in Saudi Arabia because in Islam generally, monarchy is not allowed because the country should be ruled by the *khalifah*, the caliph, essentially an Islamic state, and the caliph should be elected, and should be 'the best of the best'. It is supposedly un-Islamic to have a monarchy line. So the Wahhabis granted legitimate means for the Saudi royal family to rule the country. In return the Saudi government and the ruling family granted favours to the Wahhabi leaders. Part of that means unlimited amounts of money. The Wahhabis run six thousand schools in Pakistan and Bangladesh alone. If each school produces one terrorist, you can see what kind of world they are planning for us.[46]

For many Sunnis, Iraq's Shia elite derived their power and authority from Iran, not from ordinary Iraqis. Many Sunnis believed they were being persecuted by Iranian-backed militia and excluded by Iranian-backed politicians. They resented Tehran's enormous influence and felt that for all intents and purposes, Iran was running Iraq. These fears were given credence somewhat later in March 2015 when a senior Iranian presidential adviser, Ali Younisi, was quoted as saying that 'Baghdad is now capital of the Iranian empire'.[47] Younisi's outburst was later 'clarified' by an embarrassed Iranian government statement emphasizing Iran's recognition of Iraq's sovereignty,[48] but the damage had been done in any event. Ordinary Iraqis and powerful forces beyond its borders had long believed that Iran, once a deadly enemy, had been the puppet master of Baghdad, and that ISIS would be the best device to cut the strings.

12
Car bombs and other expenses
2013–2015

You may imagine that a car bomb is a poor man's WMD, perfect for terrorists, because an old car with a tank full of petrol sounds like it could already be a bomb of sorts in the wrong hands, but nothing could be further from the truth. In reality, a car bomb is an expensive weapon and some experts believe you need the resources of a state to mass-produce them, particularly in the way ISIS was able to in 2013, the year which saw a strong ISIS resurgence especially in the Iraqi capital.

In late 2013, I was being driven around Baghdad with a security consultant who told me:

> You might hear on the news that a vehicle bomb containing fifty kilos of C4 plastic explosive went off or even a hundred kilos of C4. But people don't realize that just one kilo of this C4 explosive could cost you two thousand to three thousand dollars. So if you do the calculation for fifty or a hundred kilos, you realize that a huge amount of money is going on one vehicle bomb.

Sometimes you can have seventeen going off in one day, or twenty or thirty. So it's running into millions of dollars. I think it means it's not just an organization; there are countries funding them.[1]

According to the 2013 edition of *Al-Naba*, the ISIS annual report, the group carried out a total of 615 vehicle bombings, including 78 suicide attacks. The bill just for those assaults alone would total approximately $61.5 million, based on the security consultant's lower-end calculation for both the amount used and the supposed lower-end black-market cost of fifty kilos at $2,000 per kilo. Alongside that, the group laid claim to a further 4,639 bombings for 2013, including 4,465 improvised explosive devices, 160 suicide-vest attacks and 14 MCBIEDs, or motorcycle-borne improvised explosive devices.[2] It begs the question: how could Abu Bakr al-Baghdadi afford all this horror?

Relatively early in its history, it appeared that the group was surviving on its own financing independently of al-Qaeda. In his July 2005 letter admonishing Abu Musab al-Zarqawi for his excesses,[3] the then deputy al-Qaeda leader Ayman al-Zawahiri also begged his supposed subordinate for funds. Al-Qaeda's money problems had become acute, particularly following the Americans' capture of the organization's number three and suspected head of finance, Abu Faraj al-Libbi.[4] Zawahiri wrote:

The brothers informed me that you suggested to them sending some assistance. Our situation since Abu al-Faraj is good by the grace of God but many lines [of finance] have been cut off. Because of this, we need a payment while new lines are being opened. So if you are capable of sending a payment of approximately one hundred thousand [dollars], we'll be very grateful to you.[5]

Zarqawi may have received money from outside sources, possibly countries or organizations, but he was also a hardened criminal and his organization became wealthy by engaging in a number of successful criminal activities. For example in Anbar, Zarqawi and Abu Omar al-Baghdadi muscled in on the sheikhs' various smuggling rackets.[6] A US intelligence report leaked to the *New York Times* in November 2006 estimated that insurgents in Iraq were raising between $70 million and $200 million a year from illegal activities. Around $25 million to $100 million came from oil smuggling, aided by 'corrupt and complicit' Iraqi individuals. As much as $36 million was raised through ransoms paid for kidnap victims. 'If accurate,' the report said, then the estimates showed that 'these sources of terrorist and insurgent finance within Iraq – independent of foreign sources – are currently sufficient to sustain the group's existence and operation.' It went on, 'In fact, if recent revenue and expense estimates are correct, terrorist and insurgent groups in Iraq may have surplus funds with which to support other terrorist organizations outside of Iraq.'[7] Early in 2006, the oil ministry in Baghdad had estimated that between ten and thirty percent of Iraq's annual $4 billion fuel imports was smuggled back out of the country for resale. At that time, the Iraqi finance minister estimated that half of all the smuggling profits were going to the insurgents, including Zarqawi and Abu Omar al-Baghdadi.[8]

The anonymous source Wikibaghdady, who intelligence services believe has been leaking information from within Islamic State's leadership, revealed how the group under Baghdadi's leadership raised money to maintain its terror campaign in the years before the declaration of the caliphate in four ways, mainly through extortion, 'collecting funds from the Shia, Christians and other minorities' and 'gaining control over the oil fields and energy sources and government funding'. Any company in receipt of a government contract should be blackmailed. 'If the owner of the company doesn't agree, then he/she should be threatened to be killed or destroy the company,' reported Wikibaghdady. The last source of revenue mentioned was armed checkpoints that would take up to two hundred dollars at a time from drivers.[9] Wikibaghdady's revelations about the group's fund raising ring true. Over the years, the group had lived extremely well 'off the land' through extortion and blackmail. At heart it was a criminal organization, which, like organized crime syndicates, raised millions through protection rackets. Often, as in Raqqa, it would describe this money as *jizya* when demanded from Christians,[10] the word applied to the tax that the Prophet Muhammad asked of non-Muslim communities in return for protection back in the seventh century.[11] Other 'taxes' were demanded of businesses from garages to telecommunications companies. The deal was always the same: you pay, or you die.

Wikibaghdady revealed, 'The State started gaining a lot of money and this led to an increase in the salaries and funds to carry out military operations. This also led to more people wanting to join the State especially when they found out how much some members were getting paid.'[12]

It was clear that, particularly from 2012 onwards, a resurgent Islamic State of Iraq had growing access to resources and funds as it increased its terror. During 2012, it claimed to have carried out 3,156 bombings, including 352 car bombs.[13] In 2013, the total number of bombings claimed was 5,254, including the 615 car bombs.[14] The attacks were part of two distinct campaigns launched by Abu Bakr al-Baghdadi. The first campaign, 'Breaking the Walls', was targeted against the Shia and aimed at augmenting Baghdadi's ranks by breaking into prisons to free jihadis; the second campaign, 'Soldiers Harvest', was a classic exercise in the management of savagery, striking at important government infrastructure, security targets and naturally, of course, the Shia.

The 'Breaking the Walls' campaign began on 21 July 2012 and consisted of twenty-four major multiple-car-bomb 'spectaculars' and no fewer than eight prison break-ins.[15] The campaign culminated on 21 July 2013 in the astonishing success of Baghdadi's Abu Ghraib operation, which led to the escape of five hundred or more prisoners.[16] The assault involved suicide bombers, car bombs and rocket-propelled grenades. The ministry of justice later confirmed that sixty-eight Iraqi soldiers and security officers had died in the break-in.[17] By July 2013, the number of violent deaths had reached one thousand per month, for the first time since April 2008.[18]

Baghdadi announced the start of 'Soldiers Harvest' with a 'spectacular' of fifteen car bombings on 29 July 2013 that targeted a hospital, a restaurant and markets. Ten of the bombings were in Baghdad, mainly in Shia areas, killing more than fifty people and injuring another hundred.[19] An authoritative investigation by a former US army intelligence official called Jessica D. Lewis, for the think-tank the Institute for the Study of War, observed that the group's campaign 'showcases the depth of a multi-echelon military organization with well-established command and control that can design and implement coordinated attacks across Iraq'.

Lewis also said ominously, 'This organization enjoys unconstrained communication among teams as well as unconstrained access to human capacity and materiel.'[20] The 29 June spectacular to mark the start of 'Soldiers Harvest' may have cost Baghdadi between $3 million and $4.5 million.

Terrorism finance has always been a murky business, often involving secretive individuals, charities and intelligence agencies. On top of that, funds can often be laundered through different countries and via a wide variety of different methods, including exchange companies.[21] Few individuals and bodies ever own up to funding terrorism, and the merest hint of support for terrorist organizations can lead to economic sanctions, the closing or freezing of bank accounts and imprisonment. That is why there has been so much mystery and speculation about the source of any monies ISIS received outside its own criminal enterprises.

The CIA gained a significant insight into ISIS wealth following the discovery in June 2014 of 160 USB memory sticks belonging to a senior ISIS commander called Abdulrahman al-Bilawi. Bilawi, then head of Baghdadi's military council, had been betrayed by a senior ISIS courier called Abu Hajjar and killed in an operation not long afterwards. The flash drives discovered at Bilawi's hideout near Mosul provided a treasure trove of information about the group's finances, disclosing cash and assets worth approximately $875 million.[22] However, that was before the capture of Mosul, which took place just a few days following Bilawi's death. On 11 June 2014, it was reported that ISIS had taken some $429 million from the central bank in Mosul, which would have pushed its net worth to more than $1.3 billion.[23] Later Iraqi bankers and officials denied that the jihadis had stolen so much from the bank in Mosul,[24] but, thanks to a range of criminal activities, the group was unquestionably wealthy. Later it would even diversify into the sale of stolen antiquities, or at least those it had not destroyed.

There has been a degree of mythologizing around the group's wealth, although its net worth was estimated by Forbes Israel in October 2014 at around $2 billion, including the $1 million to $3 million a day it was said to earn from selling crude oil on the black market. The sum of $2 billion would make IS easily the richest terror organization in the world. Second-placed Hamas, with a reputed $1 billion, comes a long way behind.[25]

Wikibaghdady revealed how Baghdadi and Haji Bakr had gone about revolutionizing the group's finances, but aside from its own criminal activities, who or what was helping to fund the group in the decade before the fall of Mosul? Or was it self-financing and self-supporting? Individuals and countries have all denied helping ISIS, for obvious reasons, but many observers find it hard to believe that the group has been totally self-sufficient.

In February and March 2014, Nouri al-Maliki explicitly accused Saudi Arabia and Qatar of funding and supporting ISIS. In a speech he accused both countries of recruiting fighters in Fallujah, and in an interview with France 24 TV on 8 March 2014, the Iraqi prime minister said, 'I accuse them [Saudi Arabia and Qatar] of inciting and encouraging the terrorist movements. I accuse them of supporting them politically and in the media and by buying weapons for them.'[26]

Not only did Saudi Arabia vehemently deny any support for ISIS, its embassy in London also denied any links between the group and the Wahhabis, the Islamist sect which gives the monarchy its authority. In a statement issued to the London-based Saudi daily *Asharq al-Awsat* in August 2014, an embassy spokesman said, 'Saudi Arabia wants the defeat and destruction of ISIS... There have been suggestions that ISIS followers are members of some sort of Wahhabi absolutist sect. Indeed, certain UK media outlets often refer to Muslims within Saudi Arabia as Wahhabists. The unsubstantiated use of this inverted connotation must end because it is untrue.'[27] The Wahhabis may be Islamist extremists and share many of the intolerant beliefs of Islamic State, but they have never supported the idea of a caliphate and indeed rebelled against the authority of the Ottoman sultan, who was also the caliph.[28]

There may not be concrete proof of the Saudis' direct funding of ISIS but the US certainly believed there was credible evidence of terrorism funding emanating from Saudi Arabia and that this money was going to Sunni terrorists. In September 2007, Stuart Levey, then the US treasury department undersecretary tasked with tracking terror financing, said, 'If I could somehow snap my fingers and cut the funding off from one country, it would be Saudi Arabia.'[29] The Saudi government has always denied direct funding of ISIS in Syria, dismissing the claims of an unnamed official from Qatar who once told *The Atlantic* magazine in 2014, 'ISIS has been a Saudi project.'[30] The key phrase when it comes to funding terrorists is 'emanating from', which suggests funding is coming from individuals and charities, and that it is not necessarily authorized by the government. ISIS has declared that it wants Saudi Arabia as part of its caliphate and Baghdadi has even appointed *wali* (governors) for the holy Saudi cities of Mecca and Medina.[31] The 'caliph' himself has denied the legitimacy of the Saudi royal family, referring to it as 'the serpent's head' and 'the stronghold of the disease'.[32] Baghdadi has declared his intention to destabilize Saudi Arabia and on 23 May 2015, IS claimed responsibility for a suicide attack on a mosque in the Kingdom's predominantly Shia eastern city of Qatif, killing twenty-one people, and even identified the bomber as one Abu Amer al-Najdi. It appeared a classic management of savagery technique to foment sectarian strife between Saudi Arabia's majority Sunnis and its Shia minority, which makes up just ten percent of the population.[33]

Saudi Arabia followed events in post-invasion Iraq keenly, which is understandable as the two countries share a border of approximately five hundred miles and Saddam had presented a real security threat to the kingdom for years. The kingdom had felt deeply threatened by Saddam's invasion of Kuwait in 1990. The Saudis had allowed the US to station thousands of troops within their borders prior to the conflict. During the fighting they had seen the Iraqis attempt to take one of their towns, Khafji, on the border with Kuwait and were forced into a battle to save it. As a predominantly Sunni country, Saudi Arabia has always taken a keen interest in the regional ambitions of Iran. Relations between the two countries have often been strained and it is clear that the Saudi government grew increasingly alarmed at the growing Iranian influence in Iraq.

According to a secret US cable on 2 January 2006, at a meeting in his capital, Riyadh, Saudi King Abdullah had bitterly complained that whereas in the past the US, Saudi Arabia and Saddam Hussein had agreed 'on the need to contain Iran', US policy had handed Iraq to Iran as a 'gift on a golden platter'.[34] Later in 2006, the Saudis offered to broker a meeting between the US and 'disaffected' Iraqi Sunni leaders. The American ambassador to Iraq told the Saudis that such meetings would be possible 'provided the Iraqis involved were not affiliated with terrorists like Zarqawi or with Saddam'. According to the secret cable, the Saudis 'laughed' at such a suggestion, claiming that 'Saddam's people are our enemies and we are looking for Zarqawi'.[35]

Professor Madawi al-Rasheed is a prominent Saudi Arabian scholar and historian of her native country, and is based at King's College London. She said:

The Saudi position on the American-led invasion of Iraq was contradictory. Saudi Arabia wanted to see Saddam Hussein go because it saw him as a regional threat, especially after he invaded Kuwait in 1990. But at the same time Saudi Arabia did not anticipate that the American invasion would actually lead to the expansion of Iranian influence. Saudi Arabia rejoiced over the overthrow of Saddam but it did not see what was going to come. As a result, Saudi Arabia had to live with the aftermath and manage the outcome of that American invasion.

First they refused to readmit Iraq into the Arab community or the Arab League. They immediately saw the appointment of a Shia majority government as a threat but also Iran had an incredible opportunity after the removal of Saddam in the sense that it initially had a huge number of Iraqi exiles who were expelled by Saddam in the 1980s. At the same time it had religious links with Iraq and Iraqi cities and it immediately penetrated Iraqi society through religious and political channels.

Saudi Arabia saw that as a problem, and from that moment the regional rivalry between Iran and Saudi Arabia started to take place in Iraq and later it spilled over into Syria and Lebanon, and later into Yemen.[36]

I asked Professor Rasheed whether she thought that either Saudi Arabia or entities and organizations from there had funded the jihadis from the time of Zarqawi onwards. She said:

> The funding is a very difficult thing. We know that after 2003 there were quite a lot of calls in Saudi Arabia to help Iraqi refugees who were mainly Sunnis who fled certain areas of Baghdad and Iraq in general and moved to Syria and Jordan.
>
> In terms of funding, I think governments know what and who is funding. As an outside observer I cannot say there was Saudi funding. But I do know there were campaigns to raise money and when we are talking about funding, we have to distinguish between state actors and non-state actors. Also, in a country like Saudi Arabia, the line between the two is very blurred. So in an opaque situation like Saudi Arabia, even that can be very difficult when we don't know who is with an NGO [non-governmental organization] and who isn't.

Of course, Saudi nationals have played a prominent role in terrorism in Iraq and elsewhere. Osama bin Laden was Saudi, as were fifteen of the nineteen hijackers participating in the 9/11 attacks. The Islamic State of Iraq records discovered in 2007[37] revealed that Saudi Arabia contributed the largest number of jihadis by far to the group, around forty-one percent of the total from August 2006 onwards.[38] Until Baghdadi made clear his threat to Saudi Arabia, there was support for ISIS in the kingdom and the group actively targeted Saudis with fundraising campaigns.[39] The anonymous source Wikibaghdady revealed that Baghdadi had deployed a media team to Saudi Arabia to promote ISIS and defend its reputation. Another team of Saudi media operatives would operate inside Syria.[40] Wikibaghdady also disclosed the identity of another close adviser to Baghdadi, a Saudi officer called Bandar bin Shaalan, who was asked to be the representative of the 'state' in Saudi Arabia. Wikibaghdady added, 'Bandar has had a great relationship with Abu Bakr al-Baghdadi.' Bin Shaalan also introduced Baghdadi to another Saudi, called al-Abu Bakr al-Qahtani, who later became head of Baghdadi's religious department.[41] Qahtani had links to what are described as 'religious leaders from Saudi Arabia',[42] although there is no evidence that this is a reference to the wealthy Wahhabis. 'Al-Qahtani was also responsible for bringing religious leaders from Saudi Arabia,' said Wikibaghdady, 'especially the ones who truly cared about Syria and are against al-Zawahiri [Ayman al-Zawahiri, leader of al-Qaeda]'.[43]

Yet another secret US cable in late 2009 made clear that, as far as the Obama White House was concerned, donors in Saudi Arabia constituted 'the most significant source of funding to Sunni terrorist groups worldwide'.[44] By then, of course, Islamic State of Iraq, as ISIS was known then, was regarded by the Pentagon as somewhat of a busted flush, or was rather lazily lumped in with al-Qaeda. A cable authorized by the then secretary of state, Hillary Clinton, also said rather damningly, 'While the Kingdom of Saudi Arabia takes seriously the threat of terrorism within Saudi Arabia, it has been an ongoing challenge to persuade Saudi officials to treat terrorist financing emanating from Saudi Arabia as a strategic priority.'

In 2008, the United States went as far as to deploy a treasury official to Riyadh specifically to help the Saudis deal with terrorism funding. 'Despite this presence more needs to be done,' the secret memo continued. 'Saudi Arabia remains a critical financial support base for al-Qaeda, the Taliban…and other terrorist groups including Hamas, which probably raise millions of dollars annually from Saudi sources often during Hajj and Ramadan.'[45]

The annual Hajj pilgrimage was a particular problem for the Saudis as many pilgrims arrived in Mecca with large amounts of cash. The Saudis had passed a law requiring arriving travellers to declare cash above a certain level, but the Hajj remained 'a vacuum in our security', as they admitted to the US.[46] However, only in March 2014 did Saudi Arabia formally designate ISIS as a terrorist entity, along with al-Nusra Front and Hezbollah.[47]

Social media funding has also presented problems for Saudi officials in tracing and blocking private donations. Furthermore, Saudi donors are encouraged to funnel any monies through Kuwait, long considered to be 'one of the most permissive terrorism environments in the gulf'.[48] Two other predominantly Sunni countries, Turkey and Qatar, have also been accused of supporting ISIS. Again Turkey, Qatar and Kuwait have all denied the allegations.

I went through the list of prime terror-funding suspects with Dr Afzal Ashraf, consultant fellow and leading terrorism expert with the influential defence think-tank the Royal United Services Institute. He said:

I haven't come across any evidence of these countries' direct involvement. There are a lot of claims but that region is full of claims and counterclaims and rumours.

There is no doubt that al-Qaeda certainly and possibly ISIS

gained some private support from individuals in those countries and from countries beyond. There are some people who support al-Qaeda to varying degrees in all of these countries. Very few are hard-core supporters and would actually pay al-Qaeda. Only rich individuals would do so. There are conspiracy theories, with some people even thinking al-Qaeda for example was created by the West.

I'm not sure at all, though, about state support. I certainly cannot imagine that the countries that you have listed, Saudi Arabia, Qatar and Kuwait, would dare to support al-Qaeda after 9/11. They just would not because they are totally beholden to the US. They know the price of funding and supporting any organization that is a declared enemy of the US. So those leaders would never ever allow that to happen knowingly.[49]

Former US Ambassador to Iraq, James Jeffrey, agreed with Dr Ashraf. 'We found no evidence of direct funding for ISIS,' he said. 'We had concerns about individual citizens but that's really hard to crack down on. Even we would have a really difficult time cracking down on it.'[50] However, allegations of Qatari meddling in the internal affairs of its neighbours are rife throughout the region. In the summer of 2013, Libyan army generals, including the acting chief of the general staff, spoke angrily to me of their suspicion that Qatar was helping to destabilize the country by funding and supporting certain militias, notably the powerful Libya Dawn group.[51] In May 2013, protestors in the Libyan capital, Tripoli, protested against Qatari interference and even burned the Qatari flag.[52]

In August 2014, the German development minister, Gerd Müller, went as far as accusing Qatar of past funding of ISIS. 'You have to ask who is arming, who is financing ISIS troops,' Müller said. 'The key word here is Qatar.'[53] The German government later distanced itself from Müller's remarks.[54] Again there is no evidence of official funding, but the suspicions of Qatari involvement in both ISIS and al-Nusra Front have remained.

Long before the fall of Mosul another Gulf state, Kuwait, had emerged as a financing and organization centre for charities and individuals supporting the many groups fighting Syria's President Assad. In December 2013, an authoritative report by the Brookings Institution think-tank said, 'These donors have taken advantage of Kuwait's unique freedom of association and its relatively weak financial rules to channel money to some of the estimated thousand rebel groups now fighting against Syrian President Bashar al-Asad [*sic*].'[55] In mid-2013, Kuwait enacted laws that for the first time criminalized terrorist financing. But according to the Brookings Institute, 'much work is needed to fully implement the new law and Kuwait's unique freedoms of assembly and association make it difficult to halt religious charities' activities'.[56]

Turkey has also been accused of helping to fund and supply ISIS, again, allegedly, as part of the bulwark against Iranian dominance of the Middle East. The country's hard-nosed president, Recep Tayyip Erdoğan, formed an alliance with Saudi Arabia to confront Iran and its 'expansionist and sectarian attitude'.[57] Professor Yasin Aktay is a leading member of Turkey's ruling Justice and Development Party (AKP) and sits on its ruling executive.[58] When we met in London, I asked Professor Aktay whether Turkey had been helping ISIS. He said:

The claim is completely ridiculous. Logically, it is impossible for us to support ISIS because ISIS is very dangerous for Turkey and it would be like playing with a bomb. Turkey has never approached ISIS and helped it.

The criticism of Turkey comes from within Turkey. There is a

very dangerous political interplay in Turkey. Our political opponents have tried to destroy our party's image. Turkey has very
openly and obviously and deliberately supported the Free Syrian
Army and the FSA is the only legitimate ally we have in Syria.
Britain has also supported the FSA. ISIS has been the enemy of
the Free Syrian Army.

What we in Turkey understand is that ISIS emerged out of the
very dangerous discrimination against the Sunni people in Iraq.
After America withdrew from Iraq they left the government to
the Shia group and this Shia group was playing with Iran. The
Nouri al-Maliki government very dangerously and violently discriminated against the Sunni and tried to make Iraq a Shia state,
and there were also many murders and massacres of Sunnis. This
created too much upset among the Sunnis and out of this
emerged a mood of revenge. This created two enemies as far as
the Sunnis were concerned: the US and the West, and the Shia.
ISIS has nothing to do with Islam; it is all to do with revenge
against the Shia. That is not to legitimize it but to try and understand it.[59]

Islamic State became financially independent thanks to theft,
extortion and selling oil on the black market. Snarling ferociously,
the group went on to bite the hands of those countries accused of
feeding and sustaining it with fighters, arms and money. According
to Baghdadi, all of the countries mentioned as his secret state
backers must, in any event, be absorbed into his caliphate. None of
Iraq's neighbours in the Middle East have ever admitted culpa-
bility for the rise of ISIS nor are they ever likely to. What is certain
is that the ISIS monster emerged from a poisonous witches' brew
of sectarianism, proxy wars and competing national and international interests. In the past, the law of unintended consequences
led the US and Saudi Arabia to fund the Mujahidin in the fight

against the Soviet Union, and that led ultimately to the creation of both the Taliban and al-Qaeda. If countries such as Saudi Arabia or Kuwait used ISIS, then ISIS used them right back in return. They say the path to Hell is paved with good intentions, but it can be paved with bad intentions too.

13
'Long live death!' – Inside the caliphate

2014–

We know a lot about the Prophet Muhammad's vision for an Islamic state because he described it in a document called the Constitution of Medina. Exiled from his home city of Mecca by his own Quraysh tribe, the Prophet was given refuge by the people of Medina, a town little more than two hundred miles directly north up the Hijaz peninsula of what is now Saudi Arabia. In 622 CE, the people of Medina asked Muhammad to write the constitution. The result was a social-military contract for the city's population, a third of whom were Jews.

The constitution was drawn up to recognize the rights of the city's minorities, namely the Jews, as well as to deal with the military threat posed by the bellicose Quraysh from Mecca. The document consisted of sixty-three articles, of which ten specifically related to the religious rights of the nine main Jewish tribes of Medina. Article 30, for example, stated, 'The Jews of Banu Awf shall be considered a community among the believers [Muslim]. They shall be guaranteed the right of religious freedom among the Muslims.'[1] The Jews were required to pay a 'proportionate liability of war expenses along with the believers' in the ongoing struggle against the Quraysh, 'so long as they [the Jews] continue to fight in conjunction with them'.[2]

As an Islamic scholar, Abu Bakr al-Baghdadi would know a great deal about the Constitution of Medina; his Islam-based cult purports to recreate the earliest days of the Prophet and the two golden generations that followed him. So it seems curious that the apparent vision of tolerance and inclusion incorporated in the Constitution of Medina more than 1,300 years ago should be so at odds with the misery and destruction that Islamic State has inflicted on the territories it has controlled.

Baghdadi's caliphate is not a static creation. Islamic State seeks to conquer what it sees as the Muslim world before the 'caliph' eventually turns his full wrath on the lands of the *kuffar*, the hated apostates. However, in Iraq at least, in the year following the fall of Mosul, IS already started to yield some of the towns and territory it had captured to Iraqi militias and military only to conquer elsewhere, such as Ramadi in the west of the country. In 2013–14, its campaign of conquest and even its war crimes were familiar and recognizable enough to most people with a little knowledge of warfare. However, as this military campaign appeared to stall, the expansion of Baghdadi's Islamic State took unorthodox and unfamiliar forms, as IS suddenly appeared in other troubled lands.

In March 2015, the Islamist group in Nigeria known as Boko Haram pledged allegiance or *bay'ah* to Baghdadi, therefore recognizing him as caliph.[3] Boko Haram, also known as Jama'at Ahlis-Sunnah, has almost equalled IS in brutality and ferocity. The group acquired worldwide opprobrium in April 2014 when it kidnapped more than two hundred schoolgirls during an attack on a secondary school. In the eyes of Baghdadi, this crime was something to be applauded. A 2015 edition of his propaganda magazine *Dabiq* says, 'They [Boko Haram] did not fear the blame of any critic when they captured and enslaved hundreds of Christian girls, even as the Crusader media machine put the brunt of its strength into focusing the world's attention on the issue.'[4]

Elsewhere, in late 2014, IS announced its presence amid the chaos of Libya in the country's eastern city of Derna, not far from the Egyptian border and just a 200-mile boat ride across the Mediterranean to Crete and Europe.[5] In early 2015, IS suddenly appeared hundreds of miles to the west, in Colonel Muammar Gaddafi's hometown of Sirte, fighting militias, and carrying out the gratuitous beheadings of twenty-one innocent Egyptian Coptic Christians[6] who happened to be working in Libya as builders.[7] Thirteen were from one village in Egypt, el-Aour, a majority Christian village in the Nile valley.[8] After the beheadings on a beach near Sirte, the masked leader of the killers pointed his knife towards the freshly bloodied waters of the sea and said, 'We will conquer Rome, by Allah's permission.'[9] In April 2015, IS murdered another thirty Christians in Libya, this time from the Ethiopian Church. IS footage showed one group of men being shot in the desert and another group being beheaded on a beach.[10] The post-revolutionary chaos provided the ideal opportunity for IS to establish a small but menacing presence in both eastern and western Libya.[11] It was textbook 'management of savagery' stuff. IS boasted pledges of allegiance from affiliate 'mujahidin' in Algeria, the Sinai in Egypt, Yemen and the 'Arabian peninsula'.[12]

Islamic State's reach proved to be long and deadly. In September 2014, the IS franchise in Algeria decapitated its French hostage, the tourist Hervé Gourdel, after the expiration of its ultimatum to France to halt air strikes against IS in Iraq.[13] In April 2014, Baghdadi engaged in more aggressive poaching from his humbled jihad competitors when he received pledges from nine former al-Qaeda emirs from Afghanistan, Turkmenistan and Iran, an area

IS calls 'Khorasan' and hopes one day to conquer.[14] Again the world was taken by surprise when IS gained control over the Palestinian refugee camp at Yarmouk just six miles from the centre of Damascus. A supposed haven became a deadly killing ground as the jihadis terrorized the camp's remaining 16,000 or so inhabitants and beheaded captives.[15]

To write a definitive account of this Islamic state, Baghdadi's 'caliphate', feels rather like building a house on foundations of jelly. Very few reporters have been allowed into the caliphate to describe what they see, and even then their movements have been tightly controlled by IS. The broiling ferocity, which initially sustained the caliphate's giddying expansion, may burn itself out; the 'state' may suddenly collapse under the onslaught from land and air by the global coalition arrayed against it. It may expand its territories in ways that cannot be predicted. The group has always taken the world by surprise and few people can say with any confidence what will happen next. However, most governments and experts think IS will not disappear any day soon and believe that its virulent and intolerant form of Islam will prove extremely difficult to eradicate.

By July 2014, the IS caliphate stretched approximately 415 miles from northern Syria to the town of Sulaiman Bek not far from the Iranian border. Its mainly captive population was numbered at anything between five and six million; around two million lived in Mosul alone. It has often been stated in the media that IS occupied an 'area larger than the United Kingdom'.[16] By the spring of 2015, it had shrunk somewhat since those heady days and may shrink significantly further should it lose Mosul and other towns. Whatever the reality on the ground, Islamic State continued to portray its caliphate as inevitable and enduring.[17]

Digitally, the caliphate stretches as far as the eye can see, from Twitter to Tango, and on to Snapchat. It projects an image of invincibility through 'Muja tweets', 'Facebooking' and 'Whatsapping', and even when it leaks, it does so through Wikibaghdady. IS uses terror to control its temporal caliphate and seeks to intimidate a vastly more powerful outside world via the Internet with its many snuff movies depicting its massacres and decapitations of innocent journalists and aid workers, and even the burning to death of a Jordanian pilot. The public 'executions' – whether they are women stoned to death for adultery or men beheaded for 'sorcery' – are designed to terrorize the group's captive millions into submission, and cow the rest of the world into leaving the caliphate alone.

The second part of the strategy proved to be an abject failure, because all it did was provoke the coming together of an unlikely coalition of more than 60 nations including Iran, Syria, Saudi Arabia and United States, Russia and even Switzerland[18] which is determined to destroy Islamic State. To many experts, this demonstrated a lamentable misunderstanding of the West. There are also signs that the first part of the strategy, of subjugating its captive population, may start to unravel. IS faces its own internal insurgency from a number of small groups, including the Raqqa Rebels Brigade, or also known as Thuwar Raqqa. In late January/early February 2015, IS killers publicly 'executed' five men and a seventeen-year-old youth who had confessed to having links to the Raqqa Rebels.[19] Naturally the murders were videoed by IS and the film posted on the Internet with the title 'The Liquidation Process of a Sleeper Cell'. This 'process' involved handcuffing the six and gunning them down in front of a large crowd. They had been accused of attempting to bomb IS headquarters in Raqqa. In October 2014, IS attempted to kidnap the leader of the Raqqa Rebels, Abu Issa, in Turkey and smuggle him across the Syrian border into the caliphate. IS militants ambushed Abu Issa in the Turkish town of Urfa, which lies not far from the Syrian border.

Eventually the jihadis realized they were not going to get past the Turkish border guards, abandoned the attempt to get Issa into Syria, and decided not to kill him. Instead they dropped him off at a Turkish hospital with a gunshot wound in his side.[20]

In Anbar, IS has faced uprisings from old Awakening enemies. The Albu Nimr tribe, also Sunni, desperately fought IS in October 2014 but ran out of ammunition, food and fuel. Eventually, IS captured their village of Zauiyat Albu Nimr and carried out a general massacre in which an estimated 322 men, women and children died.[21] There have been frequent reports from Anbar of Sunni tribesmen, many of them former Awakening members, courageously fighting IS. On 10 December 2014, IS captured twenty-one former Awakening fighters near the town of Baghdadi and shot them two days later.[22]

Islamic State has fondly portrayed the caliphate as the land of plenty. Happy pastoral scenes of people gathering fruit and vegetables from their fields or cheerfully shopping in the markets are abundant on its websites and elsewhere. The truth on the ground is somewhat different. By April 2015, images of long food queues began to emerge from Raqqa,[23] as did reports of epidemics, including five hundred cases of the flesh-eating disease leishmaniasis,[24] spread by a type of sandfly and often symptomatic of poverty, pollution and malnutrition. The pictures of deprivation and poverty[25] were completely at odds with the portrayal of the caliphate by the supposedly slick propaganda machine of media 'sheikh' Abu Mohammed al-Adnani. Hunger has proved a powerful threat to tyranny down the ages, as many a toppled dictatorship or monarchy could confirm.

The terror and cruelty experienced by ordinary people in the 'Islamic State' will come as no surprise to anyone with knowledge of the group's previous attempts at a caliphate. The horror stories of murder and mayhem sound depressingly similar to those emanating from areas of Iraqi Kurdistan terrorized by Abu Musab al-Zarqawi and the group Ansar al-Islam in 2001,[26] and from Anbar when it groaned under the tyranny of Zarqawi and Abu Omar al-Baghdadi in 2006 and 2007.[27] Each time, the story was the same, a macabre farce where savagery and fear constitute the weft and warp of the so-called 'state'.

The caliphate announced in July 2014 was unquestionably on a greater scale than its nasty and pathetic predecessor regimes. After all, there are an estimated five to seven million people said to be living under IS, far in excess even of the one million Anbaris the group terrorized in 2006–7. However, the one defining achievement of each 'caliphate' or 'emirate' has been the same – death, and plenty of it. The caliphate has not delivered security, human dignity, happiness and the promise of eventual peace, let alone basic services, but it has produced piles of corpses and promises to produce piles more. The IS factory line of death is the one piece of machinery that manages to work through the many electricity stoppages experienced on a daily basis by the caliphate's population: fuel is cheap but so is life.

In that sense, IS is immediately recognizable as one of the 'apocalyptic and death-obsessed' mass movements described by the American writer Paul Berman in his book *Terror and Liberalism*, written not long after the 9/11 attacks. He included both the Islamists and the Ba'ath Party on his list, and it is hard not to think of 'Khalifah' Abu Bakr al-Baghdadi in Berman's description of the typical leader of such a movement:

> The Leader was a superman. He was a genius beyond all geniuses. He was the man on horseback who, in his statements and demeanour was visibly mad and who, in his madness, incarnated the deepest of the anti-liberal impulses, which was the revolt against rationality.

For the Leader embodied a more than human force. He wielded the force of History (for the Bolsheviks and Communists); or the force of God (for the Catholic fascists); or the force of the biological race (for the Nazis). And, because his person exercised a power that was more than human, he was exempt from the rules of moral behaviour, and he showed his exemption, therefore his divinelike quality, precisely by acting in ways that were shocking.[28]

This also works as a description of Saddam Hussein, and it is worth remembering that the violent Islam-based *takfirism* of Islamic State is only one side of the IS coin. The former Ba'athist army officers and intelligence officials were always on the flip side and if anything, they and their methods became more prominent with the setting up of the caliphate. Both the Ba'athists and the jihadis know how to terrorize people and how to spy on them. Totalitarianism comes naturally to both wings of Islamic State. Insidiously, their 'state' has infiltrated family life, forced women into marriage and taken away children and turned them into killers.

'Raqqa is being slaughtered silently'

Baghdadi believed that all Muslims had a duty to come to the new caliphate. 'And we call on every Muslim in every place to perform hijrah [to journey to a place of refuge] to the Islamic State,' implored Baghdadi in his audio message released in May 2015, although he never explained how all 1.6 billion of the Ummah were going to fit into his still modestly sized caliphate.[29] Mosul was Islamic State's greatest prize, but its de facto capital was always Raqqa. Raqqa was the first city to fall under the sway of IS and the group battled to prevent it falling into the hands of its opponents, including Nusra Front.[30] It was the fall of Raqqa initially to Nusra in late March 2013[31] that inspired Baghdadi to travel to Syria and make his ill-fated attempt to take back control of Nusra. In all likelihood, if and when it happens, the last stand of Islamic State will take place in Raqqa.

Raqqa is situated in northern Syria on the north bank of the river Euphrates and has a population of around 220,000. One of the best sources for what has been happening in the city under IS control is a website called Raqqa Is Being Slaughtered Silently (RBSS). Communicating with the outside world has proved to be an extremely hazardous business for anyone living in the caliphate. For example, in April 2015, a Facebook page called Mosul Eye issued a dire warning to the people of Mosul: 'You are advised to totally avoid using the social networking platform "Line" in your social communication as this networking platform is penetrated by ISIS. A man was beheaded recently [after being] accused with treason for using this software for communicating with government forces and exchanging information with them.'[32]

RBSS has been run by a group of extraordinarily brave young people. IS has so far murdered at least three of the team for working for the site. I have been in contact with one of the site's most important founders and writers. He likes to be known as Abu Mohammed, but of course that is not his real name. He comes from Raqqa and lived there when Baghdadi seized control in the autumn of 2013. Abu Mohammed remembered the city before IS:

> My family was just like any other family from the city of Raqqa; we had our own customs and traditions, all of us were studying in schools and universities. We are not secularists, we are moderate Muslims, we are not militants.
>
> I smoke, as does my father too, but we do not drink alcohol. Sometimes I'd go dancing and of course I listen [to] music. We

dressed in normal clothes and our women did not cover their faces. Most of them did not like to wear the burqa or anything like that. Life was good.[33]

Obviously, life in Raqqa worsened rapidly with the onset of the Syrian civil war. Abu Mohammed said, 'Raqqa changed a lot. There has been so much damage. Bashar al-Assad's forces made random arrests; there was a lot of injustice.' First Raqqa fell to Nusra.[34] 'Al-Nusra resembled ISIS a lot,' said Abu Mohammed, 'but they were less brutal in Raqqa.

'ISIS first arrived in Raqqa on 4 September 2013, and later lost it. When it retook the city on 12 January 2014, it was brutal. They executed approximately two hundred people and after that exercised indiscriminate arrests, kidnapped activists and carried out beheadings and hand amputations.'

Abu Mohammed said the city's women had probably suffered more than anyone else since the occupation by IS, 'The situation of women in Raqqa has been very bad. Many of them were forced to marry ISIS fighters. In at least one case, a woman has committed suicide. ISIS also took a decision preventing any woman under fifty from leaving Raqqa except in serious medical cases.' Again, as in Anbar in 2006 and 2007, the group was seeking to insinuate itself in the fabric of Raqqa and throughout the 'caliphate' through forced marriage.[35]

Women were the subject of constant harassment and arbitrary arrest, according to Abu Mohammed, who added, 'A woman friend of mine was arrested and tortured. She was detained for fifteen days and suffered beatings and humiliation. Other Syrian women and even some immigrant women tortured her. After her release, she bore the marks on her body for months and for a long time afterwards she would wake screaming and terrified every night from her nightmares.' In April 2015, in the town of Tabaqa, not far from Raqqa, women were effectively prohibited from receiving dental treatment, by official decree. IS raided dental clinics to prevent male dentists treating women patients, which the militants considered 'contrary to Islam'.[36]

In particular, Yazidi women captives have suffered grievously at the hands of IS since the group's invasion during August 2014 of their homelands in Iraq's Nineveh province. Around 200,000 Yazidis managed to escape Baghdadi's genocidal onslaught[37] but the United Nations later confirmed that around 5,000 mainly male refugees were massacred and bulldozed into mass graves while around 7,000 Yazidi women were literally enslaved and many were used for sex.[38] In late 2014, IS distributed a pamphlet entitled *Su'al wa-Jawab fi al-Sabi wa-Riqab*, or 'Questions and Answers on Taking Captives and Slaves'. It is little more than a justification for systematic rape and paedophilia in a series of rhetorical questions and answers. For example, question 5 asks, 'Is it permissible to have intercourse with a female captive immediately after taking possession [of her]?' The answer is, 'If she is a virgin, he [her master] can have intercourse with her immediately after taking possession.' Question 13 asks, 'Is it permissible to have intercourse with a female who has not reached puberty?' The answer is, 'It is permissible to have intercourse with the female slave if she is fit for intercourse; however, if she is not fit for intercourse, then it is enough to enjoy her without intercourse.'[39]

Like the Christians and the Shia, the Yazidis had suffered years of murder and persecution at the hands of the group, including the devastating bomb attacks on their villages in August 2007.[40] Following the tragedy it inflicted at Sinjar IS boasted about its horrendous treatment of Yazidi women in *Dabiq*, the glossy periodical produced by 'Sheikh' Adnani. In an editorial entitled 'The Revival of Slavery before the Hour', *Dabiq* described the Yazidis as a 'pagan minority' and their creed as 'deviant'. 'Even cross-worshipping Christians for ages considered them devil worshippers and Satanists,' *Dabiq* claimed.[41]

The Yazidis were given an ultimatum: 'repent or face the sword'.[42] The article continued: 'Also their women could be enslaved…After capture, the Yazidi women and children were then divided according to the Shari'ah amongst the fighters of the Islamic State who participated in the Sinjar operations, after one fifth of the slaves were transferred to the Islamic State authority to be divided as *khums* [a traditional Islamic twenty-percent tax on war booty].'[43] The Yazidi women were to be used as concubines in perpetuity, but any offspring would be free, unlike their mother, so 'the slave girl gives birth to her master'.[44]

In April 2015, a report by the charity Human Rights Watch detailed the systematic rape and sexual violence committed by IS jihadis against Yazidi women. The report was based on interviews conducted by the charity in the town of Dohuk in Iraqi Kurdistan with twenty women and girls who had escaped from IS. Half, including two twelve-year-old girls, said they had been raped.[45] Separately, a local doctor said that of the 105 women and girls she had examined, 70 appeared to have been raped in IS captivity.

For the Human Rights Watch investigators, the rapes and abuses of Yazidi women captives went beyond just being 'widespread'. This abuse was 'systematic', even a 'methodical plan'. The report added, 'ISIS public statements concerning enslavement, forced marriage, and abuse of captured women, as well as the organized sale of Yezidi [*sic*] women and girls, indicate a widespread practice and a systematic plan of action by ISIS.'[46]

After death, sex seems to be the next great obsession of Islamic State fighters. In February 2015, local doctors in Raqqa were reporting that IS fighters were demanding Viagra 'to have more sex'. According to RBSS 'the fighters take numerous wives to satisfy their demand for sex, and spend large amounts of time searching for "sabaya" – kidnapped women and children, some of them as young as nine, sold into slavery'. Doctors disclosed to the site's reporters that 'a large section of ISIS members suffer from sexual anomalies and [a] brutal instinctive desire for sex'.[47] Many women in Raqqa dare not venture outside in case of falling into the hands of IS militants. If they do, they are forced to cover not only their body but their face and hands as well. The jihadis have taken advantage of the poverty sweeping Raqqa to force local families into effectively selling their daughters for between $2,000 and $5,000.[48]

There is a strange contradiction at the heart of the 'state'. There are its many crimes and then there is the elaborate bureaucracy that commits them. Based on documents discovered at an IS hideout, the *Telegraph* website published what was then a definitive organization plan for the group in July 2014.[49] For example, one Abu Suja (real name Auf Abdulrahman Elefery) was given the job of 'coordinator of prisoners and women's affairs', an apposite and ominous-sounding portfolio if ever there was for the beleaguered women of Raqqa.[50] One of the more curious IS job titles must surely be the position apparently held by Abdulla Ahmad al-Mishhadani as of January 2015, that of 'coordinator of guest houses and suicide bombers'.[51] Baghdadi's chief adviser, Haji Bakr, also played an enormous role in drawing up the terror management blueprint of the caliphate, according to documents discovered at his house. Each district and region would have its own 'security emir'. At a regional level, the emir would lead a team that would include two deputy emirs, a secret service boss, and separate departments for surveillance and security and training spies. At a district level, the emir would oversee a structure including heads of departments for weapons, prisons and interrogation, 'economic targets', 'intelligence cells' and the training of Sharia judges.[52]

Islamic State is undeniably 'an impressively managed and

obsessively bureaucratic organization', as described by the terrorism expert Charles Lister.[53] Hierarchical plans for IS tend to look rather out of date fairly rapidly because IS commanders have a habit of getting killed pretty often. Baghdadi lost several important lieutenants during 2014. In January, Haji Bakr, the old Ba'athist colonel who had acted as kingmaker to Baghdadi in 2010[54] and had helped eliminate any rivals, was himself assassinated probably by another jihadi group.[55] The role of 'coordinator of prisoners and women's affairs' fell vacant when Abu Suja was killed in a coalition air strike in November 2014.[56] Baghdadi was reportedly injured in the same attack.[57] Former Ba'athist colonel Abu Muslim al-Turkmani (real name Fadel Ahmad Abdullah al-Hiyali) was deputy to his caliph[58] and charged with overseeing the Iraqi provinces of IS until he was reportedly killed in a separate air strike in early December 2014.[59]

The head of IS controls its two powerful bodies, the cabinet, consisting of around seven members, and the war council. The war council, known as the *shura*, is made up of three senior IS commanders, responsible for everything from the management of warehouses where arms are stored, to the direction of suicide bombers and the planning of military operations, including bombings and assassinations. One deputy controls the twelve governors or *wali* in Syria, while the other is responsible for the twelve governors in the group's Iraqi provinces. Then there are eight separate councils dealing with a plethora of other issues.

The group's varied income streams, from hostage ransoms to the sale of black-market oil, are dealt with by the financial council, which also oversees the IS treasury department, known as the *Bayt al-Mal*, the 'House of Money'. In November 2014, the Bayt al-Mal issued a statement announcing that the caliphate would soon be minting its own coins, at the demand of none other than the 'caliph' himself:

Based on the directive of the Emir of the Believers in the Islamic State, caliph Ibrahim, may Allah preserve him, to mint currency for the Islamic State, as it is far removed from the tyrannical monetary system that was imposed on the Muslims and was a reason for their enslavement and impoverishment, and wasting the fortunes of the Ummah, making it easy to fall into the hands of the Jews and Crusaders, the Treasury Department studied the matter and presented a comprehensive project, by the grace of Allah, to mint a currency based on the inherent value of the metals gold and silver.[60]

The new currency, called the dinar, would have seven coins, two gold, three silver and two copper. The largest-value coin, containing 21.25 grams of gold, would have been worth around $694 in mid-November 2014.[61] The smallest copper coin would be worth a few cents.[62] It wasn't clear how Islamic State would obtain the necessary precious metals but the group announced in September 2015 that it had started minting its new coins.

The legal council administers what passes for justice in the 'state' while the security council manages internal policing and the many executions.[63] Islamic State has made no secret of its killing; much of it has been done in public places in front of crowds and recorded for posterity. Men and children have been crucified and beheaded, homosexuals thrown to their deaths from high buildings and women stoned to death in main squares. Most of the terror is orchestrated by the IS 'morality police', the much-feared al-Hisbah, whose name is taken from the word *hisbah*, meaning the divinely sanctioned duty for Muslims to intervene when another Muslim is violating Sharia.[64]

Minor offences such as smoking in public can be punished with amputation or worse. In March 2015, IS made it clear that it considered professional soccer to be 'a product of the decadent West' and threatened to give eighty lashes to anyone caught watching a match between Real Madrid and Barcelona.[65] In January 2015, the group caught thirteen teenagers in Mosul watching the Asian Cup match between Jordan and Iraq on TV and publicly executed them by firing squad.[66] This massacre must have been approved by their football loving 'caliph', once considered a superb goal scorer, the 'Messi of our team'.[67] A recent United Nations report stated, 'ISIS has committed torture and murder as part of an attack on a civilian population in Aleppo, Ar-Raqqah [Raqqa], Dayr Az-Zawr and Al-Hasakah governorates [all in Syria], amounting to war crimes and crimes against humanity.'[68]

Abu Mohammed witnessed many atrocities in Raqqa, including beheadings and the stoning to death of a woman accused of adultery. He told me, 'It is difficult to talk about executions without mentioning the subject of the stoning of women. I saw this happen in the municipal yard in Raqqa. They threw stones at her until she died. Watching it, I felt my heart had stopped and I did not hear anything but the voice of the woman saying "I am innocent".'[69]

The municipal yard in Raqqa is Islamic State's favourite place for stoning women to death, and it was here that Abu Mohammed watched the killing of Faddah al-Sayed. On 18 July 2014, at around 11 p.m., a truck arrived at the yard and dumped a large pile of stones. A cleric read out the sentence and then the jihadis brought in Sayed, who was clad head to toe in black. The residents who gathered in the yard refused to help IS carry out the sentence so the jihadis, mainly foreign fighters, carried out the sentence themselves.[70]

Abu Mohammed added, 'There are young people who have been crucified at the hands of ISIS. I've seen and heard them screaming with pain. ISIS always claims that they are infidels or apostates or working with Bashar al-Assad. But I knew some of them – they were good people.' IS has also targeted the group behind RBSS. Abu Mohammed said:

> My friend Mo'taz was executed because he was working with our team. They are killing anyone who disagrees with them. Anyone who says a word they do not like must be punished. People are living in fear even when they are in their own homes. ISIS does things you cannot imagine. They are just a group of criminals who have been trained to kill and intimidate people. There is nothing good in ISIS; everything about them is bad.
>
> Everyone thinks of escaping but a lot of people cannot get out and do not have the money to live outside Raqqa.

The situation has been especially bad for the *kuffar* minorities. Abu Mohammed said, 'Now there are approximately thirty Christian families in Raqqa and they are forced to pay ISIS a sum of money called a "tribute", but if Shia and other minorities are caught then they are executed immediately on charges of blasphemy.'

The Lion Cubs of the Khalifa

Many of the most sinister images to emerge from Raqqa have been of children. In one video, a boy aged around eleven with black shoulder-length hair points a pistol at two suspected Russian spies, who are kneeling on the ground in front of him with their hands tied behind their backs, and shoots them in the back of the head. Shortly before the murders are carried out, a heavily armed jihadi announces that the suspects were now at the mercy of a new force in the caliphate, the caliph's growing child army: 'By Allah's grace, they are now in the custody of the Lion Cubs of the Khalifa.'[71]

Images have also emerged of another young boy executing a third man accused of spying, this time supposedly for Israel's Mossad intelligence network. One picture shows the dead-eyed child looking coldly ahead, with his victim lying at his feet.[72] The child army known as the 'Lion Cubs of the Khalifa' is one of the most disturbing developments in the caliphate. In recent decades, the world has witnessed the phenomenon of child soldiers from South Sudan to Colombia. According to the charity War Child, children are used as soldiers because 'they are easier to condition and brainwash', adding, 'They don't eat much food, don't need paying much and have an undeveloped sense of danger so are easier to send into the line of fire.'[73]

Baghdadi started to meddle with Raqqa's education system from the beginning of his occupation. Schools and universities were closed and Islamic State started to enrol a large number of the children into boot camps. Some were simply kidnapped while others joined the Lion Cubs as a result of the widespread poverty, either for food or in return for money paid to their parents. According to sources within Raqqa, more than thirty children and forty-five young men from Raqqa were killed in Islamic State battles in the three months between early October 2014 and early January 2015.[74] 'As the mujahidin of the Islamic State continue their march against the forces of kufr [non-belief],' proclaimed *Dabiq*, 'there is a new generation waiting in the wings...these are the children of the Ummah of jihād, a generation raised in the lands of malāhim (fierce battles) and nurtured under the shade of Sharī'ah.'[75]

The children have been taken to the Sharia training camp outside Raqqa for one of two types of training. The slow training course includes an initial forty-five days of indoctrination followed by three months of military training in the use of bombs and guns. The children are then considered to be battle ready.

They are then segregated into separate groups, including the suicide bombers cadre and the bomb-making department.[76] Some children are used in supportive tasks, such as delivering food and medicine to IS fighters. On 28 August 2014, IS decided to murder 420 Syrian soldiers it had captured from three Syrian military bases.[77] Approximately one hundred of the soldiers were handed over to the Cubs for beheading, a precondition of their graduating, and they did not disappoint their caliph. The severed heads were later taken to Raqqa and displayed all around the city on walls, on pavements and even on spiked railings.

So-called 'flash training' is held when IS needs fighters quickly during major battles, such as the group's attack, beginning in mid-September 2014, on the Kurdish town of Kobani in the far north of Syria on the Turkish border. IS has also attempted to press-gang captured Yazidi children into joining the Cubs. Two boys, Habib Kalajasa and his brother Farage, aged fourteen and eleven in April 2015, survived and escaped IS to tell their tale to the BBC World Service. Habib said:

> They took us to a school and they took us to the top floor. Boys and girls. Small ones like us. They began to teach us religious and military lessons.
>
> First thing in the morning, whoever didn't wake up was beaten with a black stick. They saw that we didn't learn and they got angry and said we were laughing at their religion. After three days, they thought it was useless and [they said] 'You're not capable children.' They separated the younger and older boys and took them to do fighting and left us younger kids at school.[78]

Both boys spoke to the BBC from the sanctuary of a refugee camp in the Iraqi Kurdistan capital of Erbil, but hundreds of others suffered the loss of either their life or their childhood.

Another of the more disturbing images to emerge from Raqqa appeared in February 2015. At first sight, there is nothing remarkable about it. Again the picture is of a boy, this time aged around eight or nine, and it was taken at night. He is wearing a blue woolly hat and a wide rapturous smile, as he looks skywards.[79] It is just the sort of expression you see when children are looking up at a fireworks display…but the boy was not watching a fireworks display. He is staring up at a huge screen of the image of a pilot being burned alive in a cage. The IS propaganda film in which the boy appeared was called *The Muslims' Delight at the Burning of the Pilot*. It purports to shows the people of Raqqa looking up at big screens erected in the city showing the footage of the immolation of the pilot. The lovingly produced film of the murder, that was watched with such apparent joy by the people of Raqqa, was called *Healing the Believers' Chests*.[80]

The twenty-six-year-old pilot, Moaz al-Kasasbeh, had been captured by IS after his F-16 jet developed mechanical problems and crashed near Raqqa on 24 December 2014.[81] Kasasbeh had parachuted out in time but was quickly captured by the militants. At one time there was a proposal to trade Kasasbeh and a Japanese journalist also kidnapped by IS, Kenji Goto, for Sajida Atrous al-Rishawi, the Zarqawi woman terrorist who had helped carry out the bombing on the Radisson SAS Hotel in the Jordanian capital, Amman, in November 2005.[82] In a strange twist of fate, the original mentor of Abu Musab al-Zarqawi, Abu Muhammad al-Maqdisi, was employed by the Jordanians as a negotiator to try to negotiate the release of Kasasbeh. At the time of his involvement in the talks, the influential cleric was in a Jordanian prison on charges of inciting terrorism.[83]

Apparently Maqdisi's jihadi contacts were so formidable that he was able to reach intermediaries of Baghdadi and his media sidekick Adnani in an attempt to broker Kasasbeh's release.[84] In his letter to Baghdadi, Maqdisi begged the 'caliph' – who he addressed as 'Emir of the Islamic State' – to show leniency to Kasasbeh in order to save Rishawi, 'one of our sisters, a fellow monotheist and jihad fighter', adding, 'I ask you, oh Sheikh, in the name of Allah the Almighty, who suspended the heavens without support, not to squander this opportunity to save your and our sister and not to throw away this tremendous chance that [if acted upon], will cause the Muslims to praise you in prayer, in thanks, and in gratitude.'[85]

However, both the cleric and the world were cruelly hoaxed. Baghdadi held out the hope of a swap with Rishawi, who after all had once been an a willing servant of his old friend and leader Zarqawi, but in fact the 'caliph' had ordered the burning of Kasasbeh some weeks earlier, shortly after the pilot's capture. Abu Mohammed of RBSS told me, 'We had information about the burning of the pilot at the beginning of 2015.'[86]

On 3 February 2015, IS posted its grim film of Kasasbeh's burning, which was every bit as ritualistic as the horrifying defining scene of the cult movie *The Wicker Man*. Kasasbeh was filmed walking among the ruins of Raqqa, apparently caused by coalition air strikes against IS. The pilot, dressed in an orange jumpsuit soaked in fuel accelerant, was then placed in a cage. A jihadi in khaki brown with a blazing torch lit a fuel trail to the cage and Kasasbeh was swiftly engulfed in flames. His last moments were spent on his knees gripping the bars of the cage. A bulldozer then appeared and buried his charred remains beneath a pile of rubble, to re-enact the death of someone in an air strike, burned and buried, alive or dead. At dawn the day after the film was posted, the Jordanians hanged Sajida al-Rishawi along with an Iraqi al-Qaeda operative called Ziyad Karboli.[87] Rishawi had hoped to escape the noose and had appealed against her death sentence long before the capture and murder of Kasasbeh.[88] In the end everyone died horribly, Kasasbeh, Rishawi, and the courageous Japanese war reporter Kenji Goto, who was beheaded.[89]

It is difficult to know what to make of Maqdisi's television performance in the wake of the tragic fiasco. The cleric, who had helped to inspire Zarqawi on his path of terror, appeared on Jordanian television spluttering with indignation. He fulminated:

> They came up with the practice of immolation. People will now follow them in this practice. Immolation? The Prophet Muhammad said, 'Only the Lord of Fire torments with fire.' Is this Jihadi Salafism?! Jihadi Salafism has nothing to do with such practices. The Prophet Muhammad considered immolation to be reprehensible. He said, 'Only the Lord of Fire torments with fire.' What interest did the burning of the pilot serve? Did they think this would bring an end to the bombardments and the war?

Maqdisi also demonstrated his obvious distress at the damage IS was doing and had already done to the one thing he really cared about, jihad. He said, 'They have painted Islam, the jihadi movement, in red. They have made people think that jihad can be waged only by killing and slaughter…If anyone purports to have a caliphate but cannot provide the fruits of a caliphate he leads the Muslims to dispersal. They have presented Islam in the image of slaughter and immolation.'[90]

Maqdisi had exposed the painful truth behind the jihad to which he had devoted his life. The cleric had warned Baghdadi that failure to heed his advice and save the life of the failed suicide bomber Rishawi would 'damage your prestige and that of your state'[91] but the 'caliph' had played him for a fool. Baghdadi was convinced that his vision of the 'state' was the only one and he probably thought that Maqdisi would have been wiser to have addressed him in his pointless begging letter as 'caliph' rather than as a mere emir.

Thousands of desperate or desperately committed or confused would-be jihadis would continue to make their way to the 'state' despite its excesses but Maqdisi had been forced to recognize Baghdadi's caliphate for the disaster it was. Maqdisi and Salafi clerics like him had failed to control the dogs of holy war they had unleashed, and they had ended up with Baghdadi and his vision of an Islamic state with its systematic rapes, its slaves and concubines, child soldiers, murder, torture and genocide. This was not the return of the golden days of the Prophet and his Islamic state but a charnel house containing the remains of many innocent victims as well as the dreams of Sheikh Abu Muhammad al-Maqdisi.

In late October 2015, I was in Jordan and visited the father of Moaz al Kasasbeh, Safi Yousef al Kasasbeh, at the family home in the hills overlooking the Dead Sea, not far from the city of Karak. He told me the Kasasbeh tribe had lived in the area for centuries. 'I love all my children but Muath [Moaz] was my favourite son,' he told me as we sipped mint tea in a reception room filled with photos and mementos of his dead son. 'He was the most precious, the most handsome and the most clever. He was always the top of his class and knew the Koran by heart. I wanted him to become a doctor but he wanted to be a pilot. His death struck us like light-ning and we still have not come to terms with it.'

14
Killing the caliphate
2015

Islamic State never left Baghdad in peace, not even while the group was on its death rampages around Syria and northern Iraq. By 2015, the terror campaign begun by Abu Musab al-Zarqawi had entered its twelfth year and still the Iraqi capital was not part of the caliphate, and neither did that seem remotely possible. Baghdad had long become the forgotten front in the life and death struggle against the jihadis. By then, IS had become a cloying miasma in the Iraqi capital, one that had the power to turn – in a flash – the most humdrum domestic street scene into one of horror and tragedy. Those people who could not take the stress left Baghdad. Those who remained, and an estimated seven million did, voluntarily or simply because they could not leave, grew fatalistic and decided to get on with their lives as normally as possible. Most people have felt under a sentence of death from Islamic State to a lesser or greater extent. Reprieve comes when they are back at home with the front door shut securely behind them. Dawn brings a deadly new day, back out on death row.

Rarely if ever was there an opportunity to glimpse the human faces behind the slaughter. The IS bombers either died deliberately in their explosions, or if they detonated them from a distance they vanished. My close encounter with the jihadis came, of all places, at one of Baghdad's principal morgues, in October 2014. I had gone there to interview the people whose grim task it is to identify the victims of the bombings, often working from mere fragments of human flesh and bone.

We had arrived at the morgue when suddenly a truck stopped nearby and several armed men emerged. In the back of the vehicle were half a dozen prisoners in orange pyjama-type out-fits, blindfolded and with their hands secured behind their backs by plastic ties. Their custodians were from the much-feared Shia militia, Asa'ib Ahl al-Haq, the so-called League of the Righteous. The captives were then frogmarched into the morgue and forced to kneel outside the DNA testing labs. If the suspicions held about these men were true, they were the faces of IS terror in Baghdad.

Doctors at the morgue's labs then had the opportunity to take DNA from the suspects to see if it matched any of the explosive material found at the scene. In many ways it was heartening because the Iraqis were evidently trying to get to the bottom of the many bomb outrages taking place. It showed they had not been completely overwhelmed by IS terror. I spoke to one young doctor, Sana, who worked in the DNA labs. She had not become inured to the horror despite her work. The fear had wormed its way inside her too.

'We know what these [bombs] do. They can turn people into smithereens and little pink clouds. We are only too well aware.' She explained how the fear worked and how people in Baghdad dealt with it: 'It is alive in the subconscious of your brain, but there's also a part of your brain that tells you have to continue and keep living. You can't just hide in your home because there's a car bomb that can go off.

'You expect a car bomb to go off in any street. What's stopping it from going off in this street or that street? It's quite at random all the time. So, you just shut those feelings off. You just tell yourself "I'm not going to die today. Perhaps I'm going to die some other day, but not today."'[1]

The city's emergency services are often the first on the scene of a bombing and sometimes secondary devices await them. We visited a fire crew in downtown Baghdad in late 2014, only to find that they were attending a suicide bombing at a mosque we had passed only moments after the explosion. The men returned an hour later, seemingly unperturbed and unflustered and ready to talk about their work. An IS bomber in a suicide vest had walked into the mosque and blown himself up killing people attending midday prayers. 'I wouldn't even feed his body to the dogs,' said one of the firemen. He spoke quietly; no histrionics, but rather a genuine anger when I asked what he thought about the jihadi who had carried out the attack. The bomber's remains and those of his victims were all taken to the morgue for DNA testing and identification. One of the paramedics insisted on showing me the blood-spattered interior of his ambulance.

Thanks to IS, every attempt to live life normally is an act of courage in Baghdad. The victims at the Shia mosque, the Husseiniyat al-Khayrat in the Sinak area of the capital, were just leaving the building when they were attacked. Eleven people were killed and a further twenty-six injured.[2] The previous day had seen another attack on a Shia mosque, this time killing twenty-two.[3]

People in Baghdad seem to have an almost intense desire to obliterate any signs of an IS attack, an instinct as strong as the IS desire to annihilate them. I have visited shops, car salesrooms and hotels a few hours after an IS bombing to find the clear-up already under way.

One night in late 2014, we heard an enormous explosion. An IS suicide bomber had exploded his truck bomb on the road in front of a hotel in central Baghdad killing guests and people eating in restaurants nearby. Within half an hour, security sources had estimated the death toll at around thirty. By the time we arrived on the scene the following morning, the clean-up had started. A road gang was fixing the enormous hole in the road left by the suicide bomber. Others were clearing away the debris, the rubble and broken glass. While all this was going on, hotel guests were checking out and nonchalantly wheeling their suitcases from what was left of the hotel's reception. Clearly they had stayed in the rooms at the back, while a number of guests at the front had died. The hotel's owner took the time to talk to me with his mobile phone glued to his ear, no doubt waiting to get through to his insurers while at the same time barking instructions at the workers clearing up the mess. 'Da'esh [Islamic State] obviously,' he said very matter-of-factly when I asked him who he blamed for the bombing.

After the fall of Mosul a powerful international coalition had formed in support of the Iraqi army and militias. The fightback by land and air against IS was critical, but almost as important would be the economic and propaganda battles to come. In the counter-offensive, the coalition would attempt to degrade IS financially as well as militarily; after all, their opponent is widely believed to be the richest-ever terrorist organization.

In October 2014 Islamic State was still trying to attack towards Baghdad from the north near Samarra and from the west at the strategically important city of Amiriyah, once the temporary caliphate capital of Islamic State of Iraq, but it seemed increasingly unlikely they would march into the capital and we could not find anyone in Baghdad who felt under threat from the IS army. By then the group had also met fierce opposition in the battle for Kobani, the Syrian Kurd city in the north of Syria on the Turkish border.

At one stage, in early November 2014, IS controlled more than half of this strategically important town, and its capture would have given the group control along an important stretch of the border with Turkey, as well as a direct link to its positions in the Syrian provinces of Aleppo and Raqqa. On 3 November 2014, IS posted a new propaganda video of a British hostage, the photo-journalist John Cantlie, in Kobani. In the film, Cantlie, clearly placed by IS under immense personal duress, claimed that most of Kobani had fallen under the control of IS. He presented the film in the manner of a TV war reporter, 'The battle for Kobani is coming to an end,' Cantlie said, clearly reading from an IS script. 'The Mujahidin are just mopping up now, street-to-street and building-to-building. You can occasionally hear sporadic gunfire in the background as a result of those operations. But contrary to what the Western media would have you believe, it is not an all-out battle here now; it is nearly over.'[4]

Fast forward nearly three months later to 26 January 2015, and the Kurdish fighters of the People's Protection Units (YPG) announced that IS had been driven out of the city of Kobani altogether.[5] It had been an extremely important victory, supported by air strikes by the US-led coalition and won with great sacrifice by the Syrian Kurds, along with their brother Kurds from Iraqi Kurdistan and elements of the Free Syrian Army. The four-month battle had cost more than 1,300 lives[6] and turned an estimated 180,000 Syrian Kurds into refugees, most of them displaced to Turkey.[7]

The hawks and their quarry

Early 2015 would see further defeats for IS, but the group would also make important gains. At the end of March 2015, the Iraqis recaptured the city of Tikrit, a necessary prelude to the all-important advance on Mosul. During the battle, the militias killed Saddam's old deputy, Izzat al-Douri, who had played such an important supporting role alongside Baghdadi in the taking of Mosul.

The coalition had also taken out important IS leaders and came close to killing the caliph himself. The 'Hawks Cell', a specialist Iraqi anti-terrorism unit dedicated to targeting and killing the IS leadership,[8] carried out an air strike in the al-Baaj area of Nineveh near the village of Umm al-Rous. On 18 March 2015, according to an exclusive report in the *Guardian* (some sources say February 2015),[9] three men died in the attack.[10] Baghdadi was badly wounded in his back and leg, according to well-placed intelligence sources.

On 23 April 2015, security sources in Iraq confirmed that Abu Ala al-Afri, Islamic State's Head of the Shura Council, had been appointed as 'emir' of IS to fulfil many of Baghdadi's duties.[11] Little is known about Afri other than that he was born in 1955 and he is a former physics teacher from the Alchkhlar tribe in Fadel village, near the Iraqi city of Tal Afar, around forty miles west of Mosul.[12] He was apparently a founder member along with Baghdadi of the Mujahidin Shura Council established by Zarqawi as the successor group to al-Qaeda in Iraq.[13]

The title 'emir' is below that of caliph, and the sources added that Afri, whose real name is Abdul Rahman Mustafa Mohammed, would be a sort of 'acting caliph' while Baghdadi recovered. No sooner had Afri's appointment been announced than the Iraqis claimed he had been killed in a US-led coalition air strike on a mosque near Tal Afar. But the 'kill' could not be verified.[14] It was understood that al-Baghdadi would still retain personal command of IS 'military operations'.[15]

The group's history is littered with examples of false claims of its leaders being killed or injured. Baghdadi had been the subject of such reports in November 2014 when speculation mounted that he had been killed near Mosul in a US-led air strike on a convoy of at least ten vehicles.[16] The self-proclaimed caliph's close companion, Abu Suja (real name Auf Abdulrahman Elefery), was killed in the strike[17] along with twenty others,[18] but Baghdadi survived.

The appointment of a temporary emir was at last confirmation that the coalition had clearly come close to killing the IS boss, and it indicated that he may have been severely incapacitated. In May 2015, the *Guardian* reported that Baghdadi had suffered serious spinal damage in the air strike and was being treated by two doctors from Mosul.[19] The outside world had no sight of Baghdadi in the nine months from the time of his dramatic appearance in Mosul to the news of Afri's promotion to IS emir. In May 2015, IS released an audio message from Baghdadi in which he referenced recent events in Yemen and implored his jihadis to continue fighting, saying, 'your Lord has made jihad for the cause of Allah obligatory upon you and has commanded you to fight His enemies so that He may forgive your sins, raise you in the rank, take from among you martyrs, purify the believers and destroy the disbelievers.'[20]

According to my information, the Iraqis and other coalition forces have come close to killing or capturing Baghdadi on at least four separate occasions, including three times during the course of 2014. Baghdadi's near misses from drones and fighters may explain his particularly horrific treatment of the Jordanian pilot Kasasbeh, although the man needed few excuses for his cruelty towards his many enemies and the *Kuffar*.

In late 2014, I interviewed General Saad Maan from the Iraqi interior ministry about the Iraqis' repeated attempts to capture or kill al-Baghdadi. Maan was adamant that the Iraqis had also almost captured the IS leader in March or April of 2014: 'Six months ago we almost reached him. We killed one of his drivers and captured the others. Our troops were only one hour away from capturing him but he succeeded in running away.'

I also asked the general about his claims in July 2014 that al-Baghdadi had been killed in an air strike in Qaim shortly before the IS leader's appearance in Mosul.[21] Again Maan defended his claims and asserted that Baghdadi had been injured in the strike and that the evidence is there in the video of his speech in Mosul. 'There was an airstrike and some of al-Baghdadi's colleagues and assistants were killed. As for Baghdadi, he was injured and if you notice when you look at the footage of his declaration in the mosque in Mosul, he was hardly able to move.' Maan seemed to be right. Watching the start of the footage, Baghdadi moves very stiffly and strangely as he ascends the steps of the minbar. Of course, he may have just pulled a muscle stepping out of the shower, or it could confirm Maan's claims. When I asked the rather obvious reporter's question, 'Is it the government's aim to kill Baghdadi?' the general chuckled and looked at me as if I had taken leave of my senses, responding only: 'It is the aim of humanity.'[22] The odds are against Baghdadi making old bones, as they proved to be in the cases of Zarqawi, Abu Omar al-Baghdadi, Douri, Haji Bakr and many others besides.

Islamic State will of course find a replacement for its caliph, but experts say his loss would be devastating to the group. Following speculation about his death in November 2014, Professor Fawaz Gerges of the London School of Economics told me:

> Everything about the jihadi movement is about legitimacy, about legitimation and about theology. You have to use theology even to legitimize your actions. You cannot just kill for the sake of killing. Think of how much Osama bin Laden went to great lengths to try to rationalize his killing of Americans in the eyes

of Muslims. He called it defensive jihad, even though it was not defensive jihad.

In Islam the institution of jihad has so many rules and regulations. You have to have a legitimation. ISIS is the opposite. Abu Bakr al-Baghdadi's strategy has been to rely on military action, on savagery, on deliverance and on victory. Victory basically convinces the Ummah [worldwide community of Muslims] that "I am the Caliph." He has not nourished any ideas and that is why if Abu Bakr al-Baghdadi is killed this would represent truly a shattering blow both psychologically and also in terms of leadership.[23]

Professor Gerges was dismissive of some of the possible alternatives to al-Baghdadi. 'His death would leave a huge vacuum,' he added. 'Abu Mohammed al-Adnani [IS media chief] for example is a psychopath. He is not a person that could lead ISIS as a movement in the next one or two years, given the existential threat facing ISIS in this particular moment of its history.'

Al-Sadoun Street is one Baghdad's best-known thoroughfares and dotted along its length are many shops selling wheelchairs and aids for disabled people. I stopped to talk to some of the shop owners who explained that many of their customers were people who survived a bombing, maimed and badly injured in some way. It is an ill wind that doesn't blow someone some good. Although the shops had benefitted from Islamic State's campaign of violence, they had been badly affected in other ways. IS controlled territory north of the capital, making it impossible to import the Chinese-made wheelchairs by land. Instead, all the wheelchairs had to come by sea via the crucial Iraqi port of Basra. The shop owners were complaining bitterly that they had to pay much more for their wheelchairs and that it was hurting their businesses.

The same story could be heard elsewhere. Communications

between northern Iraq and Iraqi Kurdistan and the rest of the country were severely disrupted thanks to the 'caliphate'. To avoid IS and its lethal checkpoints, many lorries had to travel via Iran. The prices of everything from food to fuel were rocketing in Baghdad. This life and death struggle for Iraq was not just about territory. It was an economic war as well. IS attempted to take control of key oil installations in Iraq as it had in Syria, to help fund its expansion. In July 2014, IS had taken the large al-Oar oilfield in the eastern Syrian province of Deir Az Zor.[24] Across the border into Iraq, there was an all-important battle over Iraq's biggest oil refinery at Baiji, north of Baghdad. IS was said to be in control of most of the refinery but at the time of writing both city and refinery are hotly contested. In mid-June 2014 the jihadis had taken the refinery[25] but the Iraqis carried on fighting, determined to push them out of this vital facility. Iraq's budget was based on oil but IS occupation had played havoc with production, not least because it controlled the main pipeline from the northern city of Kirkuk to Turkey. Output was down from the required 3.4 million barrels a day to 2.3, and this was at a time of falling oil prices.[26]

The man charged with saving Iraq from going bankrupt, as well as waging economic war on the apparently super-rich jihadis an hour's drive up the road from Baghdad, was an affable Kurd called Hoshyar Zebari. Zebari was Iraq's finance minister and deputy prime minister. Like most of Iraq's senior politicians he was based within the comparatively secure confines of Baghdad's green zone, which is where he received me. For years, Zebari was the government's foreign minister, helped by his accentless and flawless English honed by his years studying at Essex University.

He was convinced that IS was trying to destroy Iraq, not only militarily, but economically. 'You just have to look at their tactics,' said Zebari. 'They are trying to deprive Iraq of some of its key strategic assets, the oil refineries, the oil pipes and some of the industries and factories Iraq or state companies have in those areas under their control.'

He added, 'It has impacted every aspect of life, including oil, industry, agriculture and even payment of salaries for all these civil servants for whom the government is responsible to pay. Also there is the cost of maintaining security to face this existential threat by IS to the whole state of Iraq.'[27]

Zebari also talked about the caliphate's own economy, increasingly based on oil, and he revealed how IS was selling oil to the Syrian government of Bashar al-Assad.

> ISIS was selling oil to the Syrian authorities in Syria. They were smuggling oil to Iraq and to Turkey and different parts of the region through a web and a network of smugglers. There has been a focus to dry up these resources to attack these oil fields by airstrikes. It is a battle and a serious challenge to deny ISIS its financial resources.
>
> This is a multi-faceted confrontation. It is not only military. It's about the hearts and minds of people. It is ideological and theological and economic, and of course it's military and security.

In mid May 2015, not long after Tikrit was recaptured, Iraq and its coalition allies suffered a series of serious setbacks. After a blistering offensive, including a series of suicide bombings, IS took control of Ramadi from superior numbers of Iraqi troops which abandoned the city, provoking serious US questioning of Iraq's willingness to fight.[28]

Across the border in Syria, Islamic State found itself getting richer the more territory it took. Some observers believed that the IS capture of the Palmyra gas fields would force President Assad to essentially fund the very organization trying to destroy his country by having to purchase electricity from it. Peter Ford, the former UK Ambassador to Syria, and a critic of Western policy towards the country, told me, 'I think that [possibility] is very plausible and again we only had ourselves to blame by preventing the Syrian government from taking action, such as repairing its generators for one thing. We are making it possible for Assad to do nothing else but buy electricity from IS and possibly even oil to prevent his government from collapsing. Given the choice Syria would much rather do things legitimately on the open market and not be forced to cut its own throat.'[29]

'Islamic State in Regent Street'

Shoppers and tourists wandering around the West End of London quickly get used to people thrusting leaflets and pamphlets into their hands, offering everything from cut-price golf clubs to membership of some religious cult. On 13 August 2014 a group of men set up a stall in Regent Street handing out leaflets inviting the recipients to travel to the new caliphate. 'O Ummah of Muhammad!' the leaflet said, 'Congratulations and good tidings. The Khilafah has been re-established. The dawn of a new era has begun.'[30]

The police and the Crown Prosecution Service failed to see the funny side, although no joke was intended, and two British men were charged with soliciting support for Islamic State, a proscribed terrorist organization.[31] This was not some Baghdadi outreach team but yet another stunt courtesy of a minuscule group of London-based Islamist extremists who attract far more newspaper headlines than followers. The men were associates of Anjem Choudary, a British Muslim who is habitually described in the British press as a 'firebrand cleric'[32] or a 'hate preacher'.[33]

If he is not a man with a voracious appetite for self-publicity then he is clearly doing something wrong.

I met Choudary in a baklava shop in east London to ask him why he wanted to take his family to live in the 'caliphate' and why he was unable to do so. The answer to the second question was straightforward. The British security services had confiscated his passport, and on the last raid had even removed the air rifle he used for apparently harmless recreation in the back garden.

For Choudary, Baghdadi's 'caliphate' embodied some wonderful Islamic idyll. 'I have friends who are in Syria and Iraq and they are living the life of luxury and they are so happy. They're getting free food and accommodation. They are getting salaries. Gas, electricity and water are being given free of charge. They feel secure. There's no one cheating in the market and there's no bribery or usury. This is the society we dream about.' Choudary was not interested in hearing any criticism of the 'caliph' and his 'caliphate'. He denied being involved in the Regent Street stunt but he defended the distribution of the leaflets. I asked him about the footage of all the massacres and murders posted by IS on the internet. 'Actually I don't look at them and I don't watch the videos,' said Choudary. 'They're not doing it in my name; they're doing it in God's name. I don't look at those videos for the simple reason that people get arrested for less than that these days, for downloading videos, and so the only information I get is from the Western media and I don't believe the Western media.'[34]

So far the British government has banned at least eight of the Islamist organisations involving Choudary, although he stresses, 'I'm engaged in an ideological and political struggle. We don't have any military camps here and I'm not training anyone for jihad, and I haven't been arrested even once for any terrorism related offence.' Choudary blithely admits knowing Michael

Adebolajo, the man convicted along with Michael Adebowale for the murder of British soldier Drummer Lee Rigby in London in 2013. The two men ran Rigby down in a car and then hacked him to death with knives and a cleaver. Choudary described Adebolajo as 'an absolutely wonderful guy. He's the kind of person you'd marry your daughter to. He's such a nice person with such a nice personality.' Choudary insisted he parted company with Adebolajo when it came to extending the jihad to the UK but I was struck by his use of the present tense to describe someone who was in jail for butchering an innocent young man in broad daylight.

Choudary is widely regarded in the British Muslim community and elsewhere as an absurd and misguided figure, but despite that his desire to travel to Syria with his wife and five children still baffled many people. In 2013, I met a group of young men in an impoverished district in Tunis who wanted to go to Syria and fight with the jihadis. It was understandable in some ways because clearly uppermost in their minds was a desire to escape a life of grinding poverty and long-term unemployment. What has been more difficult to understand is why people with apparently good prospects in Britain would want to be part of Islamic State. As for Choudary, he was arrested in August 2015 and charged with inviting support for Islamic State, as well as encouraging terrorism..

Jihadi John and others

A trickle of British Muslims has made it to the caliphate. Hardly a month goes by in the UK without another story of individual British Muslims or a handful of them either making it to Syria or being arrested in Turkey before they could cross the border. In February 2015, two young British Muslim girls, academically bright and popular, made it into Syria via Turkey. Kadiza Sultan, who was sixteen, and Shamina Begum, fifteen, travelled there with a third girl from Germany who has not been named for legal reasons. Their families did not know about their plans and were devastated when they found out where the girls had gone. It is a common reaction of families who have lost loved ones to Baghdadi. At that time British authorities believed that up to five hundred or so young Britons had made it to the caliphate.[35] However, a British security source believed the figure was nearer two thousand. He added that the UK authorities do not know for sure because until 2015 they did not count people leaving the country, only those arriving.[36]

Mohammed Emwazi is the best-known Briton to have made it to Syria. He gained worldwide notoriety as 'Jihadi John' when he appeared in a number of videos in late 2014 beheading Western hostages, including the reporters James Foley and Steve Sotloff and the aid workers Peter Kassig, and David Haines and Alan Henning.

Henning, a taxi driver from Salford, was working as a volunteer when he was captured by the jihadis in Syria. Before his murder by Emwazi, many had campaigned for clemency from IS, including none other than Abu Mohammad al-Maqdisi, who wrote an open letter:

The issue is to defend Islam and Jihad from being deformed... This British man came to Syria as a volunteer with a humanitarian organization that's run by Muslims. Those Muslims promised him safety and they should be respected. He also entered Syria with the permission of the Syrians who also gave him safety. Is it reasonable that his reward is kidnapping and beheading?!! He came to assist Muslims in need and for this alone, he should be received with thanks and gratitude, not with beheading and injustice which Allah does not approve of.[37]

A British organization called CAGE had also campaigned for the safety and release of Alan Henning. CAGE is a London-based advocacy group with what it describes as 'an Islamic focus'. It campaigns against state policies designed as part of the 'war on terror'. As such CAGE seeks to help those it sees as the victims of the 'war', including people who feel harassed by the security services as well former detainees. Its director, Moazzam Begg, is a former detainee at Guantanamo Bay who was released without charge in 2005 by President George W. Bush, apparently despite the protestations of the CIA and the FBI.[38]

I met Cerie Bullivant, a film-maker and journalist who is Begg's friend as well as being a senior figure at CAGE. Years earlier Bullivant himself fell foul of British security services when he tried to travel to Syria apparently to learn Arabic. He was placed under a control order that resulted in him having an electronic tag and having to sign in each day at a police station. After breaking the control orders several times, Bullivant ended up in Belmarsh prison in south-east London for six months before his eventual release without charge.[39] Bullivant struck me as a sincere and articulate man who genuinely felt the security services often did more harm than good when dealing with individuals they suspected of possible terrorist sympathies and associations. He told me how CAGE had made strenuous efforts to get Henning released through contacts in Syria and how they were deeply shocked by his murder at the hands of Jihadi John.

By a horrible coincidence, CAGE had also tried to help Henning's killer, Emwazi, in the years before he joined IS. Bullivant claimed that Emwazi's life had been ruined by his interaction with the British security services, who had allegedly tried to hire him as a spy. CAGE has alleged that when Emwazi refused to cooperate it resulted in him being harassed, in two engagements being destroyed and in him being unable to travel. '[But] it's no excuse for the terrible things Emwazi has done which I completely condemn,' said Bullivant emphatically.

CAGE caused a media storm as a result of the press conference the group held in February 2015 after Emwazi's full identity was revealed by the *Washington Post*. During the press conference, Bullivant's colleague at CAGE, Asim Qureshi, described Emwazi as 'an extremely kind, gentle, beautiful young man'.[40] Qureshi had last spoken to Emwazi three years previously in January 2012 in London when CAGE was trying to help the young Londoner over his entanglements with the security services. 'Look, the press conference could have been handled better,' said Bullivant.

> From my point of view, Asim to this day still finds it difficult to reconcile the Emwazi he knew with the guy in the videos ['Jihadi John']. He could see how it was possible when certain things were pointed out. I think Asim's really disconnected the two people and that came across in the press conference. That's because he really liked Emwazi and he's spoken about that. He thought he was a really nice person and a good guy, and he's got a complete disconnect that he can't put together the person he knew with the guy in the video. He can see how in the way he speaks and so on that it could be him but can't see how it would be him. Even Emwazi's family are in denial that it is him. My personal belief is that it is clearly is him.

Bullivant told me that he believed young Muslims went to Syria because they genuinely felt under threat in the West, mainly due to Islamophobia. 'In Islam we call it Hijrah, the flight to safety. It takes its name after the Prophet Muhammad's own flight to sanctuary from Mecca to Medina. It is not to justify people going to Syria, just to help explain it.'

He said some Britons had gone to Syria and had not found Hijrah. Instead they had recoiled from what they found there and have tried to come home. However, they know that there is a high chance of being arrested and jailed for a long time if they do return to the UK. At the time of writing, according to Bullivant, CAGE is in contact with forty Britons who are hiding in Turkey afraid to return to their own country. Some British Muslims go to Syria and are horrified at what they find and that it is not the land of milk and honey described by Anjem Choudary. They get across the border to Turkey but feel marooned there, worried about returning to the UK in case they arrested. 'It's a terrible position to be in,' said Bullivant. As for 'Jihadi John', the 'caliphate' proved no refuge. Mohammed Emwazi's own personal 'Hijrah' ended in Raqqa in a successful US drone strike on the night of 12 November 2015.

Dabiq

It always seemed unlikely that Islamic State would confine its violence to its caliphate and surrounding regions. It had already threatened to visit its terror on the West. On 8 April 2015, IS started a campaign accompanied by a video on social media with the hashtag #WeWillBurnUSAgain, threatening America with a repeat of the 9/11 attacks.[41] In fact, through the British hostage John Cantlie, Islamic State threatened the US with an attack that would dwarf 9/11. In the group's glossy periodic magazine, *Dabiq*, in late May 2015, Cantlie speculated how IS would 'purchase a nuclear device through weapons dealers with links to corrupt officials in the region, which would then be smuggled into the US via Libya, Nigeria and finally Mexico.' 'And if not a nuke, then what about a few thousand tons of ammonium nitrate explosive?' The Brit added, 'The Islamic State make [sic] no secret of the fact they have every intention of attacking America on its home soil…They'll be looking to do something big, something that would make any past operation look like a squirrel shoot…' Cantlie added in his article, doubtlessly approved and probably scripted in advance by Adnani, 'it will only be a question of time before the Islamic State reaches the Western world.'[42] Other countries face similar threats, and that is why Iraqi politicians say that their war is a Western concern too. It is indeed. Both the US and the UK are involved with air strikes, military advice and no doubt with secret intelligence help.

Iraqi deputy prime minister Hoshyar Zebari believed IS must be defeated in Iraq, and that it will collapse upon losing Mosul: 'ISIS needs be defeated in Iraq. The fall of ISIS would be in Mosul. Not Raqqa in my view. It was in Mosul where the Iraqi army collapsed and it was in Mosul where Abu Bakr al-Baghdadi declared his caliphate, and it would be in Mosul where the announcement of victory would be made.'[43]

However, few people predict the imminent end of Islamic State. If Baghdadi dies, there will be another Baghdadi to take his place. The leading American Middle East scholar Professor John Esposito told me:

Even if you take out ISIS another group is going to come along. Unless you change the conditions in the region, another group is going to come along. When people talk about Western governments addressing this problem, they reduce it too much to the ideology and theology, and then they say "Let's get some Muslim religious guys to sign up to a new project, and then let's use drones."

But that's not gong to work unless we address the problems in the region, issues such as governance. The governments are getting stricter in the region. Authoritarian governments are becoming even more so. Tougher with their own people. You have to address the underlying conditions. Otherwise all you are doing is putting a lid on the pressure cooker. In the end the pressure's going to blow.[44]

Some observers believe that the strategy of the US-led coalition of combating IS is not working. Former US Ambassador to Iraq, James Jeffrey, said America had to decide on whether to contain IS or destroy IS:

IS is not containable in my view. Time is not on our side. This is a really dangerous moment, and I would have been saying this four or five years ago but at least we always had a policy of keeping a lid on things. But no longer it seems.

The real danger would be a cataclysmic Shia-Sunni war in the region and the collapse of whole states, including Iraq and possibly Lebanon and Jordan. All of those things could lead to Sunni and Shia turning to the biggest thing with the most guns, and for the Sunnis that could be Islamic State, and for the Shia, that would be Iran.[45]

Dr David Kilcullen, the counter-insurgency expert who helped to nearly destroy Islamic State of Iraq back in 2007, has a grim prognosis for the future. He said:

If we don't defeat ISIS there are two dangerous things that can happen. The first thing is that you will have a state that starts to gobble up other states in the region and that will have real destabilizing effects. The other is more counter-intuitive. Unless we defeat these guys on the ground in Iraq and Syria, saying "let's just pull up the drawbridge and protect our societies and just leave them [ISIS] alone" is tantamount to saying "let's turn the UK or the US into a police state," because you would really have to do that to protect yourself against these guys. There's the cliché from Vietnam that we had to fight them over there so we don't have to fight them over here. Here there's a nuance to that which says "we need to fight them over there so we don't have to destroy our societies to make our societies safe."

In November 2015, France became the first country in the West to face a direct challenge from Islamic State to its own society and way of life when the group attacked Paris, killing at least 129 people and wounding more than 300. The government's immediate response was to deploy thousands of troops to protect France's towns and cities.

Dabiq is the name of Islamic State's glossy periodical, but it is also the name of a town in the Aleppo province in Syria. For Islamic State, Dabiq is the equivalent of Armageddon, the place where the last epic battle will take place between Muslims and Christians. IS propaganda often yearns for this final conflagration and it has certainly already brought destruction and insecurity to much of the region. The group may end up destroying itself or being destroyed by its many enemies. However, whatever happens, its virulent ideology looks likely to survive in a Middle East now riven by sectarian division, injustice, war and authoritarianism. For Kilcullen, how we've dealt with Islamic State has been a failure of the collective imagination, the failure to predict what might happen if too little was done to bring security, justice, human dignity and peace to a deeply troubled region. 'ISIS may eventually be destroyed,' says David Kilcullen, 'but don't imagine something worse cannot come along to take its place.'

15
Masters of mayhem
2016–

On 24 November 1989, Sheikh Abdullah Yusuf Azzam and two of his sons were heading to a mosque in western Peshawar in Pakistan for Friday prayers. As their car approached a petrol station, some forty pounds of TNT were detonated by a man spotted standing discreetly outside a nearby sewage plant. According to one lurid account, 'pieces of [Azzam's] sons were discovered up to a hundred metres away. One of his son's legs was suspended on an overhanging telephone line.' Not all was immediately lost in the carnage, however, according to a mysterious group of scholars calling themselves 'the Brothers in Ribatt', who later translated one of the sheikh's most famous theses. In the foreword to this thesis, the 'Brothers' observed of the immediate aftermath of the bombing, 'Allah be glorified, the Sheikh was found intact, except for an internal haemorrhage, that caused his death. Many attest to the musk that emanated from his body.'[1]

Sheikh Dr Abdullah Azzam was one of the most important jihadi scholars, an enormous influence on al-Qaeda, the Taliban and Islamic State. Naturally, the list of suspects for the assassination was long, from the Pakistani secret service through to the CIA and even his old disciples in al-Qaeda. But now that Azzam was dead, why should anyone outside his family, friends and fanatical supporters continue to care? Put simply, the deadly legacy of Sheikh Abdullah Azzam lives on more than a quarter of a century later in the Islamic State and its obsession with establishing a caliphate, for Azzam was the first modern Sunni extremist scholar to link the concept of jihad to the conquest of territory.

A Palestinian by birth, Azzam was a Salafi and a founding member of al-Qaeda. He actually taught Osama bin Laden in Saudi Arabia and became one of his most influential mentors. Saudi Arabia gave sanctuary to Azzam and other Salafi scholars and allowed them to teach in its schools and seminaries. Here they infused their lectures with jihad, contaminating the minds of impressionable students like bin Laden. In 1979 Azzam was thrown out of the University of Jeddah and moved first to Pakistan before again preaching jihad, this time in earnest, in a bid to drive the Soviet occupying army from Afghanistan. Azzam was also a member of the Muslim Brotherhood, like his later disciple Abu Bakr al-Baghdadi, and adopted the teachings of the hugely influential Islamist scholar Sayyid Qutb.[2] Like Qutb, Azzam believed there should be a special vanguard of Muslims to wage jihad.

Azzam propagated two forms of jihad: offensive and defensive. Offensive jihad meant taking the fight to the so-called 'far enemy' on its own territory, as al-Qaeda did so successfully and so brutally on 9/11. Defensive jihad meant repelling the unbelievers from 'Muslim lands'. To Azzam this was not a choice, it was an absolute duty, which he made clear in the thesis that was translated by 'the Brothers in Ribatt': 'If a piece of Muslim land the size of a hand span is infringed upon, then jihad becomes *Fard Ayn* [a global obligation] on every Muslim male and female, where the child shall march forward without the permission of its parents and the wife without the permission of the husband.'

This paramount duty to fight the apostate *kuffar* explains not only the ghastly nature of the group's ultra-violence but also its dreams of conquest. For Islamic State, territory has always been the principal overriding objective. It also leads directly to the question: when will the caliphate be big enough?

The answer is not until Islamic State has achieved world domination. The map at the front of this book depicting the group's global ambitions caused quite a shock when it first appeared and made headlines around the world. As disturbing as it is, the map still only shows the extent of Islamic State's ambition in its first triumphant stage, as outlined in the Seven Steps plan back in 1996 by Abu Musab al-Zarqawi and Abu Muhammad al-Maqdisi to the Jordanian reporter Fouad Hussein.[3] This plan envisaged conquering all 'Muslim lands' before turning on the lands of the *kuffar*, as Abdullah Azzam also made clear in his thesis – 'this process continues until it becomes *Fard Ayn* upon the whole world'.[4]

When his Islamic State of Iraq made its definitive break with al-Qaeda in 2006, Abu Bakr al-Baghdadi's obscure predecessor, Abu Omar al-Baghdadi, explicitly stated:

> [President George W.] Bush warned ... in his last speech in front of veterans when he said, 'This region is changing into one that threatens civilization with destruction ...' This prompted the enemy of Allah – Bush – to say after the blessed rise of the Islamic State, 'They strive to establish an Islamic State stretching from China to Spain.' He spoke the truth although he is a liar.[5]

Abu Omar's military commander, Abu Ayyub al-Masri, went even further: 'We will not rest from our jihad until we are under the olive trees of Rome, after we destroy the filthy house called the White House.'[6] Neither Rome nor Washington has ever been described as a Muslim land. It is not hard to find such proclamations by the jihadis. They are not hidden away from public view in obscure jihadi texts stuck in the filing cabinets of provincial, dusty seminaries. Islamic State often lovingly reproduces them. 'We will conquer your Rome, break your crosses and enslave your women,' the senior IS media officer Sheikh Abu Mohammed al-Adnani declared in a statement in 2015.

Islamic State has held true to its dreams of conquest despite or even because of its absorption of elements of the Iraqi Ba'ath Party. Almost from the start of the US-led occupation, the ousted, predominantly Sunni, Ba'athists saw Zarqawi's violent campaign to establish a state as the best chance they had of regaining power over Iraq. Many joined Zarqawi's movement and would continue to sign up to his organization in the years following his death.

Even the physical embodiment of the Ba'ath Party after the fall of Saddam, the Iraqi dictator's red-haired vice-president, Field Marshal Izzat al-Douri, recognized Zarqawi as the ultimate leader of the insurgency. A remarkable ceremony in early 2004 was later described by witnesses:

> In an atmosphere full of enthusiasm and high spirits for everybody, with the company of his three sons and a number of Mujahideen, Izzat Ibrahim Al Douri took off to meet with Abu Musab Al Zarqawi. At their arrival, the Mujahideen greeted them amidst calls of 'Allah Akbar' (3 times) [God is Greater]. Then the sound of gunfire was heard as Zarqawi rushed out, surrounded by the Mujahideen, covered by the dust of their blessed journey.

The report added that, at the sight of Zarqawi, 'Izzat Ibrahim shouted: "You are the commander and we are your soldiers." His son Ahmad handed him a copy of the Quran. His father took it, placed his hand and the hands of his sons on it, and they made an oath to God, pledging allegiance to Zarqawi in the Jihad until victory or martyrdom, in good and bad times.'[7] It must have been an extraordinary scene. A year or so earlier, Douri had been a field marshal and second only to Saddam Hussein. Here Douri, supposedly the embodiment of Ba'athist Iraq, was pledging allegiance to a Jordanian former pimp and petty criminal, by then a notorious mass murderer, who was determined to destroy Iraq as a nation state and absorb it into his caliphate. It is hard to think of any other event that could better have illustrated the degradation of the Ba'athists or the desperation of the Sunni.

Douri would break with the jihadis over tactics and strategy in the following years but he would later join Abu Bakr al-Baghdadi in his successful military campaign of 2014.[8] By then the Ba'athists had come to accept the jihadis' version of a state. The fusion of these two totalitarian movements made Islamic State far more dangerous and ambitious than anything envisaged by al-Qaeda. In order to hold power, the Ba'athists ultimately betrayed the very thing they were created in the first place to control, the state of Iraq.

Baghdadi's onslaught meant the dismemberment of Iraq and the country's eventual absorption into the caliphate. For the Ba'athists, any state was better than no state at all.

For IS, there will be no end to the state, either in time or in territory.[9] Nothing is more important than the state, possibly not even religion because, after all, Islam needs the state to properly exist. One thing is certain. The state is more important than people.

'The ultimate betrayal'

Aylan Kurdi was found face down in the sand at the water's edge with his chubby toddler's palms pointed skywards while the sea lapped softly around his head. When an emergency worker picked him off the beach, the little boy, still in his red T-shirt and baggy long blue shorts, looked almost as if he had fallen asleep and was being gently carried off to bed by his father. Instead, Aylan was starting a journey eastwards, from one end of Turkey to the other, one which would end with his burial the following day in his hometown of Kobani. Within hours, the images taken by a local news agency photographer of the three-year-old boy would shout out an accusation to the world from every newspaper's front page.

Aylan had drowned in the Aegean off Turkey's south coast along with his five-year-old brother Galib and their mother Rehana. They had been among the fourteen people who perished when their two small boats capsized as they made the hazardous two-and-a-half-mile journey from the tip of south-west Turkey to the Greek island of Kos, and Europe. The American novelist John Steinbeck once observed ironically that 'a war always comes to someone else'.[10] Doesn't it naturally follow that these 'someone elses' might become refugees and that they may very well want to make their way to where we are, where it's safe?

Several parties would soon stand accused of aiding and abetting the sea in the murder of Aylan Kurdi, including Western leaders, owing to alleged policy failures in the Middle East along with their people's supposed indifference to the refugees. There were also the people smugglers and President Bashar al-Assad, along with his supporters in Iran and Russia. Above all of them there was Islamic State, which had been terrorizing Aylan throughout his short life, starting long before he made the fateful voyage that would guarantee him a horrible death in the waters of the Aegean.

Aylan and his family had fled Kobani in late 2014 during the onslaught by IS. They had hoped eventually to reach Canada, where Aylan's aunt, Tima Kurdi, lived. The Canadian immigration authorities had already rejected the family's applications, as the required paperwork was 'incomplete' and 'did not meet regulatory requirements for proof of refugee status recognition'.[11] As Syrian refugees in Turkey, family members had been unable to obtain either passports or work permits. IS had turned Aylan first into a non-person and then into a dead one, in a lethal process that it has perfected over time with thousands of people.

The photo of Aylan Kurdi made an enormous worldwide impact. Within days, Germany's vice-chancellor, Sigmar Gabriel, announced his country could take in half a million refugees a year for 'several years'. At the time it was estimated that Germany would have granted asylum to 800,000 people by the end of 2015, four times the number of the previous year.[12] Other countries, including the UK, also announced they would do more to accommodate the flood of human misery from Syria. A shamed world started to speak more of 'refugees' and rather less about 'migrants'. The curse of Islamic State was rippling outwards far and wide from the Middle East.

The photograph of Aylan's body also appeared prominently in another publication. *Dabiq*, the glossy periodical produced by IS, concluded that in all eventuality the souls of Aylan Kurdi and his family would now be burning in hellfire – their just reward for daring to leave the 'caliphate'. Predictably, IS could make sense of Aylan's death only in relation to the all-important state. Although it had often tried and failed to conquer Kobani, it was still considered a 'Muslim land' and therefore part of the planned utopia.

To Abu Bakr al-Baghdadi, his land-locked, war-ravaged and unstable empire was nothing less than *Dārul-Islām*, literally the 'abode of Islam'. Everywhere else is *dārul-kufr*, the 'abode of the *kuffar*'. Under the photo of Aylan's drowned corpse, *Dabiq* railed, 'Some Syrians and Libyans are willing to risk the lives and souls of those whom they are responsible to raise upon the Sharī'ah – their children – sacrificing many of them during the dangerous trip to the lands of war-waging crusaders ruled by laws of atheism and indecency.'[13] The author of the piece went on to say, 'It should be known that voluntarily leaving *Dārul-Islām* for *dārul-kufr* is a dangerous major sin, as it is a passage towards *kufr* and a gate towards one's children and grandchildren abandoning Islam for Christianity, atheism or liberalism.' For those people who leave *Dārul-Islām* and die in the attempt, 'their refuge is Hell – and evil it is as a destination'; a Muslim's duty was surely 'Hijrah', a flight to the 'state' – not away from it.

Baghdadi has been so determined to underpin the legitimacy of his 'state' that he has returned repeatedly to his obsession of establishing a new currency. He was emphatic that the new 'caliphate' must have its own money; it could not go on using the apostate US dollar. So in late August 2015, Islamic State finally announced the long-promised introduction of its new coinage. In a highly produced film laboriously entitled *Glad Tidings of the Subjects with the Gold Currency*, IS boasted about its new gold dinar.[14] The film showed the dinars being cut from thin strips of gold by coin-making machinery and then struck. The estimated worth of the most valuable 21-carat dinar in September 2015 was said to be almost $700.[15] Baghdadi baulked at the vanity of demanding his own face on the new dinar; instead an image of the entire world, which the group predicts it will one day conquer, is on one side of the coin and on the other are seven stalks of wheat, apparently to demonstrate the harvests and bounty lavished by IS on its captive millions.

Despite the propaganda over the new coins, few of the people in Baghdadi's 'caliphate' doubted that the US dollar would continue to be the 'caliphate's' de facto reserve currency, particularly when it came to paying its own fighters; nor did they believe there would be anything worthwhile to spend the new dinars on. As for the lavishing of bounty, IS was reaping what it had sowed: a harvest of suffering and death.

Innocent civilians continue to pay the heaviest price for Islamic State's conquests. Air strikes are a daily reality for people in the 'caliphate' on both sides of the Iraqi–Syrian border, but the brunt of the ferocity has been borne by Raqqa. In mid-September Sarmad al-Jilane, a journalist for the website Raqqa Is Being Slaughtered Silently (RBSS), reported that 'the people in Alraqqa [sic] are suffering of panic and fear conditions, because of raids and massacres'. IS has also had to parry attacks from the predominantly Kurdish fighting units called the People's Protection Units (or YPGs). In turn, IS introduced a curfew and began a series of arrest trawls.

During the late summer and early autumn of 2015, it became apparent that conditions were worsening within the 'caliphate' itself. Aside from the food queues and electricity shortages, the water had become 'undrinkable'. At al-Tabqa, a city to the west of Raqqa, the drinking water had turned brown and become infested with little white worms.[16] Red dust and green algae were reported in the water supply within Raqqa itself. At al-Tabqa, IS blamed one of its water engineers, Ibrahim Othman, for allegedly absconding with the funds set aside for providing clean water to the city.[17] The Red Crescent, which had been handing out water purification tablets and maintaining the water plants, had been kicked out of the 'caliphate' early in 2015. Mothers had to rely on extortionately priced bottled water for most of their household needs. According to the courageous reporting team of RBSS, cases of dysentery had gone up by 600 percent and the number of kidney ailments by 300 percent. There was growing evidence of mutiny within territories controlled by IS, particularly on the Iraqi side of the 'caliphate' border. For example, in early October 2015, IS massacred seventy men from the Albu Nimr tribe in the Khanzir area near Lake Tharthar, some eighty miles north of Baghdad.[18] The Albu Nimr had first risen up against the group during the Awakening almost a decade earlier[19] and the men had sought refuge in Khanzir after fleeing IS-occupied territory near Ramadi. Many were murdered because they had relatives in Iraq's security forces.[20]

The currency and the conquests, along with the brutal suppression of the captive populations, all have the same purpose: to demonstrate permanence and to sell the idea that the 'caliphate' is here to stay. The longer it stays, the more it seems likely to endure and the more likely it is that it will grow. It must grow and, as it does, its long list of perceived threats, both military and even cultural, must die.

Year zero

In late May 2015 the city of Palmyra, in central Syria, fell to IS. The world greeted this news with a heavy heart and the sickening feeling that its glorious ancient ruins, as one-time capital of the doomed breakaway empire of Queen Zenobia of the third century CE,[21] would certainly fall victim to Baghdadi's cultural wrecking ball.

Before capturing Palmyra on 21 May, IS had already laid waste to any ancient cities, churches and monuments it considered to have committed *shirk* – the sin of idolatry. In March 2015, IS bull-dozed the ruins of Nimrud, an Assyrian city from the thirteenth century BCE in northern Iraq twenty miles south of Mosul. 'Whenever we control a piece of land we remove the symbols of polytheism and spread monotheism in it,' one jihadi told the camera.[22] Also in northern Iraq, the group destroyed the ancient Parthian city of Hatra, a UNESCO World Heritage site sixty-eight miles south-west of Mosul. The city's fortified walls had withstood the Roman legions but they were no match for IS militants armed with TNT, hammers and drills. Irina Bokova, the head of UNESCO, said that 'the destruction of Hatra marks a turning point in an appalling strategy of cultural cleansing underway in Iraq'.[23]

Palmyra was often compared to Pompeii and was in some ways more impressive and mystical. But nothing outside Islam and the

'State' is sacred to IS and therefore the destruction of the ancient city began in earnest on 27 June 2015 with the ancient statue of the Lion of al-Lāt. The lion, consort of the goddess al-Lāt, held a gazelle between his paws to show al-Lāt's merciful qualities. No such clemency was shown to the long-redundant stone lion as the group set about its predictable and methodical ruination of the site. On 30 August 2015, it blew up the beautiful Temple of Baalshamin,[24] followed a week later with the destruction of the ancient Temple of Bel, the subject of a later *Dabiq* photo feature entitled 'Destroying the Shirk Temple of Bel'.[25] Many *shirk* Islamic monuments of great importance have also been obliterated in the group's attempt to wipe clean the historical and cultural heritage of two countries that were often referred to as the 'cradle of civilization'. Baghdadi even ordered the murder of the director of the Palmyra site, a highly respected archaeologist. Khaled al-Asaad, aged eighty-three, had bravely refused pleas from his family to leave before it was too late.[26] IS goons beheaded Asaad in a local square and then hanged his decapitated corpse with red twine from a traffic light,[27] his reward for apparently refusing to tell the group's antiquities racketeers where important treasures had been hidden. Whatever happens to IS or its 'caliphate' in the future, it has left an indelible stain on the region and is likely to be remembered more for what it has destroyed than for what it has built.

'The most shaming'

In late August 2015, the Taliban finally admitted what many people, particularly in Western intelligence, had believed for a long time: it had been covering up the death of its religious leader, Mullah Mohammed Omar. This news was of the greatest interest to Abu Bakr al-Baghdadi, who had challenged Mullah Omar's position as *Amir al-Mu'minin*, Commander or Prince of the Faithful, the title most associated with a true caliph.

Mullah Omar had also been the religious leader of Islamic State's sworn enemy, al-Qaeda. Osama bin Laden had pledged allegiance, or *bay'ah*, to him personally. Therefore, the fact that the religious leader of both al-Qaeda and the Taliban had died – apparently and perhaps surprisingly of natural causes – on 24 April 2013 was of some importance.[28] Mullah Omar had never claimed to be a caliph, but only al-Qaeda's 'utmost imam' and the bounded leader of a 'regional emirate'.[29]

Abu Bakr al-Baghdadi was particularly furious because he believed that a still-living Mullah Omar was the only obstacle not just to his annexation of al-Qaeda but to his undisputed leadership of the global community of Muslims, the *Ummah*, as he made clear through *Dabiq* in September 2015: 'Throughout this period, the various Qā'idah branches claimed they could not claim allegiance to the Qurashi Khalifah Abū Bakr al-Baghdādī because Mullā Umar was their "utmost imām".'[30] Baghdadi directed his ire for this hoax principally at the man who had orchestrated it successfully for two and a half years, Mullah Omar's successor at the head of the Taliban, Mullah Akhtar Mohammed Mansoor. Describing the ruse as 'the most shaming event' of 2015, *Dabiq* raged, 'One finds the closest precedent to be the myth of "Pope Joan", a woman who supposedly fooled the pagan church into electing her pope while disguising herself as a man. She allegedly succeeded in duping and ruling the cross-worshippers before being exposed and dying shortly afterwards.'[31]

No mention was made in *Dabiq* of the startling revelation in August 2015 that the self-proclaimed 'caliph' himself was a serial rapist who, according to authoritative reports, had repeatedly forced himself on the captive US hostage Kayla Mueller, among others.[32] Mueller had been kidnapped in August 2013 while leaving a Spanish Médecins sans Frontières hospital in Aleppo and IS had demanded a $5 million ransom. She had gone to Syria to help the victims of war and, like Alan Henning before her, was rewarded with terror and death. She was kept by IS in a house in the Syrian town of al-Shadadiya. Captive Yazidi girls were also kept there and abused as sex slaves; apparently they were gifts for IS fighters who had been victorious in battle.

One of the Yazidi girls would later reveal to US investigators the full extent of Mueller's ordeal. According to the IS media outlet Manbar, the courageous US aid worker died in a Jordanian air strike on 6 February 2015. The house in which she'd been held in al-Shadadiya was run by Umm Sayyaf, the wife of an important Tunisian IS financier, Abu Sayyaf. In May 2015 US Special Forces captured Umm Sayyaf in a raid during which her husband died. The Yazidi girl witness was rescued in the same operation.[33] Umm Sayyaf is said to be cooperating with her US interrogators in Iraq. She is believed to have corroborated the revelations made by the Yazidi girl about Kayla Mueller and the abuse she suffered at the hands of Abu Bakr al-Baghdadi.

Despite his crimes, Baghdadi remains undisputed master of his 'caliphate'. At the time of writing, the expansion of the 'caliphate' has stalled while its enemies increase in strength and numbers. In September 2015, Russian troops were dispatched to Syria in a desperate attempt to prop up the discredited regime of President al-Assad and prevent the country from falling completely to IS, a disaster that would give the group access to the Mediterranean. A report by the Royal United Services Institute (RUSI) suggested that Russia might be in danger of actually helping IS if it targets the group's enemies such as al-Nusra Front and Ahrar al-Sham.[34] The report also warned that in all probability neither Iraq nor Syria have viable futures as nation states, with Iraq in particular 'likely to split along sectarian lines'.[35]

The inviolability and sacredness of the 'state' is such that the group will strike back ruthlessly at any country that attacks it, as it did against Russia and France in the autumn of 2015. If the 'Islamic state' was vulnerable to attack from the great powers lined up against it, then their people and capitals would also suffer in turn. Demonstrating its global reach, Islamic State struck at Paris in November 2015. The assault on the French capital came as a huge shock to many people who believed that IS ultra-violence was a phenomenon confined to the Middle East. Surely the attacks would be a harbinger of more terror to come in Europe and probably elsewhere in the West. The 'state' would strike back at all enemies, whenever and wherever they could, in their bars, restaurants and concert halls. Could the group's terror survive the extinction of the 'state' and if it did, what would be the point of it?

So for IS, the ultimate answer must be the destruction of the 'state' it has built amid the wreckage of Iraq and Syria. 'Da'esh has actually defined its success through territory,' said Dr Afzal Ashraf, a consultant fellow with RUSI. 'So to defeat an organization, you have to defeat its idea of success. Al-Qaeda defined its success by its ability to hit the far enemy [the West] and that's why it became hugely successful. They said they were going to do it back in 1995. Nobody really knew about it until 2001 and suddenly we had 9/11. And then young guys started flocking to it like nobody's business.'[36]

Ashraf has been critical of the West's approach to IS and believes too many regional players have failed to deal with the IS threat. He also cited the example of Saudi Arabia using its air force over Yemen to attack the Houthis, a rebellious Shia tribe supported militarily by Iran.[37] Why weren't the Saudis apparently devoting as much effort to defeating IS? 'There's a very strange psyche going on in the Middle East,' added Ashraf. 'There's been this lack of interventionism and you've also got this conspiratorial misdirection. So ISIS is a very convenient bogeyman for everybody in the region and that's a very dangerous thing. Frankly the world is in a mess as far as this is concerned.'

On 30 October 2015, the bodies of two young men were dis-covered in the Turkish city of Urfa, not far from the Syrian border.[38] Ibrahim Abdul Qader and Fares Hammadi had been shot and beheaded. Both worked as journalists for Raqqa Is Being Slaughtered Silently, the website which has done so much to reveal the grisly reality of Islamic State. The site's founder Abu Mohammed told me from Syria that he was in no doubt IS sent the killers. 'It seems they have cells,' he said. 'It's getting worse for us'. As for people in the 'caliphate', 'it's getting worse and worse'. The murders exposed the real menace to the future of the 'State'. Despite its many enemies the one thing IS really fears is the truth.

As of autumn 2015, the 'State' persists more or less intact in the shape and size it achieved on conquering Mosul in June 2014, and that's despite the air strikes, the Iraqi army and the mainly Kurdish YPG fighting groups. So far that combination, including the US-led air campaign, has not brought about the collapse of the 'caliphate', although the enemies of IS would continue to nibble away at its conquests. In late September 2015, more than three thousand Kurdish security troops alongside Kurdish Peshmerga fighters managed to recapture ten Arab villages from IS in the district of Hawija, twenty miles south-west of Kirkuk.[39] The group had taken the villages during its triumphant rampage in June 2014 that culminated in the capture of Mosul.[40] In mid-November 2015, the Iraqi army advanced on Ramadi while Kurdish forces started to clear the important city of Sinjar in northern Iraq.[41] The Kurds know only too well how much the group's existence is completely intertwined with its obsession with territory – seizing it, holding it and expanding it. It is the group's obligation, its *Fard Ayn*. Through its resilience and utter remorselessness IS has shown that to be defeated, it cannot be left in control of any territory, even if that territory, as Abdullah Azzam once taught, ends up being no bigger than the palm of a man's hand.

Notes

Introduction

1 Author interview, February 2015.

1: The face that launched a thousand hits

1 Abu Mohammed al-Adnani, 'This the Promise of Allah', quoted in 'ISIS Spokesman Declares Caliphate, Rebrands Group as "Islamic State"', Site Monitoring Service [online], 29 June 2014 (https://news.siteintelgroup.com/Jihadist-News/isis-spokesman-declares-caliphate-rebrands-group-as-islamic-state.html) (accessed 19 March 2015).

2 Bernard Lewis, *The Political Language of Islam* (Chicago: University of Chicago Press, 1988), p. 44.

3 Ibid., p. 44.

4 Reuters, 5 July 2014.

5 'Profile: Abu Bakr al-Baghdadi', BBC News [online], 5 July 2014 (http://www.bbc.co.uk/news/world-middle-east-27801676) (accessed 19 March 2015).

6 Author interview with Lt-Col. Myles B. Caggins, US Department of Defense, 2015.

7 In *Al-Naba*, IS claimed to have carried out 1,083 assassinations during 2013 alone. Total bombings including car bombs and improvised explosive devices comes to 5,492: see Alex Bilger, 'ISIS Annual Reports Reveal Metrics-driven Military Command', Institute for the Study of War, 22 May 2014, p. 10.

8 Basheer M. Nafi, 'The Abolition of the Caliphate in Historical

Context', in *Demystifying the Caliphate: Historical Memory and Contemporary Contexts*, ed. Madawi Al-Rasheed, Carol Kersten and Marat Shterin (London: Hurst, 2013), p. 45.

9   Jason Goodwin, *Lords of the Horizons: A History of the Ottoman Empire* (London: Chatto & Windus, 1998) – a highly recommended account of the Ottoman empire and its last days.

10 Mario Ledwith, 'Terror Warlord Al-Baghdadi Denounces the West – but Is Spotted Wearing "£3,500 James Bond Wristwatch"', Mail Online, 6 July 2014 (http://www.dailymail.co.uk/news/article-2682415/Terror-warlord-al-Baghdadi-denounces-West-spotted-wearing-pricy-Western-wristwatch-resembles-expensive-Omega-Rolex.html) (accessed 19 March 2015).

11 'A Message to the Mujahidin and the Muslim Ummah in the Month of Ramadan', Al-Furqan Media Foundation, 1 July 2014.

12 Al-Adnani, 'This the Promise of Allah'.

13 Borzou Daraghi, 'Biggest Bank Robbery That "Never Happened" – $400 million ISIS heist', *Financial Times*, 17 July 2014.

14 'Energy News Update', Iraq Oil Institute, 3 November 2014.

15 'Experts: ISIS Makes up to $3 Million Daily in Oil Sales', Al Arabiya News [online], 28 August 2014 (http://english.alarabiya.net/en/perspective/analysis/2014/08/28/Experts-ISIS-makes-up-to-3-million-daily-in-oil-sales.html) (accessed 19 March 2015).

16 IS released a film showing the immolation of Muath Safi al-Kasasbeh on 3 February 2015.

17 'The Revival of Slavery: Before the Hour', *Dabiq* 4, 2014, p. 14.

18 'Foreword', *Dabiq* 4, 2014, p. 5.

19 Ned Parker and Oliver Holmes, 'Iraq Chases Baghdad Sleeper Cells as "Zero Hour" Looms over Capital', Reuters [online], 3 July 2014 (http://uk.reuters.com/article/2014/07/03/us-iraq-security-sleeper-insight-idUKKBN0F81FK20140703) (accessed 19 March 2015).

20 Jean-Charles Brisard, *Zarqawi: The New Face of al-Qaeda* (Cambridge: Polity Press, 2005), p. 72.

21 Author interview, 2015.

22 Author interview, 2015.

23 Brisard, *Zarqawi*, p. 10.

24 Ibid., p. 12.

25 Ibid., pp. 13, 50.

26 'The Islamic State', Mapping Militant Organizations [online] (http://web.stanford.edu/group/mappingmilitants/cgi-bin/groups/view/1) (accessed 19 March 2015).

27 Brisard, *Zarqawi*, pp. 5–7.

28 Ibid., p. 19.

29 Thomas Joscelyn, 'Jailed Jihadist Ideologue Says the ISIS Is a "Deviant Organization"', Long War Journal [online], 28 May 2014 (http://www.longwarjournal.org/archives/2014/05/jailed_jihadist_ideo.php) (accessed 19 March 2015).

30 Brisard, *Zarqawi*, p. 43.

31 Sayyid Qutb, *Ma'alim fi'al-Tariq* ['Milestones'] (Lahore: Kazi, [1964] 1981), p. 56.

32 Ibid., Introduction 5.

33 Ibid., Introduction 1 and 2.

34 Ibid., pp. 9–10.

35 Qutb was hanged in 1966.

36 Roxanne L. Euben and Muhammad Qasim Zaman (eds), *Princeton Readings in Islamic Thought: Texts and Contexts from al-Banna to Bin Laden* (Princeton, NJ: Princeton University Press, 2009), pp. 19–20.

37 Abu Muhammad Aasim al-Maqdisi, *Democracy Is a Religion!*, tr. Abu Muhammad al-Maleki.

38 Loretta Napoleoni, *Insurgent Iraq: Al Zarqawi and the New Generation* (London: Constable, 2005), pp. 56–7.

39 Al-Furqan Media Center, Islamic State, Audio message by Abu Bakr al-Baghdadi, posted 14 May 2015 by the Middle East Media Research Institute (MEMRI) Jihad and Terrorism Threat Monitor, 'In New Audio Speech, Islamic State (ISIS) Leader Al-Baghdadi Issues Call to Arms to All Muslims'.

2: Seven steps

1 Loretta Napoleoni, *Insurgent Iraq: Al Zarqawi and the New Generation* (London: Constable, 2005), p. 75.

2 Jean-Charles Brisard, *Zarqawi: The New Face of al-Qaeda* (Cambridge: Polity Press, 2005), p. 41.

3 Napoleoni, *Insurgent Iraq*, p. 75.

4 There are several analyses of the Hussein book. One of the better ones is Aaron Y. Zelin, 'Jihad 2020: Assessing Al-Qaida's 20-year Plan', World Politics Review [online], 11 September 2013 (http://www.worldpoliticsreview.com/articles/13208/jihad-2020-assessing-al-qaida-s-20-year-plan) (accessed 20 March 2015).

5 Ibid.

6   Author interview.

7   Sayyid Qutb, *Ma'alim fi'al-Tariq* ['Milestones'] (Lahore: Kazi, [1964] 1981), pp. 6–7.

8   Ibid., pp. 47–9.

9   Ibid., p. 97.

10 Bruce Riedel, 'Al Qaeda's Surprising New Target', Daily Beast [online], 30 July 2010 (http://www.thedailybeast.com/articles/2010/07/30/al-qaedas-ayman-zawahiri-criticizes-turkey-seeks-ottoman-restoration.html) (accessed 29 April 2015); comments attributed to Ayman al-Zawahiri, then deputy leader of al-Qaeda.

11 David Kilcullen, *The Accidental Guerrilla: Fighting Small Wars in the Midst of a Big One* (New York: Oxford University Press, 2011), p. 17.

12 Quoted in Jeffrey Pool, 'Zarqawi's Pledge of Allegiance to Al-Qaeda: From *Mu'asker al-Battar*, Issue 21', *Terrorism Monitor* 2:24.

13 Abdel Bari Atwan, *The Secret History of al-Qaeda* (Berkeley: University of California Press, 2006), p. 194.

14 Napoleoni, *Insurgent Iraq*, p. 61.

15 Mary Anne Weaver, 'The Short, Violent Life of Abu Musab al-Zarqawi', *The Atlantic*, July–August 2006.

16 Terence White, 'Flashback: When the Taleban took Kabul', BBC News [online], 15 October 2001 (http://news.bbc.co.uk/1/hi/world/south_asia/1600136.stm) (accessed 20 March 2015).

17 Atwan, *The Secret History of al-Qaeda*, p. 195.

18 Brisard, *Zarqawi*, p. 48.

19 Ibid.

20 Atwan, *The Secret History of al-Qaeda*, p. 195.

21 Zarqawi may have earned this nickname earlier on his way to Afghanistan: see Napoleoni, *Insurgent Iraq*, p. 42.

22 Weaver, 'The Short, Violent Life of Abu Musab al-Zarqawi'.

23 Ibid.

24 Brisard, *Zarqawi*, p. 48.

25 Emily Hunt, 'Zarqawi's "Total War" on Iraqi Shiites Exposes a Divide among Sunni Jihadists', PolicyWatch 1049, Washington Institute [online], 15 November 2005 (http://www.washingtoninstitute.org/policy-analysis/view/zarqawis-total-war-on-iraqi-shiites-exposes-a-divide-among-sunni-jihadists) (accessed 20 March 2015).

26 Ibid.

27 Thomas Joscelyn, 'Jailed Jihadist Ideologue Says the ISIS Is a "Deviant Organization"', Long War Journal [online], 28 May 2014 (http://

www.longwarjournal.org/archives/2014/05/jailed_jihadist_ideo.
php) (accessed 19 March 2015).

28 Weaver, The Short, Violent Life of Abu Musab al-Zarqawi.

29 Brisard, *Zarqawi*, p. 49; Atwan, *The Secret History of al-Qaeda*, p. 195.

30 Brisard, *Zarqawi*, pp. 49–50.

31 Ibid., p. 58.

32 Weaver, The Short, Violent Life of Abu Musab al-Zarqawi.

33 Ibid.

34 *Jordan Times*, 27 July 2003, based on testimony in court of Shadi
Mohammad Mustafa Abdullah. a 26-year-old Jordanian of Palestinian
origin.

35 'Al-Qaeda's New Military Chief', BBC News [online], 19 December
2001 (http://news.bbc.co.uk/1/hi/world/south_asia/1717863.stm)
(accessed 20 March 2015).

36 'Most Wanted Terrorists: Saif al-Adel', Federal Bureau of Investigation
[online]   (http://www.fbi.gov/wanted/wanted_terrorists/saif-al-
adel/view) (accessed 20 March 2015).

37 Weaver, 'The Short, Violent Life of Abu Musab al-Zarqawi'.

38 Brisard, *Zarqawi*, pp. 75–6.

39 Atwan, *The Secret History of al-Qaeda*, p. 196.

40 Ibid, p. 196. Atwan asserts Zarqawi was 'dismayed' with the attacks (p.
197).

41 Brisard, *Zarqawi*, p. 109.

42 Report by Human Rights Watch following interviews it carried out
in 2002.

43 'Ansar al-Islam in Iraqi Kurdistan', Human Rights Watch [online], 5
February 2003 (http://www.hrw.org/legacy/backgrounder/mena/
ansarbk020503.htm) (accessed 20 March 2015).

44 'Mulla Krekar: Only ISIS Can Fulfil Muslim "Ambitions and
Dreams"', Rûdaw [online], 5 February 2015 (http://rudaw.net/
english/middleeast/050220151) (accessed 29 April 2015).

45 In 2015 Norway banished Krekar, whose real name is Najmuddin
Faraj Ahmad, to a remote village: Justin Huggler, 'Norway Attempts to
Relocate Islamic Hate Preacher to Remote Village 300 Miles North
of Oslo', *Daily Telegraph*, 30 January 2015.

46 Neil McFarquhar, 'Threats and Responses: Attack on US Diplomat;
American Envoy Killed in Jordan', *International New York Times*
[online], 29 October 2002 (http://www.nytimes.com/2002/10/29/
world/threats-and-responses-attack-on-us-diplomat-american-en-
voy-killed-in-jordan.html) (accessed 20 March 2015).

47 'Jordan Hangs US Diplomat Killers', BBC News [online], 11 March 2006 (http://news.bbc.co.uk/1/hi/world/middle_east/4796280.stm) (accessed 20 March 2015).

48 Brisard, *Zarqawi*, pp. 85–7.

49 In an ABC News interview on 28 September 2005 with Barbara Walters, Powell referred to his UN speech as 'a blot', adding, 'It was painful. It's painful now.'

50 Transcript available at 'Iraq, Denial and Deception: US Secretary of State Colin Powell Addresses the UN Security Council', White House [online], 5 February 2003 (georgewbush-whitehouse.archives.gov/news/releases/2003/02/20030205-1.html) (accessed 20 March 2015).

3: Chaos theory and fact

1 Author interview, 2015

2 Michael White and Sarah Hall, 'BBC under Fire over Chaos Reports', *The Guardian*, 12 April 2003.

3 Ibid.

4 James Dobbins, Seth G. Jones, Benjamin Runkle et al., *Occupying Iraq: A History of the Coalition Provisional Authority* (Santa Monica, CA: Rand, 2009), p. xiv.

5 Chilcot Inquiry, transcript of oral evidence by Major General Tim Cross, 7 December 2009, p. 9.

6 Ibid., p. 17.

7 'Neo-cons' is short for 'neo-conservatives', an often derogatory term used at that time about the advisers of President George W. Bush.

8 Author interview, 2015.

9 Interview with Lt. Gen. (Retd.) Jay Garner, PBS, 11 August 2006. Garner had been the head of the Office for Reconstruction and Humanitarian Assistance, the first interim authority after the invasion.

10 Ali A. Allawi, *The Occupation of Iraq: Winning the War, Losing the Peace* (New Haven, CT: Yale University Press, 2007), p. 117.

11 Ibid., p. 116.

12 L. Paul Bremer, *My Year in Iraq: The Struggle to Build a Future of Hope* (New York: Simon & Schuster, 2006), p. 64.

13 Ibid., p. 64.

14 'The Future of the Global Muslim Population', Pew Research Center

[online], 27 January 2011 (http://www.pewforum.org/2011/01/27/the-future-of-the-global-muslim-population) (accessed 20 March 2015).

15 'The World's Muslims: Unity and Diversity', Pew Research Center [online], 9 August 2012 (http://www.pewforum.org/2012/08/09/the-worlds-muslims-unity-and-diversity-executive-summary/) (accessed 20 March 2015); percentages of Shia and Sunni Muslims who identify themselves as such.

16 John F. Devlin, 'The Ba'ath Party: Rise and Metamorphosis', *American Historical Review*, 96:5, 1991, pp. 1396–1404.

17 Adeed Dawisha, *Iraq: A Political History* (Princeton, NJ: Princeton University Press), p. 185.

18 Saddam Hussein was president of Iraq between 16 July 1979 and 9 April 2003.

19 Miranda Sissons and Abdulrazzaq al-Saiedi, *A Bitter Legacy: Lessons of De-Ba'athification in Iraq*, International Center for Transitional Justice, March 2013, p. 4.

20 Ibid., p. 4.

21 Ibid., p. 4.

22 Allawi, *The Occupation of Iraq*, pp. 149–50.

23 Thomas E. Ricks, *Fiasco: The American Military Adventure in Iraq* (London: Allen Lane, 2006), p. 159.

24 Ibid., p. 159.

25 Sissons and Saiedi, *A Bitter Legacy*, p. 4.

26 Devlin, *The Ba'ath Party*, p. 1407.

27 Allawi, *The Occupation of Iraq*, p. 149; Sissons and Saiedi, *A Bitter Legacy*, p. 4.

28 From letter written by Zarqawi in 2004, published in the appendix of Jean-Charles Brisard, *Zarqawi: The New Face of al-Qaeda* (Cambridge: Polity Press, 2005).

29 'Sunnis and Shia in the Middle East', BBC News [online], 19 December 2013 (http://www.bbc.co.uk/news/world-middle-east-25434060) (accessed 29 April 2015).

30 Sissons and Saiedi, *A Bitter Legacy*, p. 10.

31 Dobbins, Jones, Runkle et al., *Occupying Iraq*, p. xiii.

32 Coalition Provisional Authority Order Number 1: De-Ba'athification of Iraqi Society, CPA/ORD/16 MAY 2003/01.

33 Bremer, *My Year in Iraq*, pp. 41–2.

34 James P. Pfiffner, 'US Blunders in Iraq: De-Ba'athification and Disbanding the Army', *Intelligence and National Security*, 25:1, 2010, p. 79.

35 Bremer, *My Year in Iraq*, p. 71.

36 Ibid., pp. 50–1.

37 Ibid., p. 53.

38 Ibid., p. 42.

39 Chilcot Inquiry, transcript of oral evidence by General Sir Mike Jackson, 28 July 2010, p. 30.

40 Ricks, *Fiasco*, p. 159.

41 Bremer, *My Year in Iraq*, pp. 38–42.

42 Coalition Provisional Authority Order Number 2: Dissolution of Entities, CPA/ORD/23 MAY 2003/02.

43 Bremer, *My Year in Iraq*, p. 55.

44 Ibid., p. 55.

45 Ibid., p. 55.

46 CPA Order Number 2.

47 US–CENTCOM, list of 8,697 disqualified military officers, 29 July 2003, WikiLeaks, cryptographic identity SHA256 961def670c9597a3 51d16580872c42bd9e095f487765036267d7c4461d0146a8.

48 Ricks, *Fiasco*, p. 162.

49 Ibid., p. 60.

50 There have been repeated claims that Saddam had people fed feet first into shredders, even that his son Qusay Hussein supervised some of these murders at Abu Ghraib prison. Some found this hard to believe back in 2004; see Brendan O'Neill, 'Not a Shred of Evidence', *The Spectator*, 21 February 2004.

51 Radwan Mortada, 'Al-Qaeda Leaks II: Baghdadi Loses His Shadow', Al-Akhbar English [online], 14 January 2014 (http://english. al-akhbar.com/content/al-qaeda-leaks-ii-baghdadi-loses-his-shadow) (accessed 20 March 2015).

52 Wikibaghdady. I go into further detail about Wikibaghdady later in the book.

53 Christoph Reuter, 'The Terror Strategist: Secret Files Reveal the Structure of Islamic State', Spiegel Online International, 18 April 2015 (http://www.spiegel.de/international/world/islamic-state-files-show-structure-of-islamist-terror-group-a-1029274.html) (accessed 29 April 2015).

54 Author interview, 2015.

55 CPA Order Number 1.

56 Rajiv Chandrasekaran, *Imperial Life in the Emerald City: Inside Baghdad's Green Zone* (New York: Alfred A. Knopf, 2006), p. 85.

57 Ibid., p. 85.

58 President George W. Bush never actually used this expression; a banner saying 'Mission Accomplished' was strung across the carrier USS *Abraham Lincoln* when Bush gave his valedictory speech on 1 May 2003.

59 Author interview, 2015.

60 Maliki Reshapes the National Security System', WikiLeaks [online], 15 May 2007, canonical ID 07BAGHDAD1593_a (https://wikileaks. org/plusd/cables/07BAGHDAD1593_a.html) (accessed 26 March 2015).

61 Transcript of event to celebrate the reissue of *Every War Must End* by Dr Fred C. Iklé, Center for Strategic and International Studies, 1 March 2005, p. 18. Lehman was US navy secretary between 5 February 1981 and 10 April 1987.

4: The management of savagery

1 Author interview, 2013.

2 See Chapter 1.

3 Abu Bakr Naji, *The Management of Savagery: The Most Critical Stage through Which the Ummah Must Pass*, tr. William McCants, May 2006, p. 11, for the John M. Olin Institute for Strategic Studies at Harvard University.

4 Ibid., p. 39.

5 Ibid., p. 39.

6 Ibid., p. 46.

7 Ibid., p. 44.

8 Ibid., p. 38.

9 Ibid., p. 48.

10 Michael W. S. Ryan, 'Hot Issue: *Dabiq* – What Islamic State's New Magazine Tells Us about Their Strategic Direction, Recruitment Patterns and Guerrilla Doctrine', Jamestown Foundation [online], 1 August 2014 (http://www.jamestown.org/programs/hotissues/sin-gle-hot-issues/?tx_ttnews%5Btt_news%5D=42702&tx_ttnews%5B backPid%5D=61&cHash=e96be5e421a55fb15bec8cddb3117985) (accessed 20 March 2015).

11 See chapter 2.

12 Abu Bakr Naji was identified as the possible author by the Al Arabiya Institute for Studies.

13 The TWAR wiki says the video was released to publicize al-Qaeda's

merger with an Egyptian terrorist group, Gama'a al Islamiyya (http://totalwar-ar.wikia.com/wiki/Mohammad_Hasan_Khalil_al-Hakim) (accessed 20 March 2015).

14 Peter L. Bergen and Daniel Rothenberg (eds), *Drone Wars: Transforming Conflict, Law, and Policy* (New York: Cambridge University Press, 2015), p. 32; Amir Mir, '50th Al-Qaeda Leader Killed in 338th Drone Strike', News International (Pakistan) [online], 3 December 2012 (http://www.thenews.com.pk/Todays-News-2-146255-50th-al-Qaeda-leader-killed-in-338th-drone-strike) (accessed 20 March 2015).

15 See map.

16 Kim Gamel, 'Sunni Who Aided US Gunned Down in Iraq', *Washington Post* [online], 29 May 2006 (http://www.washingtonpost.com/wp-dyn/content/article/2006/05/28/AR2006052800108.html) (accessed 20 March 2015).

17 Charles Levinson, 'Sunni Tribes Turn against Jihadis', *Christian Science Monitor* [online], 6 February 2006 (http://www.csmonitor.com/2006/0206/p01s01-woiq.html) (accessed 20 March 2015).

18 'Iraq's Most Wanted – Where Are They Now?', BBC News [online], 1 September 2010 (http://www.bbc.co.uk/news/world-middle-east-11155798) (accessed 20 March 2015); For the full pack, see Joel Christie, 'Dead Hand, Deck of 52 Most-wanted Iraqi Playing Cards Given to Soldiers at the Start of the War Shows the Fall of Saddam "the Ace of Spades" Hussein's army', Mail Online, 18 October 2014 (http://www.dailymail.co.uk/news/article-2798050/dead-hand-deck-52-wanted-iraqi-playing-cards-given-soldiers-start-war-shows-fall-saddam-ace-spades-hussein-s-army.html) (accessed 20 March 2015).

19 Michael Knights, 'Saddam Hussein's Faithful Friend, the King of Clubs, Might Be the Key to Saving Iraq', *New Republic* [online], 24 June 2014 (http://www.newrepublic.com/article/118356/izzat-ibrahim-al-douri-saddam-husseins-pal-key-stopping-isis) (accessed 20 March 2015).

20 Leila Fadel, 'Saddam's Ex-officer: We've Played Key Role in Helping Militants', NPR [online], 19 June 2014 (http://www.npr.org/blogs/parallels/2014/06/19/323691052/saddams-ex-officer-weve-played-key-role-in-helping-militants) (accessed 20 March 2015).

21 See Ahmed S. Hashim, *Iraq's Sunni Insurgency* (Abingdon: Routledge, 2009), ch. 1 for more details on the various insurgent groups.

22 Thomas Burrows, 'The King of Clubs Is Dead: Former Saddam

Henchman on US Most-wanted List Who Became ISIS Commander Is Killed in Fighting near Former Tyrant's Home City', Mail Online, 20 April 2015 (http://www.dailymail.co.uk/news/article-3043774/ ISIS-commander-former-Saddam-Hussein-henchman-codenamed-King-Clubs-military-s-list-wanted-Iraqis-killed-near-former-tyrant-s-home-city.html) (accessed 29 April 2015).

23 See Ahmed S. Hashim, *Iraq's Sunni Insurgency* (Abingdon: Routledge, 2009), ch. 1 for more details on the various insurgent groups.

24 Bill Roggio, '1920s Revolution Brigades Turns on al Qaeda in Diyala', Long War Journal [online], 12 June 2007 (http://www.longwar-journal.org/archives/2007/06/1920s_revolution_bri.php) (accessed 20 March 2015).

25 'Ansar al-Islam', Mapping Militant Organizations [online] (http://web.stanford.edu/group/mappingmilitants/cgi-bin/groups/view/13?highlight=ansar+al-islam) (accessed 20 March 2015). Ansar al-Sunna later became known as Ansar al-Islam.

26 Harry de Quetteville, '12 Die in Baghdad Embassy Bomb Blast', *Daily Telegraph*, 8 August 2003.

27 'Results in Iraq: 100 Days toward Security and Freedom' (available at http://georgewbush-whitehouse.archives.gov/infocus/iraq/part2.html) (accessed 23 March 2015).

28 L. Paul Bremer, *My Year in Iraq: The Struggle to Build a Future of Hope* (New York: Simon & Schuster, 2006), pp. 140–1.

29 *Sergio*, HBO documentary, 2009.

30 Thomas E. Ricks, *Fiasco: The American Military Adventure in Iraq* (London: Allen Lane, 2006), p. 216.

31 'Baghdad Terror Blast Kills Dozens', BBC News [online], 27 October 2003 (http://news.bbc.co.uk/1/hi/world/middle_east/3216539.stm) (accessed 23 March 2015)

32 Riverbend, *Baghdad Burning: Girl Blog from Iraq* (New York: Feminist Press, 2005), pp. 8–9.

33 'Iraq Index: Tracking Variables of Reconstruction and Security in Post-Saddam Iraq', Brookings Institution, 13 February 2004, p. 19. The Gallup poll was based on interviews with 1,178 adults between 8 August and 4 September 2003.

34 Author interview, 2015.

35 Adam Ereli, 'Rewards for Justice: Reward Increase for Abu Mu'sab al-Zarqawi', press statement, US department of state, 30 June 2004.

36 A US state department poster declared, 'MURDER: Nairobi & Dar es Salaam bombings, 1998, 224 killed and 5,000 wounded.

MURDERER: Usama bin Laden. Up to $25 million reward.' The poster can be seen at https://www.rewardsforjustice.net/murder_murderer_ubl.pdf (accessed 29 April 2015).

In fact, the total was $27 million, including $25 million from the state department and $2 million offered by the Airline Pilots Association and the Air Transport Association. In any event, bin Laden was eliminated by the US Navy SEALs and the money was apparently never paid

37 Transcript of Zarqawi letter, US department of state archive, 2004.

38 The letter was found or intercepted by the CPA.

39 Loretta Napoleoni, *Insurgent Iraq: Al Zarqawi and the New Generation* (London: Constable, 2005), p. 159.

40 'Iraq Shias Massacred on Holy Day', BBC News [online], 2 March 2004 (http://news.bbc.co.uk/1/hi/world/middle_east/3524589.stm) (accessed 23 March 2015).

41 Transcript of Zarqawi letter, US department of state archive, 2004.

42 Amir Hassanpour, 'The Kurdish Experience', *Middle East Report*, 189, 1994.

43 'Obituary: Ayatollah Mohammad Baqir al-Hakim', *The Guardian*, 30 August 2003.

44 Aki Peritz and Eric Rosenbach, *Find, Fix, Finish: Inside the Counterterrorism Campaigns That Killed Bin Laden and Devastated Al-Qaeda* (New York: PublicAffairs, 2012), p. 118.

45 Claude Salhani, 'Hakim's Return to Iraq', *Washington Times*, 15 May 2003.

46 Bremer, *My Year in Iraq*, pp. 143–4.

47 'Blasts at Shiite Ceremonies in Iraq Kill More than 140', *International New York Times*, 2 March 2004.

48 John F. Burns, 'At Least 64 Dead as Rebels Strike in 3 Iraqi Cities', *New York Times*, 20 December 2004.

49 Author interview, 2015.

50 Author interview, 2015.

51 'Bombers Kill 35 Kids Lined Up for Candy', Associated Press, 1 October 2004.

52 Paul McGeough, 'Handicapped Boy Who Was Made into a Bomb', *Sydney Morning Herald*, 2 February 2005.

53 Ibid.

54 'Obituary: Abu Musab al-Zarqawi', *The Guardian*, 9 June 2006.

55 'VBIED ATTK ON CIV IN AL HILLAH: 166 CIV KILLED, 146 INJ, 0 CF INJ/DAMAGE', WikiLeaks [online], 28 February 2005,

report key 7DC3DD72-79A7-449D-93C1-EBD985B624A9 (https://wikileaks.org/irq/report/2005/02/IRQ20050228n1529. html) (accessed 23 March 2015).

56 Charlotte Buchen, 'The Man Turned Away', PBS Frontline [online], 16 October 2006 (http://www.pbs.org/wgbh/pages/frontline/ene-mywithin/reality/al-banna.html) (accessed 23 March 2015).

57 Aaron Y. Zelin, 'The War between ISIS and al-Qaeda for Supremacy of the Global Jihadist Movement', Research Notes 20, Washington Institute [online], June 2014 (http://www.washingtoninstitute.org/policy-analysis/view/the-war-between-isis-and-al-qaeda-for-su-premacy-of-the-global-jihadist) (accessed 23 March 2015).

58 Author interview, 2015.

59 Jean-Charles Brisard, *Zarqawi: The New Face of al-Qaeda* (Cambridge: Polity Press, 2005). p. 143.

60 Peter R. Mansoor, *Surge: My Journey with General David Petraeus and the Remaking of the Iraq War* (New Haven, CT: Yale University Press, 2013), p. 160.

61 Sewell Chan, 'Beheading Victim "Loved Adventure and Risk"', *Washington Post*, 14 May 2004.

62 'THREATENING EMAIL SENT TO CONTRACTORS IVO BAYJI: 0 INJ/DAMAGE', WikiLeaks [online], 1 July 2005, report key: 83E4A7A5-2508-480E-B67C-49EF4114D152 (https://wikileaks.org/irq/report/2005/07/IRQ20050701n2088.html) (accessed 23 March 2015).

63 Author interview, 2015.

64 Ayman al-Zawahiri, 'Letter from Ayman al-Zawahiri to Abu Musab al-Zarqawi', Council on Foreign Relations [online], 9 July 2005 (http://www.cfr.org/iraq/letter-ayman-al-zawahiri-abu-musab-al-zarqawi/p9862) (accessed 23 March 2015).

65 Ibid.

66 Author interview, 2015.

5: 632 and all that

1 Author interview, 2013.

2 Astonishingly, no one died in the Samarra bombing although many were to die as a result afterwards.

3 Christopher M. Blanchard, 'Islam: Sunnis and Shiites', Congressional Research Service, 28 January 2009, pp. 2–4.

4   Edward Wong, 'Prisoner Links Iraqi to Attack on Shi'ite Shrine, Official Says', *New York Times*, 29 June 2006.

5   Ibid.

6   Megan K. Stack, 'Iraq Loses Voice in the Wilderness with Violent Death of Journalist', *Cincinnati Post*, 15 March 2006.

7   'Gunmen Disrupt Bahjat's Funeral', *Gulf News*, 25 February 2006.

8   Robert F. Worth, 'Blast Destroys Shrine in Iraq, Setting Off Sectarian Fury', *New York Times*, 22 February 2006.

9   Iraqi Body Count.

10 Iraqi Body Count.

11 'Global Overview 2014: People Internally Displaced by Conflict and Violence', Internal Displacement Monitoring Centre, May 2014, p. 57.

12 Richard Beeston, 'Imams Put Fatwa on Carp Caught in Tigris', *The Times*, 27 June 2007.

13 Richard Engel, *War Journal: My Five Years in Iraq* (New York: Simon & Schuster, 2008), p. 361–2.

14 Ali's wife was Muhammad's daughter Fatimah.

15 See chapter 4.

16 See chapter 4.

17 Schmuel Bar, 'Sunnis and Shiites: Between Rapprochement and Conflict', *Current Trends in Islamist Ideology*, 2, 2005, 90–1.

18 Ibid., p. 92.

19 Patrick Cockburn, *Muqtada al-Sadr and the Shia Insurgency in Iraq* (London: Faber & Faber, 2009), p. 49.

20 Ian Black, '"Chemical Ali" on Trial for Brutal Crushing of Shia Uprising', *The Guardian*, 22 August 2007; for comprehensive account see Cockburn, *Muqtada al-Sadr and the Shia Insurgency in Iraq*, pp. 70–96.

21 Cockburn, *Muqtada al-Sadr and the Shia Insurgency in Iraq*, p. 34.

22 See chapter 4.

23 'The World Factbook: Iraq', Central Intelligence Agency [online] (https://www.cia.gov/library/publications/the-world-factbook/geos/iz.html) (accessed 23 March 2015).

24 Raad Alkadiri and Chris Toensing, 'The Iraqi Governing Council's Sectarian Hue', Middle East Research and Information Project [online], 20 August 2003 (http://www.merip.org/mero/mero082003) (accessed 23 March 2015).

25 Ibid.

26 L. Paul Bremer, *My Year in Iraq: The Struggle to Build a Future of Hope* (New York: Simon & Schuster, 2006), p. 101.

NOTES

27   Miranda Sissons and Abdulrazzaq al-Saiedi, *A Bitter Legacy: Lessons of De-Ba'athification in Iraq*, International Center for Transitional Justice, March 2013, p. 12.

28   Ibid., p. 15.

29   Ibid., p. 12.

30   'Unmaking Iraq: A Constitutional Process Gone Awry', Middle East Briefing No. 19, International Crisis Group, 26 September 2005, p. 2.

31   Sissons and Saiedi, *A Bitter Legacy*, pp. 15–16.

32   'Make or Break: Iraq's Sunnis and the State', Middle East Report No. 144, International Crisis Group, 14 August 2013.

33   'Unmaking Iraq', p. 1.

34   'Bodies Mutilated in Iraq Attack', BBC News [online], 31 March 2004 (http://news.bbc.co.uk/1/hi/world/middle_east/3585765. stm) (accessed 23 March 2015).

35   Loretta Napoleoni, *Insurgent Iraq: Al Zarqawi and the New Generation* (London: Constable, 2005), p. 217.

36   Iraq Body Count.

37   Timothy S. McWilliams, *US Marines in Battle: Fallujah, November–December 2004* (Quantico,VA: United States Marine Corps, 2014).

38   Thomas E. Ricks, *Fiasco: The American Military Adventure in Iraq* (London: Allen Lane, 2006), p. 401.

39   Spencer C.Tucker (ed.), *Encyclopedia of Insurgency and Counterinsurgency: A New Era of Modern Warfare* (Santa Barbara, CA: ABC-CLIO, 2013), p. 270.

40   Author interview, 2014.

41   Cockburn, *Muqtada al-Sadr and the Shia Insurgency in Iraq*, pp. 70, 190–1.

42   'Iraq Index: Tracking Variables of Reconstruction and Security in Post-Saddam Iraq', Brookings Institution, 1 October 2007, p. 16.

43   Mussab al-Khairalla, 'Iraqi Minister Plays Down Torture Bunker Allegations', *Washington Post*, 17 November 2005.

44   Steven N. Simon, 'After the Surge: the Case for US Military Disengagement from Iraq', CSR No. 23, Council on Foreign Relations, February 2007, p. 19.

45   Jakub Cerny, *Death Squad Operations in Iraq* (Swindon: Conflict Studies Research Centre, 2006), p. 2.

46   Ibid., p. 5.

47   Bill Roggio, '"Shiite Zarqawi" Returns to Baghdad from Iran', Long War Journal [online], 21 August 2010 (http://www.longwarjournal.

org/archives/2010/08/shiite_zarqawi_retur.php) (accessed 23 March 2015).

48 Based on Cerny, *Death Squad Operations in Iraq*; reported in Farah Stockman and Bryan Bender, 'Iraqi Militia's Wave of Death', *Boston Globe*, 2 April 2006.

6: The forgotten caliph

1 See Chapter 4.

2 'At 171445CMAR05 Bde G3 informed DANBAT that Al-Zarqawi was on his way to Basrah travelling south on rte 6 from Al Amarah. At 1745C Lynx discovered a suspect vehicle, which stopped at GR QV 366257 (12k', WikiLeaks [online], 18 March 2005, report key 2A5BB8F4-A335-4E2F-BF6C-28E46D842B83 (https://wikileaks.org/irq/report/2005/03/IRQ20050318n1566.html) (accessed 23 March 2015).

3 See Chapter 4.

4 'Iraq Stampede Deaths Near 1,000', BBC News [online], 31 August 2005 (http://news.bbc.co.uk/1/hi/world/middle_east/4199618.stm) (accessed 23 March 2015). An obscure Sunni group called Jaysh al-Taifa al-Mansoura ('Army of the Victorious Sect') claimed responsibility for the mortar attack.

5 '"800 Dead" in Baghdad Bridge Disaster', *The Guardian*, 31 August 2005.

6 Peter Chalk (ed.), *Encyclopedia of Terrorism* (Santa Barbara, CA: ABC-CLIO, 2013).

7 Ibid.

8 The death sentences were later overturned and reduced to life imprisonment.

9 Author interview, 2015.

10 Although Islamic State posted the film of Kasasbeh's killing on 3 February, it is believed he was murdered earlier.

11 The Long War Journal reported on 'conflicting' rumours concerning Zarqawi's possible death or injury: (Bill Roggio, 'Zarqawi Successors', Long War Journal [online], 28 May 2005 (http://www.longwar-journal.org/archives/2005/05/zarqawi_success.php) (accessed 23 March 2015).

12 Nelson Hernandez, 'Now Playing in Iraq: Zarqawi Outtakes', *Washington Post*, 5 May 2006.

13 'Iraqi Army Captures Zarqawi Aide in Baghdad – Report', Reuters, 29 May 2006.

14 'How They Got Zarqawi', *The Age*, 10 June 2006.

15 *The Hunt for Zarqawi: Target Zarqawi*, National Geographic Channel, 30 January 2007, comments attributed to General Stanley McChrystal.

16 Scott McLeod and Bill Powell, 'Zarqawi's Last Dinner Party', *Time*, 11 June 2006.

17 'How They Got Zarqawi'.

18 McLeod and Powell, 'Zarqawi's Last Dinner Party'.

19 Gil Kaufman, 'Autopsy Finds al-Zarqawi Died of Internal Injuries 52 Minutes after Bombing', MTV News [online], 12 June 2006 (http://www.mtv.com/news/1534088/autopsy-finds-al-zarqawi-died-of-internal-injuries-52-minutes-after-bombing) (accessed 23 March 2015).

20 Ibid.

21 'How Zarqawi Was Found and Killed', BBC News [online], 9 June 2006 (http://news.bbc.co.uk/1/hi/world/middle_east/5060468.stm) (accessed 23 March 2015).

22 Scott Stewart, 'Why US Bounties on Terrorists Often Fail', Stratfor Global Intelligence [online], 12 April 2012 (https://www.stratfor.com/weekly/why-us-bounties-terrorists-often-fail) (accessed 23 March 2015).

23 John F. Burns, 'US Strike Hits Insurgent at Safehouse', *New York Times*, 8 June 2006.

24 Quoted in D. Hazan, 'Al-Zarqawi: A Post Mortem Prior to His Killing, Al-Zarqawi Had Lost His Sunni Allies', Inquiry and Analysis Report No. 284, Middle East Media Research Institute, 30 June 2006.

25 Bill Roggio, 'Joining al-Qaeda, Declining al-Qaeda', Long War Journal [online], 31 January 2006 (http://www.longwarjournal.org/archives/2006/01/joining_alqaeda_decl.php) (accessed 24 March 2015).

26 Emily Hunt, 'Zarqawi's "Total War" on Iraqi Shiites Exposes a Divide among Sunni Jihadists', PolicyWatch 1049, Washington Institute [online], 15 November 2005 (http://www.washingtoninstitute.org/policy-analysis/view/zarqawis-total-war-on-iraqi-shiites-exposes-a-divide-among-sunni-jihadists) (accessed 20 March 2015).

27 Bill Roggio, 'The Iraqi Insurgent Divide Widens', Long War Journal [online], 26 January 2006 (http://www.longwarjournal.org/archives/2006/01/the_iraqi_insurgent.php) (accessed 24 March 2015).

28 Hazan, 'Al-Zarqawi'.

29 David Kilcullen, *The Accidental Guerrilla: Fighting Small Wars in the Midst of a Big One* (New York: Oxford University Press, 2011), p. 3; Qiao Liang and Wang Xiangsui, *Unrestricted Warfare* (Beijing: PLA Literature and Arts Publishing House, 1999).

30 Jason Burke, Peter Beaumont and Mohammed al-Ubeidy, 'How Jordanians Hunted Down Their Hated Son', *The Observer*, 11 June 2006.

31 Bill Roggio, 'The Abu Omar al-Bagdadi Saga', Long War Journal [online], 10 March 2007 (http://www.longwarjournal.org/archives/2007/03/the_abu_omar_albagda.php) (accessed 24 March 2015).

32 Bill Roggio, 'Unconfirmed Report: Abu Omar al Baghdadi Killed; al Qaeda's Information Minister Confirmed Killed', Long War Journal [online], 3 May 2007 (http://www.longwarjournal.org/archives/2007/05/unconfirmed_report_a_1.php) (accessed 24 March 2015).

33 Bill Roggio, 'Islamic State of Iraq Leader Reported Captured', Long War Journal [online], 23 April 2009 (http://www.longwarjournal.org/archives/2009/04/islamic_state_of_ira_1.php) (accessed 24 March 2015).

34 'Responding to the Doubts', *Dabiq* 7, 2015, p. 25.

35 CBS News, 7 May 2008.

36 Martin Chulov, 'My Husband the al-Qaida Kingpin', *The Guardian*, 16 July 2010.

37 Michael R. Gordon, 'Leader of Al-Qaeda Group in Iraq Was Fictional, US Military Says', *New York Times*, 18 July 2007.

38 Bill Roggio, 'Al Qaeda Continues Attacks on Awakening Security Forces', Long War Journal [online], 25 December 2007 (http://www.longwarjournal.org/archives/2007/12/al_qaeda_continues_a.php) (accessed 24 March 2015).

39 Chulov, 'My Husband the Al-Qaida Kingpin'.

40 'Iraq Sentences al-Qaeda Chief's Widow to Life', AFP, 29 June 2011.

41 Bernard Lewis, *The Political Language of Islam* (Chicago: University of Chicago Press, 1988), pp. 50–1.

42 Quoted in Nibras Kazimi, 'The Caliphate Attempted', *Current Trends in Islamist Ideology*, 7, 2008, pp. 17–18.

43 Quoted in Nibras Kazimi, 'Would-be Caliph's Inaugural Address to the Islamic 'Ummah', Talisman Gate blog, 23 December 2006 (http://talismangate.blogspot.co.uk/2006/12/would-be-caliphs-inaugural-address-to.html) (accessed 24 March 2015).

44   Ibid.

45   Fred Kaplan, *The Insurgents: David Petraeus and the Plot to Change the American Way of War* (New York: Simon & Schuster, 2013), p. 247.

46   Ibid., p. 247.

47   The *Washington Post* received the leaked Devlin report: Dafna Linzer and Thomas E. Ricks, 'Anbar Picture Grows Clearer, and Bleaker', *Washington Post*, 28 November 2006.

48   Nibras Kazimi, 'Al-Baghdadi Names Pseudonyms – for Ministerial Portfolios', Talisman Gate blog, 19 April 2007 (http://talismangate. blogspot.co.uk/2007/04/al-baghdadi-names-pseudonymsfor.html) (accessed 24 March 2015).

49   Chulov, 'My Husband the al-Qaida Kingpin'.

50   Martin Chulov, 'Al-Qaida Terrorist's Widow to Be Hanged', *The Guardian*, 9 May 2011.

51   Jim Garamone, 'Masri Now Leads Iraq Al Qaeda, Coalition Officials Say', US Department of Defense [online], 16 June 2006 (http://www.defense.gov/news/newsarticle.aspx?id=16029) (accessed 24 March 2015).

52   Ibid.

53   Aaron Y. Zelin, 'The War between ISIS and al-Qaeda for Supremacy of the Global Jihadist Movement', Research Notes 20, Washington Institute [online], June 2014 (http://www.washingtoninstitute.org/policy-analysis/view/the-war-between-isis-and-al-qaeda-for-supremacy-of-the-global-jihadist) (accessed 23 March 2015).

54   See Chapter 4.

55   Letter from Adam Gadahn, Combating Terrorism Center at West Point [online], January 2011, SOCOM-2012-0000004, pp. 7–9 (https://www.ctc.usma.edu/posts/letter-from-adam-gadahn-original-language-2) (accessed 24 March 2015).

56   Ibid.

57   Letter from Hafiz Sultan, Combating Terrorism Center at West Point [online], 28 March 2007, SOCOM-2012-0000011 (https://www.ctc.usma.edu/posts/letter-from-hafiz-sultan-original-language-2) (accessed 24 March 2015).

58   Giles Burnham, Riyadh Lafta, Shannon Doocy et al., 'Mortality after the 2003 Invasion of Iraq: A Cross-sectional Cluster Sample Survey', *The Lancet*, 11 October 2006.

59   Iraq Body Count.

60   Peter Beaumont, '135 Die in Bombing as "Civil War" Grips Iraq', *The Observer*, 4 February 2007.

61 Austin Long, 'The Anbar Awakening', *Survival: Global Politics and Strategy*, 50:2, 2008, p. 75.

62 Quoted in Kazimi, 'Would-be Caliph's Inaugural Address to the Islamic 'Ummah'.

63 Author interview, 2015.

7: Wake-up call

1 Gary W. Montgomery and Timothy S. McWilliams (eds), *Al-Anbar Awakening, Volume II: Iraqi Perspectives – From Insurgency to Counterinsurgency in Iraq 2004–2009* (Quantico, VA: Marine Corps University Press, 2009), pp. 20–1, testimony of Miriam relating to her cousin's husband.

2 Najim Abed Al Jabouri and Sterling Jensen, 'The Iraqi and AQI Roles in the Sunni Awakening', *Prism*, 2:1 (2011), p. 9.

3 Montgomery and McWilliams (eds), *Al-Anbar Awakening, Volume II*, p. 35.

4 See chapter 2.

5 Austin Long, 'The Anbar Awakening', *Survival*, 1 April 2008; author interview with Dr David Kilcullen, 20 February 2015.

6 Montgomery and McWilliams (eds), *Al-Anbar Awakening, Volume II*, p. 140, testimony of Sheikh Sabah al-Sattam Effan Fahran al-Shurji al-Aziz.

7 Ibid., p. 140, testimony of Sheikh Sabah al-Sattam Effan Fahran al-Shurji al-Aziz.

8 Author interview, 2015.

9 Loulla-Mae Eleftheriou-Smith, 'British "Vicar of Baghdad" Claims Isis Beheaded Four Children for Refusing to Convert to Islam', *The Independent*, 8 December 2014.

10 Robin Perrie, 'You've Just Eaten Your Son: IS "Served Kidnap Victim to His Mum"', *The Sun*, 2 March 2015.

11 Peter BetBasoo, 'Incipient Genocide: The Ethnic Cleansing of the Assyrians of Iraq', Assyrian International News Agency, 12 June 2007, revised 3 September 2014.

12 Ibid., p. 5. The story is also told in Dr Patrick Sookhdeo, 'Iraq: Is Any Suffering like Our Suffering?', Barnabas Aid, January–February 2007.

13 Author interview, 2015.

14 Combatting Terrorism Center Archives, West Point Military Academy, AQI document (http:/ctc.usma.edu/aq/pdf/IZ-060316-01-Trans.pdf).

15   Fred Kaplan, *The Insurgents: David Petraeus and the Plot to Change the American Way of War* (New York: Simon & Schuster, 2013), p. 247.

16   Author interview, 2015.

17   See chapter 6 and also Peter R. Mansoor, *Surge: My Journey with General David Petraeus and the Remaking of the Iraq War* (New Haven, CT: Yale University Press, 2013), pp. 121–2.

18   George W. Bush, *Decision Points* (London: Virgin, 2011), p. 367.

19   James A. Baker III and Lee H. Hamilton (co-chairs), *The Iraq Study Group Report: The Way Forward – A New Approach* (New York: Vintage, 2006) (aka Baker–Hamilton report), p. 30.

20   Ibid., p. 15.

21   Ibid., p. 30.

22   Mark Tran, 'Iraq Study Group Urges Troop Withdrawal', *The Guardian*, 6 December 2006.

23   Speech by George W. Bush on the Surge, 10 January 2007.

24   Author interview, 2015.

25   Adam Strickland, 'Meet FFFA Partner Jassim Suwaydawi, the Lion of Sofia, Part 1', Fund for Fallen Allies [online], 7 August 2013 (http://fundforfallenallies.org/news/2013/08/07/meet-jassim-suwayda-wi-lion-sophia-part-i) (accessed 25 March 2015).

26   Mansoor, *Surge*, pp. 132–3.

27   Ibid., pp. 44–6.

28   Author interview, 2015.

29   Ibid., pp. 137–8.

30   Kaplan, *The Insurgents*, p. 262.

31   Author interview, 2015.

32   Linda Robinson, *Tell Me How This Ends: General Petraeus and the Search for a Way out of Iraq* (New York: PublicAffairs, 2008), pp. 320–1.

33   Ibid., p. 254.

34   Bill Roggio, 'Al-Qaeda's Chlorine Attacks: The Dirty War in Anbar', Long War Journal [online], 17 March 2007 (http://www.longwar-journal.org/archives/2007/03/al_qaedas_chlorine_a.php) (accessed 25 March 2015).

35   '"Chlorine Bomb" Hits Iraqi Village', BBC News [online], 16 May 2007 (http://news.bbc.co.uk/1/hi/world/middle_east/6660585.stm) (accessed 25 March 2015).

36   Letter from Hafiz Sultan, Combating Terrorism Center at West Point [online], 28 March 2007, SOCOM-2012-0000011 (https://www.ctc.usma.edu/posts/letter-from-hafiz-sultan-original-language-2) (accessed 24 March 2015).

37 Abdelhak Mamoun, 'Urgent: ISIS Kills 300 Iraqi Soldiers by Chlorine Gas Attack in Saqlawiyah', Iraqi News [online], 22 September 2014 (http://www.iraqinews.com/iraq-war/urgent-isis-kills-300-iraqi-soldiers-chlorine-gas-attack-saqlawiyah) (accessed 25 March 2015).

38 Brian Fishman (ed.), 'Bombers, Bank Accounts and Bleedout: Al-Qaida's Road in and out of Iraq', Combating Terrorism Center at West Point, July 2008, pp. 32–41.

39 Ibid., p. 42.

40 Ibid., pp. 55–6.

41 Ahmed S. Hashim, *Iraq's Sunni Insurgency* (Abingdon: Routledge, 2009), pp. 44–5.

42 Kevin Drum, 'The Myth of AQI', *Washington Monthly* [online], 6 September 2007 (http://www.washingtonmonthly.com/archives/individual/2007_09/012011.php) (accessed 25 March 2015).

43 Mansoor, *Surge*, pp. 137–8.

44 Jonathan Steel, 'Baghdad's Day of Sectarian Death: Five Car Bombs, 160 Killed', *The Guardian*, 24 November 2006.

45 Toby Dodge, *Iraq: From War to a New Authoritarianism* (Abingdon: Routledge, 2012), p. 39.

46 See Chapter 6.

47 Mansoor, *Surge*, p. 67.

48 Author interview, 2015.

49 Rod Nordland, 'Some Progress Seen in Baghdad', *Newsweek*, 17 November 2007.

50 Author interview, 2015.

51 Nordland, 'Some Progress Seen in Baghdad'.

52 Patrick Cockburn, 'Iraq: Violence Is Down – but Not Because of America's "Surge"', *Independent on Sunday*, 14 September 2008.

53 'Operation Phantom Thunder', Institute for the Study of War [online] (http://www.understandingwar.org/operation/operation-phantom-thunder) (accessed 25 March 2015).

54 'Operation Arrowhead Ripper', Institute for the Study of War [online] (http://www.understandingwar.org/operation/operation-arrowhead-ripper) (accessed 25 March 2015).

55 Letter from Hafiz Sultan, 'Dear Brother Adnan', Combating Terrorism Center at West Point [online], 28 March 2007, SOCOM-2012-0000011 (https://www.ctc.usma.edu/posts/letter-from-hafiz-sultan-original-language-2) (accessed 24 March 2015).

56 Bill Roggio, 'Samara Mosque Bombing Suspects Identified; Reports of Violence', Long War Journal [online], 13 June 2007 (http://www.

longwarjournal.org/archives/2007/06/samarra_mosque_bombi.
php) (accessed 25 March 2015).

57   Mansoor, *Surge*, p. 160.

58   Author interview, 2015.

59   Bill Roggio, 'Letters from al Qaeda Leaders Show Iraqi Effort Is in
Disarray', Long War Journal [online], 11 September 2008 (http://
www.longwarjournal.org/archives/2008/09/letters_from_al_qaed.
php) (accessed 25 March 2015).

60   'Operation Phantom Thunder', Institute for the Study of War [online].

61   'Death Toll from Suicide Bombings in NW IRAQ RISES to 500',
Xinhua news agency, 15 July 2007.

62   Bill Roggio, 'USAF Kills al Qaeda Emir behind Yazidi Villages
Attacks', Long War Journal [online], 9 September 2007 (http://www.
longwarjournal.org/archives/2007/09/usaf_kills_al_qaeda.php)
(accessed 25 March 2015).

63   'Tribal Chiefs Killed in Baghdad Hotel Blast', Al Arabiya News [online],
25 June 2007 (http://www.alarabiya.net/articles/2007/06/25/35867.
html) (accessed 30 April 2015).

64   Anthony H. Cordesman, *Iraq's Insurgency and the Road to Civil Conflict,
Volume 2* (Westport, CT: Praeger Security International, 2008), p. 517.

65   Joshua Partlow, Ann Scott Tyson, and Robin Wright, `Bomb Kills a
Key Sunni Ally of US', *Washington Post*, 14 September 2007.

66   Montgomery and McWilliams (eds), *Al-Anbar Awakening, Volume II*, p.
48.

67   'Operation Phantom Phoenix', Institute for the Study of War [online]
(http://www.understandingwar.org/operation/operation-phan-
tom-phoenix) (accessed 25 March 2015).

68   Iraq Body Count, based on database 2007–10.

69   Bill Roggio, 'Al-Qaeda in Iraq Uses Disabled Women in Baghdad
Bombings', Long War Journal [online], 1 February 2008 (http://
www.longwarjournal.org/archives/2008/02/al_qaeda_in_iraq_use.
php) (accessed 25 March 2015).

70   'Twin Bombings Kill Scores in Baghdad', CBS News [online], 1
February 2008 (http://www.cbsnews.com/news/twin-bombings-
kill-scores-in-baghdad) (accessed 25 March 2015).

71   Roggio, 'Al-Qaeda in Iraq Uses Disabled Women in Baghdad
Bombings'.

72   Roggio, 'Letters from al Qaeda Leaders Show Iraqi Effort Is in
Disarray'.

73   Ibid.

74 Zawahiri refers to the letter of 25 January 2008 in a later missive he wrote and signed on 6 March 2008: see Bill Roggio, Daveed Gartenstein-Ross and Tony Badran, 'Intercepted Letters from al-Qaeda Leaders Shed Light on State of Network in Iraq', Foundation for Defense of Democracies [online], 12 September 2008 (http://www. defenddemocracy.org/media-hit/intercepted-letters-from-al-qaeda-leaders-shed-light-on-state-of-network-in) (accessed 25 March 2015).

75 Ibid.

76 Otaibi was eventually killed during a battle in Paktia province, Afghanistan, in May 2008, according to Bill Roggio, 'Pakistani Taliban, Iraqi al Qaeda Operatives Killed in Afghanistan', Long War Journal [online], 11 May 2008 (http://www.longwarjournal.org/archives/2008/05/pakistani_taliban_ir.php) (accessed 30 April 2015).

77 Roggio, 'Letters from al Qaeda Leaders Show Iraqi Effort Is in Disarray'.

78 Author interview, 2015.

79 Author interview, 2015.

8: Savagery under new management

1 Nicholas A. Heras, 'Former al-Qaeda in Iraq (AQ) "Governor" Executed by Iraqi Government', *Militant Leadership Monitor*, 4:4, 2013.

2 Scott Stewart, 'Jihadists in Iraq: Down for the Count?', Stratfor Global Intelligence [online], 29 April 2010 (https://www.stratfor.com/weekly/20100428_jihadists_iraq_down_count) (accessed 25 March 2015).

3 Martin Chulov, Isis: The Inside Story, *The Guardian*, 11 December 2014.

4 Martin Chulov, 'My Husband the al-Qaida Kingpin', *The Guardian*, 16 July 2010; Chulov, 'Isis'.

5 'Iraq Sentences al-Qaeda Chief's Widow to Life', AFP, 29 June 2011.

6 Martin Chulov, 'Al-Qaida Terrorist's Widow to Be Hanged', *The Guardian*, 9 May 2011.

7 Stewart, 'Jihadists in Iraq'.

8 'Iraq: A Bleak Future for the Islamic State of Iraq?', WikiLeaks, email ID 1324208, 18 October 2012 (https://wikileaks.org/gifiles/

docs/13/1324208_iraq-a-bleak-future-for-the-islamic-state-of-iraq-.html) (accessed 25 March 2015).

9 Mike Mount, 'Reward for Wanted Terrorist Drops', CNN [online], 13 May 2008 (http://edition.cnn.com/2008/WORLD/meast/05/13/pentagon.masri.value) (accessed 25 March 2015).

10 Ibid., remark attributed to Jamie Graybeal, spokesman for US Central Command.

11 Author interview, 2015.

12 'Re: [CT] New AQI Leadership: al-Qurashi and al-Qurashi', WikiLeaks, email ID 381027, 17 May 2010 (https://wikileaks.org/gifiles/docs/38/381027_re-ct-new-aqi-leadership-al-qurashi-and-al-qurashi-.html) (accessed 25 March 2015).

13 Letter from Osama bin Laden to 'Sheikh Mahmud', Combatting Terrorism Centre at West Point [online], SOCOM 2012-0000019-HT, 4 July 2010 (https://www.ctc.usma.edu/posts/letter-from-ubl-to-atiyatullah-al-libi-4-original-language-2) (accessed 25 March 2015).

14 BBC News, Al-Qaeda 'military leader' Abu Suleiman killed in Iraq', 25.2.11.

15 'Fw: [CT] [OS] IRAQ – Al Qaeda Members in Iraq, Shaving Their Beards, Wearing Jeans and Pledging Allegiance to Their Caliph by Mobilemessaging', WikiLeaks, 28 May 2010, email ID 386943 (https://wikileaks.org/gifiles/docs/38/386943_fw-ct-os-iraq-al-qaeda-members-in-iraq-shaving-their-beards.html) (accessed 25 March 2015).

16 Kieran Corcoran, 'ISIS Terror Chief "Believed Dead": Iraqi Military Confirm Warlord WAS Injured in US-led Airstrike as Speculation Grows Feared Jihadist Perished in Attack', Mail Online, 10 November 2014 (http://www.dailymail.co.uk/news/article-2827728/ISIS-terror-chief-believed-dead-Iraqi-military-confirm-warlord-injured-led-airstrike-speculation-grows-feared-jihadist-perished-attack.html) (accessed 30 April 2015).

17 Martin Chulov and Kareem Shaheen, 'Isis Leader Abu Bakr al-Baghdadi "Seriously Wounded in Airstrike"', The Guardian, 21 April 2015.

18 Confidential source, 2015

19 Author interview, 2014.

20 Peter Beaumont, 'Abu Bakr al-Baghdadi: The Isis Chief with the Ambition to Overtake al-Qaida', The Guardian, 12 June 2014.

21 Bill Roggio, 'ISIS Confirms Death of Senior Leader in Syria', Long War Journal [online], 5 February 2014 (http://www.longwarjournal.

org/archives/2014/02/isis_confirms_death.php) (accessed 25 March 2015).

22 See chapter 5.

23 See further Aaron Y. Zelin, 'Abu Bakr al-Baghdadi: Islamic State's Driving Force', BBC News [online], 31 July 2014 (http://www.bbc.co.uk/news/world-middle-east-28560449) (accessed 25 March 2015).

24 Ibid.

25 *The Biography of Khalifa Abu Bakr al-Baghdadi, Amir Ul Mu'minin (Commander of the Believers)*, written, it is thought, by a Bahraini ideologue named Turki al-Binali under the pen name Abu Humam Bakr bin Abd al-Aziz al-Athari and originally published in July 2013.

26 Zelin, 'Abu Bakr al-Baghdadi'.

27 Author interview, 2014.

28 *The Biography of Khalifa Abu Bakr al-Baghdadi.*

29 'Kopf des Kalifats', *Süddeutsche Zeitung* [online], 18 February 2015 (http://www.sueddeutsche.de/politik/is-anfuehrer-al-baghdadi-kopf-des-kalifats-1.2356920) (accessed 25 March 2015).

30 Ibid.

31 Al Monitor, The many names of Abu Bakr al-Baghdadi, by Ali Hashem, 23.3.15.

32 *The Biography of Khalifa Abu Bakr al-Baghdadi.*

33 Ibid.

34 Author interview, 2014.

35 Ruth Sherlock, 'How a Talented Footballer Became World's Most Wanted Man, Abu Bakr al-Baghdadi', *The Telegraph* [online], 11 November 2014 (http://www.telegraph.co.uk/news/worldnews/middleeast/iraq/10948846/How-a-talented-footballer-became-worlds-most-wanted-man-Abu-Bakr-al-Baghdadi.html) (accessed 25 March 2015).

36 Ibid.

37 Author interview, 2014.

38 'Youssef Qaradawi Says ISIS Leader Abu Bakr al-Baghdadi Was Once Muslim Brotherhood; First English Translation of Statement', Global Muslim Brotherhood Daily Watch [online], 21 October 2014 (http://www.globalmbwatch.com/2014/10/21/featured-youssef-qaradawi-isis-leader-abu-bakr-al-baghdadi-part-muslim-brotherhood-english-translation-statement) (accessed 25 March 2015). The article includes a link to the Qaradawi interview.

39 Musa Kahn Jalalzai, 'Abu Bakr al-Baghdadi in Afghanistan', *Daily Times* (Pakistan), 20 January 2015.

40 'Lashkar-e-Jhangvi: Incidents and Statements involving Lashkar-e-Jhangvi', South Asia Terrorism Portal [online] (http://www.satp.org/satporgtp/countries/pakistan/terroristoutfits/lej.htm) (accessed 25 March 2015).

41 See chapter 2. The group was then known as Sipah-e-Sahaba before a split.

42 Syed Ali Abbas Zaidi, 'ISIS Links with Pakistan: Past and Present', Laaltain [online], 9 July 2014 (http://www.laaltain.com/isis-links-pakistan-past-present) (accessed 25 March 2015).

43 Sherlock, 'How a Talented Footballer Became World's Most Wanted Man'.

44 Zeerak Fahim, 'ISIS Chief Lived in Kabul During Taliban Rule', Pajhwok Afghan News [online], 11 July 2014 (http://www.pajhwok.com/en/2014/07/11/isis-chief-lived-kabul-during-taliban-rule) (accessed 25 March 2015).

45 Ibid.

46 *The Biography of Khalifa Abu Bakr al-Baghdadi.*

47 Bill Roggio, 'Joining al-Qaeda, Declining al-Qaeda', Long War Journal [online], 31 January 2006 (http://www.longwarjournal.org/archives/2006/01/joining_alqaeda_decl.php) (accessed 24 March 2015).

48 Detainee personnel record for Abu Bakr al-Baghdadi.

49 Author interview, 2014.

50 Author interview, 2015.

51 Email from James Skylar Gerrond, former US police captain at Camp Bucca, to author on 22 January 2015. Author interviewed Gerrond in 2014.

52 Richard Barrett, 'The Islamic State', Soufan Group, November 2014. This report lists many of the ex-Bucca inmates in senior IS positions.

53 Author interview, 2014.

54 Peter R. Mansoor, *Surge: My Journey with General David Petraeus and the Remaking of the Iraq War* (New Haven, CT: Yale University Press, 2013), pp. 151–3.

55 Ibid.

56 Author interview, 2015.

57 Author interview, 2014.

58 Lamiat Sabin, 'Abu Bakr al-Baghdadi Profile: The Mysterious Leader

of Isis – and Why He Is Called the 'Invisible Sheikh', *Independent on Sunday*, 9 November 2014.

59 See chapter 7.

60 Quoted in 'A Jaysh al-Mujahideen Amir's Testimony on Abu Bakr', Aymenn Jawad al-Tamimi's blog, 12 December 2014 (http://www. aymennjawad.org/2014/12/a-jaysh-al-mujahideen-amir-testimony-on-abu-bakr) (accessed 26 March 2015).

61 'Kopf des Kalifats', *Süddeutsche Zeitung* [online], 18 February 2015 (http://www.sueddeutsche.de/politik/is-anfuehrer-al-baghda-di-kopf-des-kalifats-1.2356920) (accessed 25 March 2015).

62 Quoted in Roggio, 'Joining al-Qaeda, Declining al-Qaeda'.

63 *The Biography of Khalifa Abu Bakr al-Baghdadi*.

644 Martin Chulov, 'Isis: The Inside Story', *The Guardian*, 11 December 2014.

65 Jethro Mullen, Greg Botelho and Nic Robertson, 'Source: Wife of ISIS Leader al-Baghdadi Arrested in Lebanon', CNN [online], 3 December 2014 (http://edition.cnn.com/2014/12/02/world/meast/leba-non-isis-leader-family/index.html) (accessed 26 March 2015).

66 Al Monitor, the many names of Abu Bakr al-Baghdadi, by Ali Hashem, 23 March 2015.

67 *The Biography of Khalifa Abu Bakr al-Baghdadi*.

68 Author interview, 2014.

69 Christoph Reuter, 'The Terror Strategist: Secret Files Reveal the Structure of Islamic State', Spiegel Online International, 18 April 2015 (http://www.spiegel.de/international/world/islamic-state-files-show-structure-of-islamist-terror-group-a-1029274.html) (accessed 29 April 2015).

70 Translation of Wikibaghdady, collected by Yousef bin Tashfin, 14–15 December 2013.

71 Reuter, 'The Terror Strategist'.

72 Ibid.

73 Ibid.

74 Bill Roggio, 'Al-Qaeda in Iraq's Security Minister Captured in Anbar', Long War Journal [online], by 1 December 2010 (http://www.long-warjournal.org/archives/2010/12/al_qaeda_in_iraqs_se_1.php) (accessed 26 March 2015).

75 Sam Jones, 'Opaque Structure Adds to Challenge of Defeating Isis', *Financial Times*, 24 August 2014.

76 Iraq Body Count, the average of the three annual deaths totals for 2010 to 2012.

77 Translation of Wikibaghdady, 15 December 2013.

78 'Terrorist Designation of Ibrahim Awwad Ibrahim Ali al-Badri', media note, US Department of State [online], 4 October 2011 (http://m.state.gov/md174971.htm) (accessed 26 March 2015).

79 Author interview, 2015.

80 Martin Chulov, 'Baghdad Church Siege Survivors Speak of Taunts, Killings and Explosions', *The Guardian*, 1 November 2010.

81 Anthony Shadid, 'Church Attack Seen as Strike at Iraq's Core', *New York Times*, 1 November 2010.

82 Author interview, 2014.

83 Raffi Khatchadourian, 'Azzam the American: The Making of an al-Qaeda Homegrown', *New Yorker*, 22 January 2007.

84 Letter from Adam Gadahn, Combating Terrorism Center at West Point [online], January 2011, SOCOM-2012-0000004 (https://www.ctc.usma.edu/posts/letter-from-adam-gadahn-original-language-2) (accessed 24 March 2015).

85 'Iraq's Qaeda Pledges Support to Zawahiri, Vows Attacks', Reuters, 9 May 2011.

86 Quoted in Bill Roggio, 'Al-Qaeda Suicide Bomber Kills 28 Iraqis in Attack in Baghdad Mosque', Long War Journal [online], 28 August 2011 (http://www.longwarjournal.org/archives/2011/08/al_qaeda_suicide_bom_4.php) (accessed 26 March 2015).

87 Ibid.

88 'String of Baghdad Attacks Kills at Least 69', CBS News [online], 22 December 2011 (http://www.cbsnews.com/news/string-of-baghdad-attacks-kills-at-least-69) (accessed 26 March 2015).

89 Rania Abouzeid, 'The Jihad Next Door: The Syrian Roots of Iraq's Newest Civil War', Politico [online], 23 June 2014 (http://www.politico.com/magazine/story/2014/06/al-qaeda-iraq-syria-108214.html#.VRPd-_ysX9V) (accessed 26 March 2015).

9: Shia folly

1 See Chapter 1.

2 Author interview with Brigadier General Saad Maan, recorded in Baghdad on 23 October 2014.

3 Author interview, 2015.

4 'Fake Bomb Detector Seller James McCormick Jailed', BBC News

[online], 2 May 2013 (http://www.bbc.co.uk/news/uk-22380368) (accessed 26 March 2015).

5   Caroline Hawley and Meirion Jones, 'Export Ban for Useless "Bomb "Detector"', BBC Newsnight [online], 22 January 2010 (http://news.bbc.co.uk/1/hi/programmes/newsnight/8471187.stm) (accessed 26 March 2015).

6   Author interview, 2015; 'James McCormick Guilty of Selling Fake Bomb Detectors', BBC News [online], 23 April 2013 (http://www.bbc.co.uk/news/uk-22266051) (accessed 30 April 2015).

7   *The Guardian*, Fake bomb detector conman jailed for 10 years, by Robert Booth, 2 May 2013.

8   Suadad al Salhy, 'Iraq Police Official Charged in Bomb Device Scandal', Reuters, 17 February 2011.

9   'Iraq Orders "Corruption" Arrests', BBC News [online], 11 October 2005 (http://news.bbc.co.uk/1/hi/world/middle_east/4329686.stm) (accessed 26 March 2015).

10 Dispatch filed by Caroline Hawley for BBC News on 11 October 2005.

11 Ibid.

12 'Corruption by Country/Territory: Iraq', Transparency International [online] (http://www.transparency.org/country#IRQ) (accessed 26 March 2015).

13 Anthony H. Cordesman, Sam Khazai and Daniel Dewit, 'Shaping Iraq's Security Forces', Center for Strategic and International Studies, 16 December 2013, p. 29.

14 Anthony H. Cordesman and Sam Khazai, *Iraq in Crisis* (Lanham, MD: Rowman & Littlefield, 2014), p. 134.

15 Ibid., p. 135.

16 Alexandra Zavis, 'Iraqi Troops Not Ready to Go It Alone', *Los Angeles Times*, 1 September 2008.

17 Sam Dagher, 'Iraqi Report on Corruption Cites Prosecutors' Barriers', *New York Times*, 5 May 2009.

18 Fred Lambert, 'Iraqi PM: Bagdad Govt. Paying Salaries of 50,000 Non-existent Iraqi Soldiers', UPI [online], 30 November 2014 (http://www.upi.com/Top_News/World-News/2014/11/30/Iraqi-PM-Baghdad-govt-paying-salaries-of-50000-non-existent-Iraqi-soldiers/1821417385384/?spt=sec&or=tn) (accessed 26 March 2015).

19 Author interview, 2015.

20 Author interview, 2015.

21 See chapter 5.

22 Author interview, 2015.

23 Quoted in Dexter Filkins, 'What We Left Behind', *New Yorker*, 28 April 2014.

24 Author interview, 2015.

25 'Severe Abuse at Ministry of Interior Site 4 Detention Facility', WikiLeaks [online], 10 June 2006, canonical ID 06BAGHDAD1960_a (https://wikileaks.org/plusd/cables/06BAGHDAD1960_a.html) (accessed 26 March 2015)

26 Seymour M. Hersh, 'Torture at Abu Ghraib', *New Yorker*, 10 May 2004. This is a particularly thorough piece on the affair, based on a leaked official report into what happened.

27 Duncan Gardham and Paul Cruickshank, 'Abu Ghraib Photos "Show Rape"', *The Telegraph* [online], 27 May 2009 (http://www.telegraph. co.uk/news/worldnews/northamerica/usa/5395830/Abu-Ghraib-abuse-photos-show-rape.html) (accessed 30 April 2015). Quote attributed to Major General (Retd.) Antonio Taguba, the former army officer who conducted an inquiry into the Abu Ghraib jail in Iraq in 2004.

28 See also 'Demarche to Iraqi Interior Minister on Site 4', WikiLeaks [online], 7 August 2006, canonical ID 06BAGHDAD2842_a (https:// wikileaks.org/plusd/cables/06BAGHDAD2842_a.html) (accessed 26 March 2015).

29 'Maliki Reshapes the National Security System', WikiLeaks [online], 15 May 2007, canonical ID 07BAGHDAD1593_a (https://wikileaks. org/plusd/cables/07BAGHDAD1593_a.html) (accessed 26 March 2015).

30 Ibid.

31 'Majority Government Needed, PM Maliki Tells Codel McCain', WikiLeaks [online], 11 July 2007, canonical ID 07BAGHDAD2298_a (https://wikileaks.org/plusd/cables/07BAGHDAD2298_a.html) (accessed 26 March 2015).

32 Andrew Slater, 'The Monster of Mosul: How a Sadistic General Helped ISIS Win', Daily Beast [online], 19 June 2014 (http://www. thedailybeast.com/articles/2014/06/19/iraq-put-a-death-squad-commander-and-torturer-in-charge-of-mosul-no-wonder-isis-is-winning.html) (accessed 26 March 2015).

33 'Part 2 of 2: Sectarian Violence Forces Major Shift in Baghdad', WikiLeaks [online], 12 July 2007, canonical ID 07BAGHDAD2318_a (https://wikileaks.org/plusd/cables/07BAGHDAD2318_a.html) (accessed 26 March 2015).

34 Arwa Damon, 'Shadowy Iraq Office Accused of Sectarian Agenda', CNN [online], 1 May 2007 (http://edition.cnn.com/2007/WORLD /meast/05/01/iraq.office/index.html) (accessed 26 March 2015).

35 Linda Robinson, *Tell Me How This Ends: General Petraeus and the Search for a Way out of Iraq* (New York: PublicAffairs, 2008), pp. 156–7.

36 Ibid, pp. 156–7.

37 'Maliki Reshapes the National Security System', WikiLeaks [online], 15 May 2007, canonical ID 07BAGHDAD1593_a (https://wikileaks. org/plusd/cables/07BAGHDAD1593_a.html) (accessed 26 March 2015).

38 Author interview, 2015.

39 Ibid.

40 Ali Khedery, 'Why We Stuck with Maliki and Lost Iraq', *Washington Post*, 3 July 2014.

41 Robinson, *Tell Me How This Ends*, p. 260.

42 Peter R. Mansoor, *Surge: My Journey with General David Petraeus and the Remaking of the Iraq War* (New Haven, CT: Yale University Press, 2013), p. 215.

43 'Loose Ends: Iraq's Security Forces between US Drawdown and Withdrawal', Middle East Report No. 99, International Crisis Group, 26 October 2010, p. 28.

44 Ibid., p. 28

45 Martin Chulov, 'Iraq Disbands Sunni Militia That Helped Defeat Insurgents', *The Guardian*, 2 April 2009.

46 Rod Nordland, 'Arrests of Sunni Leaders Rise in Baghdad', *New York Times*, 29 July 2009.

47 Author interview, 2015.

48 Author interview, 2015.

49 'Iraq's Secular Opposition: The Rise and Decline of al-Iraqiya', Middle East Report No. 127, International Crisis Group, 31 July 2012.

50 Author interview, 2015

51 'Iraq's Secular Opposition: The Rise and Decline of al-Iraqiya', p. 22.

52 Quoted ibid.

53 Cordesman and Khazai, *Iraq in Crisis*, p. 96.

54 Author interview, 2015.

55 Lara Jakes and Rebecca Santana, 'Iraq Withdrawal: US Abandoning Plans to Keep Troops In Country', AP, 15 October 2011.

56 Martin Chulov, 'Saddam Hussein Deputy Tariq Aziz Calls for US Forces to Stay in Iraq', *The Guardian*, 5 August 2010.

57 'Iraqi General Says Planned US Troop Pull-out 'Too Soon', BBC

News [online], 12 August 2010 (http://www.bbc.co.uk/news/world-middle-east-10947918) (accessed 26 March 2015).

58 Author interview, 2015.

59 Kareem Raheem, 'Iraq Blasts Kill 100 as Fugitive VP Gets Death Sentence', Reuters [online], 9 December 2012 (http://uk.reuters.com/article/2012/09/09/us-iraq-hashemi-idUKBRE88806O20120909) (accessed 26 March 2015).

60 Ibid.

61 Author interview, 2015.

62 Sinan Salaheddin and Adam Schreck, 'Iraq Confirms Arrest of Minister's Bodyguards', *The Washington Post*, 21 December 2012.

63 Patrick Markey and Raheem Salmani, 'Protests Erupt after Iraqi Minister's Staff Detained', *Daily Star* (Lebanon), 22 December 2012.

10: Scourge of Syria

1 Author interview.

2 In Arabic, ISIS is often referred to as Da'esh, which is an acronym for the full name of the group between April 2013 and June 2014, ad-Dawlat al-Islamiyah fi al-Iraq wash-Sham.

3 Author interview, 2015.

4 Al-Manarah al-Bayda Foundation for Media production, audio message from Abu Muhammad al-Jawlani, rejection of merger of Nusra with ISI to form ISIS, 10 April 2013; in it Jawlani suggests it was he who suggested to Baghdadi the idea of heading a team to Syria in 2011.

5 Bill Roggio,'Al Nusrah Front Claims Credit for Suicide Bombing in Damascus', Long War Journal [online], 30 April 2012 (http://www.longwarjournal.org/archives/2012/04/al_nusrah_front_clai_1.php) (accessed 30 March 2015).

6 'Jabhat al-Nusra', Mapping Militant Organizations [online] (http://web.stanford.edu/group/mappingmilitants/cgi-bin/groups/view/493) (accessed 30 March 2015).

7 Jennifer Cafarella, 'Jabhat al-Nusra in Syria: An Islamic Emirate for al-Qaeda', Middle East Security Report 25, Institute for the Study of War, December 2014.

8 Author interview, 2015.

9 'The Collapse of Syria's "Moderate" Rebels', Soufan Group [online], 3 March 2015 (http://soufangroup.com/tsg-intelbrief-the-collapse

-of-syrias-moderate-rebels) (accessed 30 March 2015) estimates 1,600 rebel groups.

10 Bill Roggio, 'Al Nusra Front Claims Complex Suicide Assault on Syrian Army HQ', Long War Journal [online], 28 September 2012 (http://www.longwarjournal.org/archives/2012/09/al_nusrah_front_clai_5.php) (accessed 30 March 2015). This article reveals that by late September 2012, Nusra had 'claimed responsibility' for twenty-four of the thirty-one suicide attacks in the Syrian civil war.

11 Bill Roggio, 'Al Nusrah Front Seizes Control of Syrian City of Raqqah', Long War Journal [online], 8 March 2013 (http://www.longwarjournal.org/archives/2013/03/al_nusrah_front_seiz_1.php) (accessed 30 March 2015).

12 See Chapter 8 and Bill Roggio, 'ISIS Confirms Death of Senior Leader in Syria', Long War Journal [online], 5 February 2014 (http://www.longwarjournal.org/archives/2014/02/isis_confirms_death.php) (accessed 25 March 2015).

13 Christoph Reuter, 'The Terror Strategist: Secret Files Reveal the Structure of Islamic State', Spiegel Online International, 18 April 2015 (http://www.spiegel.de/international/world/islamic-state-files-show-structure-of-islamist-terror-group-a-1029274.html) (accessed 29 April 2015).

14 Wikibaghdady, 15 December 2013.

15 Wikibaghdady, 15 December 2013.

16 Al Manarah al Bayda Foundation for Media production, audio message from Abu Muhammad al Jawlani, rejection of merger of Nusra with ISI to form ISIS, 10 April 2013.

17 Letter of Ayman al-Zawahiri, to the leaders of Islamic State of Iraq and Jabhat al-Nusra in al-Sham; see Basma Atassi, 'Qaeda Chief Annuls Syrian–Iraqi Jihad Merger', Aljazeera [online], 9 June 2013 (http://www.aljazeera.com/news/middleeast/2013/06/2013699425657882.html) (accessed 30 March 2015).

18 Ibid.

19 'Iraqi al-Qaeda Chief Rejects Zawahiri Orders', Aljazeera [online], 15 June 2013 (http://www.aljazeera.com/news/middleeast/2013/06/2013615172217827810.html) (accessed 30 March 2015).

20 Wikibaghdady, 20 December 2013.

21 Wikibaghdady, 8 January 2014.

22 Wikibaghdady, 12 January 2014.

23 Author interview, 2015.

NOTES

24 Interview with Hassan Aboud, head of the political bureau of the Islamic Front, Aljazeera, 4 December 2014.

25 'Senior FSA Opposition Commander Killed by Rival ISIL', Alalam [online], 15 March 2014 (http://en.alalam.ir/news/1576069) (accessed 30 March 2015).

26 Michael Peel, 'Syrian Rebel Infighting Grows as al-Qaeda Kills Rival Commander', *Financial Times*, 12 July 2013.

27 Valerie Szybala, 'Syrian Rebels Attack ISIS', Institute for the Study of War Syria Updates [online], 5 January 2014 (http://iswsyria.blogspot.co.uk/2014/01/syrian-rebels-attack-isis.html) (accessed 30 March 2015).

28 Richard Spencer, 'Al-Qaeda-linked Rebels Apologise after Cutting Off Head of Wrong Person', *The Telegraph* [online], 14 November 2013 (http://docs.newsbank.com/openurl?ctx_ver=z39.88-2004&rft_id=info:sid/iw.newsbank.com:UKNB:DTSTL&rft_val_format=info:ofi/fmt:kev:mtx:ctx&rft_dat=14A1869319AB9820&svc_dat=InfoWeb:aggregated5&req_dat=126A5C6AD2F04B4F-98782CE44224BC4F) (accessed 30 March 2015).

29 Aron Lund, 'Syria's Ahrar al-Sham Leadership Wiped Out in Bombing', Carnegie Endowment for International Peace [online], 9 September 2014 (http://carnegieendowment.org/syriaincrisis/?fa=56581) (accessed 30 March 2015).

30 Reuter, 'The Terror Strategist'.

31 'ISIS, Opposition Factions in Raqqa Discuss Captive Exchange', Syrian Observer [online], 11 May 2014 (http://syrianobserver.com/EN/News/26866/ISI S+Opposition+Factions+in+Raqqa+Discuss+Captive+Exchange) (accessed 30 April 2015), from a story by al-Quds al-Arabi.

32 Romain Caillet, 'The Islamic State: Leaving al-Qaeda Behind', Carnegie Endowment for International Peace [online], 27 December 2013 (http://carnegieendowment.org/syriaincrisis/?fa=54017) (accessed 30 March 2015).

33 'How Did Raqqa Fall to the Islamic State of Iraq and Syria?', SyriaUntold [online], 8 January 2014 (http://www.syriauntold.com/en/2014/01/how-did-raqqa-fall-to-the-islamic-state-of-iraq-and-syria) (accessed 30 March 2015).

34 Author interview.

35 Patrick Cockburn, 'Dozens Die as Anger Spreads over Iraq Army Raid on Protest Camp', *The Independent*, 23 April 2013.

36 See Chapter 4.

37 Author interview, 2015.

38 'Iraqi PM Warns against "Sectarian War"', Aljazeera [online], 25 April 2013 (http://www.aljazeera.com/news/middleeast/2013/04/2013425123452971800.html) (accessed 30 March 2015).

39 Author interview, 2015.

40 'Iraq Sunni Unrest Prompts TV Channel Licence Suspension', BBC News [online], 28 April 2013 (http://www.bbc.co.uk/news/world-middle-east-22329641) (accessed 30 March 2015).

41 'Iraqi PM Warns against "Sectarian War"'.

42 'Iraq Jailbreaks: Hundreds Escape in Taji and Abu Ghraib', BBC News [online], 22 July 2013 (http://www.bbc.co.uk/news/world-middle-east-23403564) (accessed 30 March 2015).

43 Iraq Body Count, 2012 and 2013; the average annual death toll in Iraq for the period 2003–14, including the 2006, 2007 and 2014 outliers, is 12,533.

44 Iraq Body Count, 2012 and 2013.

45 See Alex Bilger, 'ISIS Annual Reports Reveal Metrics-driven Military Command', Institute for the Study of War, 22 May 2014.

46 See Chapter 7.

47 'Bomb Attack Kills Officers in Iraq's Anbar Province', BBC News [online], 21 December 2013 (http://www.bbc.co.uk/news/world-middle-east-25478063) (accessed 30 March 2015).

48 'Maliki's Policies: The Quest for Salvation at Iraq's Expense', Arab Center for Research and Policy Studies [online], 9 January 2014 (http://english.dohainstitute.org/release/05adf2f2-29bc-4b67-a115-b37a0476b365) (accessed 30 March 2015).

49 Kirk H. Sowell, 'Maliki's Anbar Blunder', *Foreign Policy* [online], 15 January 2014 (http://foreignpolicy.com/2014/01/15/malikis-anbar-blunder) (accessed 30 March 2015).

50 Garrett Brinker and Nigel Cory, 'Violence, Distrust, and Instability: Iraq's Future in Uncertain Times', Georgetown Public Policy Review [online], 13 March 2014 (http://gppreview.com/2014/03/13/violence-distrust-and-instability-iraqs-future-in-uncertain-times) (accessed 30 March 2015).

51 'Iraq MP Ahmed al Alwani Arrested in Deadly Ramadi Raid', BBC News [online], 28 December 2013 (http://www.bbc.co.uk/news/world-middle-east-25534541) (accessed 30 March 2015).

52 AFP, 'Iraq Sentences Sunni Ex-MP to Death for Murder', *Daily Mail*, 23 November 2014.

53 'Maliki's Policies'.

54 Mushreq Abbas, 'Resolution of Anbar Crisis Requires Security, Political Coordination', tr. Kamal Fayad, Al Monitor [online], 3 January 2014 (http://www.al-monitor.com/pulse/originals/2014/01/iraq-anbar-protests-crisis-security-political-solution.html) (accessed 30 March 2015).

55 Thomas Joscelyn, 'Chechen-led Group Swears Allegiance to Head of Islamic State of Iraq and Sham', Long War Journal [online], 27 November 2013 (http://www.longwarjournal.org/archives/2013/11/muhajireen_army_swea.php) (accessed 30 March 2015).

56 Caillet, 'The Islamic State'.

57 Ibid.

58 Yasir Ghazi and Tim Arango, 'Iraq Fighters, Qaeda Allies, Claim Fallujah as New State', *New York Times*, 3 January 2014.

59 'Iraqi City in Hands of al-Qaida-linked Militants', Voice of America [online], 4 January 2014 (http://www.voanews.com/content/iraqi-city-in-hands-of-alqaidalinked-militants/1823591.html) (accessed 30 March 2015).

60 Author interview, 2015.

61 Brian Michael Jenkins, 'Brothers Killing Brothers: The Current Infighting Will Test al-Qaeda's Brand', Rand Corporation, 2014.

62 Aron Lund, 'Who and What Was Abu Khalid al-Suri? Part 1', Carnegie Endowment for International Peace [online], 24 February 2014 (http://carnegieendowment.org/syriaincrisis/?fa=54618) (accessed 30 March 2015).

63 Translation of statement by Ayman al-Zawahiri, acknowledging ISIS is not part of al-Qaeda, 3 February 2014.

64 Ibid.

65 Ellen Knickmeyer, 'Al-Qaeda Disavows Rebel Group Fighting Syrian Regime', *Wall Street Journal,* 3 February 2014.

66 'Global Overview 2014: People Internally Displaced by Conflict and Violence', Internal Displacement Monitoring Centre, May 2014, p. 59.

67 Ibid., pp. 13–14.

68 See Chapter 9.

69 See Chapter 9.

70 Report, 'Analysis: What We Talk about When We Talk about Iraq and Syria', Caerus Associates [online] (http://caerusassociates.com/ideas/what-we-talk-about-when-we-talk-about-iraq-and-syria) (accessed 30 March 2015); Yasir Abbas and Dan Trombly, 'Inside the Collapse of

the Iraq Army's 2nd Division', War on the Rocks [online], 1 July 2014 (http://warontherocks.com/2014/07/inside-the-collapse-of-the-iraqi-armys-2nd-division) (accessed 30 March 2015).

71 Ibid.

72 Wladimir van Wilgenburg, 'ISIS Seen as Liberators by Some Sunnis in Mosul', Al Monitor [online], 11 June 2014 (http://www.al-monitor.com/pulse/originals/2014/06/isis-mosul-takeover-residents-blame-iraqi-army.html) (accessed 30 March 2015).

73 'Iraq: Abusive Commander Linked to Mosul Killings', Human Rights Watch [online], 11 June 2013 (http://www.hrw.org/news/2013/06/11/iraq-abusive-commander-linked-mosul-killings) (accessed 30 March 2015).

74 Ned Parker, Isabel Coles and Raheem Salman, 'Special Report: How Mosul Fell – An Iraqi General Disputes Baghdad's Story', Reuters [online], 14 October 2014 (http://uk.reuters.com/article/2014/10/14/us-mideast-crisis-gharawi-special-report-idUK-KCN0I30Z820141014) (accessed 30 March 2015).

75 Ibid.

76 Ibid.

77 Hugh Naylor, 'Maliki Ignored ISIL Warnings before Mosul's Fall, Says City's Governor', *The National* [online], 18 June 2014 (http://www.thenational.ae/world/middle-east/maliki-ignored-isil-warn-ings-before-mosulx2019s-fall-says-cityx2019s-governor) (accessed 30 March 2015).

78 Author interview, 2015.

79 Office of the High Commissioner for Human Rights and United Nations Assistance Mission for Iraq (UNAMI) Human Rights Office, 'Report on the Protection of Civilians in the Armed Conflict in Iraq: 5 June to 5 July 2014', p. 11.

80 Ibid., pp. 10–12.

81 Office of the High Commissioner for Human Rights and United Nations Assistance Mission for Iraq (UNAMI) Human Rights Office, 'Report on the Protection of Civilians in the Armed Conflict in Iraq: 5 June to 5 July 2014', p. 10.

82 Author interview.

11: The furnace of war

1 'Iraq Kurdistan Independence Referendum Planned', BBC News [online], 1 July 2014 (http://www.bbc.co.uk/news/world-middle-east-28103124) (accessed 21 April 2015).

2 See Chapter 7.

3 Author interview 2014; the figure for murdered Christians in the parish of St George's Baghdad is as of 6 July 2014, the date of the interview.

4 See Chapter 8.

5 See Chapter 7.

6 Nissim Rejwan, *The Last Jews of Baghdad, Remembering a Lost Homeland* (Austin: University of Texas Press, 2004); the last Ottoman yearbook in 1917 for Baghdad numbers 80,000 Jews among the city's 202,200 inhabitants. This is also the subject of *The Last Jews of Iraq*, a programme on BBC Radio 4, broadcast on 4 December 2011 and presented by Alan Yentob.

7 Naomi E. Pasachoff and Robert J. Littman, *A Concise History of the Jewish People* (Lanham, MD: Rowman and Littlefield, 2005), p. 310.

8 Reverend Canon Andrew White, sermon to congregation of St George's Church, Baghdad, 6 July 2014.

9 Mailonline, Four young Christians brutally beheaded by ISIS for refusing to convert to Islam, says British Vicar of Baghdad forced to flee, by Tim MacFarlan, 12 December 2014. Based on the interview Canon Andrew White gave to Orthodox Christian News, Before Being Killed Children Told ISIS 'No, We Love Jesus', 28 November 2014.

10 'What Comes to You of Good Is from Allah: Message from Abu Muhammad al-Adnani al-Shami, Spokesman of Islamic State of Iraq and Sham', al-Furqan media centre, 12 June 2014.

11 AFP, 'ISIS Destroys Shrines, Shiite Mosques in Iraq', Al Arabiya News [online], 5 July 2014 (http://english.alarabiya.net/en/News/middle-east/2014/07/05/ISIS-destroys-Shiite-mosques-shrines-in-Iraq.html) (accessed 21 April 2015).

13 Author interview, 2014.

14 Tim Arango, 'Escaping Death in Northern Iraq', *New York Times*, 3 September 2014.

15 'Iraqi Teams Exhume Mass Graves of Soldiers in Tikrit', BBC News [online], 7 April 2015 (http://www.bbc.co.uk/news/world-middle-east-32197107) (accessed 21 April 2015).

15 Author interview, Canon Reverend Andrew White, July 2014.

16 'What Comes to You of Good Is from Allah'.

17 Hayder al-Khoei, 'Could Isis Take Iraqi's Capital?', *New Statesman*, 19 June 2014.

18 Daniel Howden, 'Sistani Renounces Fatwa on Gays', *The Independent*, 16 May 2006.

19 The Official Website of the Office of His Eminence Al-Sayyid Ali al-Hussein al-Sistani (http://www.sistani.org/english) (accessed 21 April 2015).

20 Mark Oliver, Laura Smith and news agencies, 'Shia Shrine Blasts Spark Reprisal Attacks', *The Guardian*, 22 February 2006.

21 Thomas L. Friedman, 'A Nobel for Sistani', *New York Times*, 20 March 2005.

22 Ali Mamouri, 'Sistani Issues Fatwa against Sectarian Violence in Iraq', Al Monitor [online], 11 October 2013 (http://www.al-monitor. com/pulse/originals/2013/10/iraqi-moderates-manage-sectarianism.html) (accessed 21 April 2015).

23 Abbas Kadhim and Luay Al Khateeb, 'What Do You Know about Sistani's Fatwa?', Huff Post Politics [online], 7 October 2014 (http:// www.huffingtonpost.com/luay-al-khatteeb/what-do-you-know-about-si_b_5576244.html) (accessed 21 April 2015).

24 Dina al-Shibeeb, 'Sistani's Disapproval of Maliki is Bad Elections News for the Premier', Al Arabiya News [online], 24 April 2014 (http://english.alarabiya.net/en/perspective/2014/04/24/Sistani-s-disproval-of-Maliki-is-bad-elections-news-for-the-premier.html) (accessed 21 April 2015).

25 Nour Malas, 'Iraqi Leader Maliki Loses Backing of Shiite Figure and Iran for New Term', *Wall Street Journal*, 22 July 2014.

26 'Iraq Crisis: Maliki Quits as PM to End Deadlock', BBC News [online], 15 August 2014 (http://www.bbc.co.uk/news/world-middle-east-28798033) (accessed 21 April 2015).

27 Farnaz Fassihi, 'Iran Deploys Forces to Fight al Qaeda-Inspired Militants in Iraq', *Wall Street Journal*, 12 June 2014.

28 Dexter Filkins, 'The Shadow Commander', *New Yorker*, 30 September 2013.

29 Bill Roggio, 'Mugniyah behind Establishment of Mahdi Army', Long War Journal [online], 23 February 2008 (http://www.longwarjournal.org/archives/2008/02/mugniyah_behind_esta.php) (accessed 21 April 2015).

30 Joseph Felter and Brian Fishman, 'Iranian Strategy in Iraq: Politics and

"Other Means"', Combating Terrorism Center at West Point, October 2008, p. 6.

31 Confidential briefing, 2014

32 Nancy Trejos and Robin Wright, 'Iranians Captured inside Iraq', *Washington Post*, 12 January 2007.

33 Bill Roggio, 'Iran Continues to Train Shia Terror Groups for Attacks in Iraq', Long War Journal [online], 15 August 2008 (http://www.longwarjournal.org/archives/2008/08/map_details_irans_op.php) (accessed 21 April 2015).

34 The five main militias are the Badr Brigades (or Badr Corps or Badr Organization), the Mahdi Army, the Saraya al-Salam (an offshoot of Mahdi Army), the Asa'ib Ahl al-Haq and the Kata'ib Hizbullah (Hizbullah Brigades), reportedly another offshoot of the Mahdi Army's 'special groups'.

35 See Chapter 4.

36 'Absolute Impunity, Militia rule in Iraq', Amnesty International, October 2014, pp. 6–7.

37 'Iraq Tikrit: Looting and Lawlessness Follow Recapture', BBC News [online], 4 April 2015 (http://www.bbc.co.uk/news/world-middle-east-32181503) (accessed 30 April 2015).

38 See Chapter 5.

39 Bill Roggio, '"Shiite Zarqawi" Returns to Baghdad from Iran', Long War Journal [online], 21 August 2010 (http://www.longwarjournal.org/archives/2010/08/shiite_zarqawi_retur.php) (accessed 23 March 2015).

40 To complicate matters further, Badr left SCIRI following the 2006–7 civil war in Iraq; SCIRI, then renamed the Islamic Supreme Council of Iraq (ISCI), established a new militia called the Knights of Hope.

41 See Chapter 5.

42 Felter and Fishman, 'Iranian Strategy in Iraq', pp. 7–8.

43 Ibid., pp. 7–8.

44 Author interview, 2013.

45 See Chapter 9.

46 Author interview, 2013.

47 'Iranian advisor clarifies "Baghdad capital of Iranian empire" remark', Al Arabiya [online], 13 March 2015 (http://english.alarabiya.net/en/News/middle-east/2015/03/13/Iranian-advisor-clarifies-Baghdad-capital-of-Iranian-empire-remark.html) (accessed 21 April 2015).

48 'Iran President's Advisor's [*sic*] Responds to Iraq Criticism', Alalam [online], 11 March 2015 (http://en.alalam.ir/news/1684363) (accessed 21 April 2015).

12: Car bombs and other expenses

1   Author interview, 2013.
2   Alex Bilger, 'ISIS Annual Reports Reveal Metrics-driven Military Command', Institute for the Study of War, 22 May 2014, p. 10.
3   See Chapter 4.
4   'Pakistan "Catches al-Qaeda Chief"', BBC News [online], 4 May 2005 (http://news.bbc.co.uk/1/hi/world/south_asia/4512885.stm) (accessed 21 April 2015).
5   Letter from Ayman al-Zawahiri to Abu Musab al-Zarqawi, 9 July 2005.
6   See Chapters 6 and 7.
7   John F. Burns and Kirk Semple, 'US Finds Iraq Insurgency Has Funds to Sustain Itself', New York Times, 26 November 2006.
8   Ibid.
9   Wikibaghdady, 14 December 2013.
10 Richard Spencer, 'Militant Islamist Group in Syria Orders Christians to Pay Tax for Their Protection', The Telegraph [online], 27 February 2014 (http://www.telegraph.co.uk/news/10666204/Militant-Islamist-group-in-Syria-orders-Christians-to-pay-tax-for-their-protection.html) (accessed 30 April 2015).
11 Joseph Thorndike, 'How ISIS Is Using Taxes to Build a Terrorist State', Forbes [online], 18 August 2014 (http://www.forbes.com/sites/tax-analysts/2014/08/18/how-isis-is-using-taxes-to-build-a-terrorist-state/) (accessed 30 April 2015).
12 Ibid.
13 Bilger, 'ISIS Annual Reports Reveal Metrics-driven Military Command', p. 10.
14 Ibid., p.10. Car bomb totals include vehicle suicide bombings known as SVBIEDs, or suicide vehicle-borne improvised explosive devices.
15 Jessica D. Lewis, 'Al-Qaeda in Iraq Resurgent', Middle East Security Report 14, Institute for the Study of War, September 2013, p. 7.
16 See Chapter 10.
17 Jessica Lewis, 'Al Qaeda in Iraq's "Breaking the Walls" Campaign Achieves Its Objectives at Abu Ghraib', Institute for the Study of War Iraq Updates [online], 28 July 2013 (http://iswiraq.blogspot.co.uk/2013/07/al-qaeda-in-iraqs-breaking-walls.html) (accessed 21 April 2015).
18 Lewis, 'Al-Qaeda in Iraq Resurgent', p. 7.
19 Duraid Adnan, 'Wave of Car Bombs Kills Dozens in Iraq', International New York Times, 29 July 2013.

20 Lewis, 'Al-Qaeda in Iraq Resurgent', p. 21.

21 Elizabeth Dickinson, 'Playing with Fire: Why Private Gulf Financing for Syria's Extremist Rebels Risks Igniting Sectarian Conflict at Home', Analysis Paper 16, Saban Centre at Brookings, December 2013, p. 12.

22 Martin Chulov, 'How an Arrest in Iraq Revealed Isis's $2 Billion Jihadist Network', *The Guardian* [online], 15 June 2014 (http://www.theguardian.com/world/2014/jun/15/iraq-isis-arrest-jihadists-wealth-power) (accessed 30 April 2015).

23 Jack Moore, 'Mosul Seized: Jihadis Loot $429m from City's Central Bank to Make Isis World's Richest Terror Force', International Business Times [online], 11 June 2014 (http://www.ibtimes.co.uk/mosul-seized-jihadis-loot-429m-citys-central-bank-make-isis-worlds-richest-terror-force-1452190) (accessed 30 April 2015).

24 Jeffrey Bender, 'Iraqi Bankers Say ISIS Never Stole $430 Million from Mosul Banks', Business Insider [online], 17 July 2014 (http://www.businessinsider.com/isis-never-stole-430-million-from-banks-2014-7?IR=T) (accessed 30 April 2015).

25 Vasudevan Sridharan, 'List of World's Richest Terror Networks Revealed', International Business Times [online], 12 November 2014 (http://www.ibtimes.co.uk/list-worlds-richest-terror-networks-unveiled-1474351) (accessed 30 April 2015).

26 'Iraqi PM Maliki says Saudi, Qatar Openly Funding Violence in Anbar', Reuters, 9 March 2014.

27 Ramtanu Maitra, 'ISIS: Saudi-Qatari-funded Wahhabi Terrorists Worldwide', *Executive Intelligence Review*, 29 August 2014.

28 Madawi Al-Rasheed, 'The Wahhabis and the Ottoman Caliphate, The Memory of Historical Antagonism', in *Demystifying the Caliphate: Historical Memory and Contemporary Contexts*, ed. Madawi Al-Rasheed, Carol Kersten and Marat Shterin (London: Hurst, 2013), pp. 118–28.

29 'Saudis Said Failing to Crack Down on al Qaeda Donors', Reuters, 12 September 2007.

30 Steve Clemons, '"Thank God for the Saudis": ISIS, Iraq, and the Lessons of Blowback', *The Atlantic*, 23 June 2014.

31 Chris Zambelis, 'To Topple the Throne: Islamic State sets its Sights on Saudi Arabia', *Terrorism Monitor*, 13:5, 2015.

32 Ibid.

33 Council on Foreign Relations, The Sunni-Shia Divide, A CFR Info Guide Presentation, HYPERLINK "http://www.cfr.org/peace-conflict-and-human-rights/sunni-shia-divide/p33176" \l "!/" http://

www.cfr.org/peace-conflict-and-human-rights/sunni-shia-divide/p33176#!/

34 'Ambassador [Zalmay] Khalilzad Seeks Post-Iraqi Elections Support from Saudi Leaders', WikiLeaks [online], 2 January 2006, canonical ID 06RIYADH7_a (https://wikileaks.org/plusd/cables/06RI-YADH7_a.html) (accessed 21 April 2015).

35 Ibid.

36 Author interview, 2015.

37 See Chapter 7 for more details.

38 Brian Fishman (ed.), 'Bombers, Bank Accounts and Bleedout: Al-Qaida's Road in and out of Iraq', Combating Terrorism Center at West Point, July 2008, pp. 34–5.

39 Lori Plotkin Boghardt, 'Saudi Funding of ISIS', PolicyWatch 2275, Washington Institute [online], 23 June 2014 (http://www.washingtoninstitute.org/policy-analysis/view/saudi-funding-of-isis) (accessed 21 April 2015).

40 Wikibaghdady, 27 December 2013.

41 'Quilliam Exclusive: Alleged Leaks from Islamic State Reveal International Network of bribery', Quilliam [online], 14 November 2014 (http://www.quilliamfoundation.org/blog/quilliam-exclusive-alleged-leaks-from-islamic-state-reveal-international-network-of-bribery/) (accessed 21 April 2015).

42 Wikibaghdady, 20 December 2013.

43 Wikibaghdady, 20 December 2013.

44 'Terrorist Finance: Action Request for Senior Level Engagement on Finance', WikiLeaks [online], 30 December 2009, canonical ID 09STATE131801_a (https://wikileaks.org/plusd/cables/09STATE131801_a.html) (accessed 21 April 2015).

45 Ibid.

46 'Saudi Interior Ministry Briefs Special Advisor Holbrooke and Treasury DAS Glaser on Terrorism Finance', WikiLeaks [online], 29 May 2009, canonical ID 09RIYADH716_a (https://wikileaks.org/plusd/cables/09RIYADH716_a.html) (accessed 22 April 2015).

47 Boghardt, 'Saudi Funding of ISIS'.

48 Ibid.

49 Author interview, 2014.

50 Author interview, 2015.

51 David Rhode, 'Libya Peace Talks May Be Doomed by Meddling Powers: US', Reuters, 8 December 2014.

52 'Qatar Pays Price for Its Generous Support to Muslim Brotherhood', Middle East Online, 11 May 2013 (http://www.middle-east-online.com/english/?id=58685) (accessed 22 April 2015).

53 'German Minister Accuses Qatar of Funding Islamic State Fighters', Reuters [online], 20 August 2014 (http://uk.reuters.com/article/2014/08/20/uk-iraq-security-germany-qatar-idUKKB-N0GK1I220140820) (accessed 22 April 2015).

54 Ibid.

55 Dickinson, 'Playing with Fire', p. 1.

56 Ibid., p. 1.

57 'Turkish–Iranian Rivalry on the Rise', Daniel Pipes [online], 25 July 2011, updated 6 April 2015 (http://www.danielpipes.org/blog/2011/07/turkish-iranian-rivalry-on-the-rise) (accessed 22 April 2015).

58 As of February 2015, Professor Aktay sat on the AKP's Central Decision and Executive Council (MKYK), which is chaired by President Erdoğan.

59 Author interview, 2015.

13: 'Long live death!'

1 See Dr Muhammad Tahir-ul-Qadri, *Constitutional Analysis of the Constitution of Madina* [*sic*], Article 30.

2 Ibid., Article 29.

3 'Islamic State "Accepts" Boko Haram's Allegiance Pledge', BBC News [online], 13 March 2015 (http://www.bbc.co.uk/news/world-africa-31862992) (accessed 22 April 2015).

4 'The Bay'ah from West Africa', *Dabiq* 8, 2015, pp. 14–15.

5 Erin Banco, 'ISIS Establishes Stronghold In Derna, Libya', International Business Times [online], 10 November 2014 (http://www.ibtimes.com/isis-establishes-stronghold-derna-libya-1721425) (accessed 30 April 2015).

6 One of the twenty-one victims, a national of Chad, is said not to have been a Christian, but chose their fate after seeing his Coptic friends die, and then refusing to reject Christ. Before being murdered he is reported to have said, 'Their God is my God.'

7 'Daesh (ISIS) Releases Video of Beheading 21 Kidnapped Egyptians + video', Alalam [online], 15 February 2015 (http://en.alalam.ir/news/1676783) (accessed 22 April 2015).

8   Maggie Michael, 'Isis Beheading of Coptic Christians: The Egyptian Village Wracked by Grief for Young Men Killed by Militants', *The Independent* [online], 17 February 2015 (http://www.independent.co.uk/news/world/middle-east/isis-beheading-of-coptic-christians-the-egyptian-village-wracked-by-grief-for-young-men-killed-by-militants-10051487.html?origin=internalSearch) (accessed 30 April 2015).

9   *A Message Signed with Blood to the Nation of the Cross*, Al Hayat Media Center, video posted on 15 February 2015.

10 'IS Releases new "Killing" Video of Ethiopian Christians', BBC News [online], 20 April 2015 (http://www.bbc.co.uk/news/world-middle-east-32373166) (accessed 30 April 2015).

11 Ruth Sherlock, 'Islamic State: Inside the Latest City to Fall under Its Sway', *The Telegraph* [online], 10 March 2015 (http://www.telegraph.co.uk/news/worldnews/africaandindianocean/libya/11460124/How-Gaddafis-home-city-in-Libya-fell-under-the-rule-of-Islamic-State-jihadists.html) (accessed 22 April 2015).

12 'Remaining and Expanding', *Dabiq* 5, 2014, pp. 22–33.

13 'French Hostage Herve Gourdel Beheaded in Algeria', BBC News [online], 24 September 2014 (http://www.bbc.co.uk/news/world-africa-29352537) (accessed 30 April 2015).

14 Radwan Mortada, 'Khorasan Pledge Splits al-Qaeda', Alakhbar English [online], 23 April 2014 (http://english.al-akhbar.com/node/19516) (accessed 22 April 2015).

15 *The Independent*, Isis accused of beheading captives in Palestinian refugee camp Yarmouk as advance towards Syrian capital Damascus continues, by Adam Withnall, 6 April 2015.

16 Graeme Wood, 'What ISIS Really Wants', *The Atlantic*, March 2015.

17 'Remaining and Expanding'.

18 *The Washington Post*, What the 60-plus members of the anti-Islamic State coalition are doing, by Sebastian Payne, 25 September 2014.

19 'ISIS Militants Execute Six Opponents in Raqqa', ARA News [online], 3 February 2015 (http://aranews.net/2015/02/isis-militants-execute-six-opponents-raqqa/) (accessed 22 April 2015).

20 Ruth Sherlock, Yilmaz Ibrahim Pasha and Magdy Samaan, 'Islamic State Foiled in Attempt to Kidnap Syrian Rebel Leader in Turkey', *The Telegraph* [online], 19 October 2014 (http://www.telegraph.co.uk/news/worldnews/middleeast/syria/11173013/Islamic-State-foiled-in-attempt-to-kidnap-Syrian-rebel-leader-in-Turkey.html) (accessed 22 April 2015).

NOTES

21 Reuters, 'Iraq Says Over 300 Tribe Members Killed by ISIS', Al Arabiya [online], 3 November 2014 (http://english.alarabiya.net/en/News/middle-east/2014/11/03/Iraq-says-322-tribe-members-killed.html) (accessed 30 April 2015).

22 Bill Roggio and Caleb Weiss, 'Islamic State Overruns Town in Anbar, Executes Awakening Fighters', Long War Journal [online], 14 December 2014 (http://www.longwarjournal.org/archives/2014/12/islamic_state_overruns_town_in.php) (accessed 30 April 2015).

23 Simon Tomlinson, 'The Caliphate's Food Queues: Hundreds Queue for Hours as They Wait for Food in ISIS Capital', Mail Online, 7 April 2015 (http://www.dailymail.co.uk/news/article-3028921/The-photographs-ISIS-WON-T-posting-propaganda-Hundreds-queue-hours-wait-food-caliphate-s-capital.html) (accessed 22 April 2015).

24 Abu Mohammed, 'Pollution Aggravates Leishmaniasis inside Raqqa', Raqqa Is Being Slaughtered Silently [online], 20 March 2015 (http://www.raqqa-sl.com/en/?p=840) (accessed 22 April 2015).

25 The photos were supplied to Mail Online and other media outlets by the website Raqqa Is Being Slaughtered Silently.

26 See Chapter 2.

27 See Chapter 7.

28 Paul Berman, *Terror and Liberalism* (New York: W. W. Norton, 2003), p. 50.

29 Al-Furqan Media Center, Islamic State, Audio message by Abu Bakr al-Baghdadi, posted 14 May 2015 by the Middle East Media Research Institute (MEMRI) Jihad and Terrorism Threat Monitor, 'In New Audio Speech, Islamic State (ISIS) Leader Al-Baghdadi Issues Call to Arms to All Muslims'.

30 See Chapter 10.

31 'How Did Raqqa Fall to the Islamic State of Iraq and Syria?', SyriaUntold [online], 8 January 2014 (http://www.syriauntold.com/en/2014/01/how-did-raqqa-fall-to-the-islamic-state-of-iraq-and-syria) (accessed 30 March 2015).

32 Mosul Eye community, Facebook, 19 April 2015.

33 Author interview, 2015.

34 See Chapter 10.

35 See Chapter 7.

36 Abu Mohammed, 'ISIS Prevents Dentists from Curing Women', Raqqa Is Being Slaughtered Silently [online], 20 April 2015 (http://www.raqqa-sl.com/en/?p=994) (accessed 22 April 2015).

37 Tim Arango, 'Sunni Extremists in Iraq Seize 3 Towns from Kurds and Threaten Major Dam', *New York Times*, 3 August 2014.

38 Steve Hopkins, 'Full Horror of the Yazidis Who Didn't Escape Mount Sinjar: UN Confirms 5,000 Men Were Executed and 7,000 Women Are Now Kept as Sex Slaves', Mail Online, 14 October 2014 (http://www.dailymail.co.uk/news/article-2792552/full-horror-yazidis-didn-t-escape-mount-sinjar-confirms-5-000-men-executed-7-000-women-kept-sex-slaves.html) (accessed 22 April 2015).

39 See 'Islamic State (ISIS) Releases Pamphlet on Female Slaves', MEMRI Jihad and Terrorism Threat Monitor [online], 4 December 2014 (http://www.memrijttm.org/islamic-state-isis-releases-pamphlet-on-female-slaves.html) (accessed 30 April 2015).

40 See Chapters 6 and 7.

41 'The Revival of Slavery before the Hour', *Dabiq* 4, 2014. p. 14.

42 Ibid., p. 15.

43 Ibid., p. 15.

44 Ibid., p. 16.

45 'Iraq: ISIS Escapees Describe Systematic Rape', Human Rights Watch [online], 15 April 2015 (http://www.hrw.org/news/2015/04/14/iraq-isis-escapees-describe-systematic-rape) (accessed 22 April 2015).

46 Ibid.

47 Abu Mohammed, 'ISIS Fighters Are Desperately Trying to Obtain VIAGRA, Spending Money on Kinky Underwear for Their "Wives"…Then Subjecting Them to "Brutal, Abnormal" Sex Acts According to Doctors in Syria', Raqqa Is Being Slaughtered Silently [online], 17 February 2015 (http://www.raqqa-sl.com/en/?p=589) (accessed 22 April 2015).

48 Ibid.

49 Hisham al-Hashimi and Telegraph Interactive Team, 'Revealed: The Islamic State "Cabinet", from Finance Minister to Suicide Bomb Deployer', *The Telegraph* [online], 9 July 2014 (http://www.telegraph.co.uk/news/worldnews/middleeast/iraq/10956193/Revealed-the-Islamic-State-cabinet-from-finance-minister-to-suicide-bomb-deployer.html) (accessed 22 April 2015).

50 Charles Lister, 'Islamic State Senior Leadership: Who's Who', available at http://www.brookings.edu/~/media/Research/Files/Reports/2014/11/profiling-islamic-state-lister/en_whos_who.pdf?la=en (accessed 22 April 2015).

51 'The Rise of ISIS', *Frontline*, PBS, 28 October 2014. Source: The Soufan Group.

NOTES

52 Christoph Reuter, 'The Terror Strategist: Secret Files Reveal the Structure of Islamic State', Spiegel Online International, 18 April 2015 (http://www.spiegel.de/international/world/islamic-state-files-show-structure-of-islamist-terror-group-a-1029274.html) (accessed 29 April 2015).

53 Charles Lister, 'Profiling the Islamic State', Brookings Doha Center, Analysis Paper 13, November 2014, p. 5.

54 See Chapter 8.

55 Bassem Mroue, 'Key al-Qaida Militant Reportedly Killed in Syria', Associated Press, 27 January 2014.

56 Ruth Sherlock and Magdy Samaan, 'Islamic State Leader Abu Bakr al-Baghdadi's Close Aide Killed in US Airstrike', *The Telegraph* [online], 9 November 2014 (http://www.telegraph.co.uk/news/worldnews/islamic-state/11219630/Islamic-State-leader-Abu-Bakr-al-Baghdadis-close-aide-killed-in-US-air-strike.html) (accessed 22 April 2015).

57 'Iraq Confirms: Islamic State Group Leader Injured, Deputy Killed', i24 News [online], 10 November 2014 (http://www.i24news.tv/en/news/international/middle-east/50331-141109-iraq-investigating-is-chief-s-fate-after-air-strikes) (accessed 22 April 2015).

58 See Chapter 3 for the Ba'athist credentials of al-Turkmani and Chapter 8 for his stay in Camp Bucca.

59 'Abu Muslim al-Turkmani: From Iraqi Officer to Slain ISIS Deputy', Al Arabiya News [online], 19 December 2014 (http://english.alarabiya.net/en/perspective/profiles/2014/12/19/Abu-Muslim-al-Turkmani-From-Iraqi-officer-to-slain-ISIS-deputy.html) (accessed 22 April 2015).

60 Syed Choudhury, 'Can ISIS Mint Its Own Currency?', Middle East Monitor [online], 19 November 2014 (https://www.middleeastmonitor.com/blogs/politics/15359-can-isis-mint-its-own-currency) (accessed 22 April 2015).

61 Borzou Daragahi, 'Isis Declares Its Own Currency', *Financial Times,* 13 November 2014.

62 Around eight cents in November 2014.

63 Hashimi et al., 'Revealed: the Islamic State "Cabinet"'.

64 Lorenzo Vidino, 'Hisba in Europe? Assessing a Murky Phenomenon', European Foundation for Democracy, June 2013, p. 9.

65 Abu Mohammed, 'ISIS Militants Threatened to Give 80 Lashes to Anybody Caught Watching El Clasico Because Game Is "Product of Decadent West"', Raqqa Is Being Slaughtered Silently [online], 26

321

March 2015 (http://www.raqqa-sl.com/en/?p=860) (accessed 22 April 2015).

66   Ibid.

67   See Chapter 8.

68   'Rule of Terror: Living under ISIS in Syria', Report of the Independent International Commission of Inquiry on the Syrian Arab Republic, United Nations, 14 November 2014, paragraph 46.

69   Author interview, 2015.

70   'Women Stoned to Death in Syria for Adultery', Associated Press, 30 June 2014.

71   'Islamic State Video Purports to Show Boy Executing Two Spies', Clarion Project [online], 13 January 2015 (http://www.clarion-project.org/news/islamic-state-young-boy-executes-two-russian-spies) (accessed 22 April 2015).

72   'The Lions of Tomorrow', *Dabiq* 8, 2015, pp. 20–1.

73   'Child Soldiers', War Child [online] (http://www.warchild.org.uk/issues/child-soldiers) (accessed 22 April 2015).

74   Abu Ibrahim Raqqawi, 'IS Boot Camps Rob Raqqa's Children of Their Childhood', Raqqa Is Being Slaughtered Silently [online], 7 January 2015 (http://www.raqqa-sl.com/en/?p=150) (accessed 22 April 2015).

75   'The Lions of Tomorrow', p. 20.

76   Raqqawi, 'IS Boot Camps Rob Raqqa's Children of Their Childhood'.

77   The men were from the 17th Syrian army division, the 93rd brigade and the al-Tabqah airbase, according to Raqqawi, 'IS Boot Camps Rob Raqqa's Children of Their Childhood'.

78   *Children on the Front Line*, BBC World Service Radio, 31 March 2015.

79   Abu Ibrahim Raqqawi, 'ISIS Followers Celebrate Jordanian Pilot Death at Outdoor Screening Party', Raqqa Is Being Slaughtered Silently [online], 4 February 2015 (http://www.raqqa-sl.com/en/?p=443) (accessed 22 April 2015).

80   Abu Mohammed, 'Jordanian Pilot Burned Alive: Moaz al-Kasasbeh Was "Heavily Drugged So He Would Not Scream",' Raqqa Is Being Slaughtered Silently [online], 12 February 2015. IS posted *Healing the Believers' Chests* on 3 February 2015.

81   'Jordan Pilot Ejected over Syria after "Technical Failure",' AFP, 26 December 2014.

82   See Chapter 6.

83   'Jordanian Pilot Was Dead before Islamic State Proposed Swap, Negotiator Says', Asahi Shimbun [online], 21 February 2015 (http://

ajw.asahi.com/article/behind_news/politics/AJ201502210049)
(accessed 22 April 2015).

84 Mohammed al-Falidat, 'Jordan's Security Services Gamble on Maqdisi', Al-Araby, 7 February 2015.

85 Quoted in 'Sheikh Abu Muhammad al-Maqdisi's Efforts to Arrange Prisoner Exchange Deal to Free Jordanian Pilot', MEMRI [online], 13 February 2015 (http://www.memrijttm.org/sheikh-abu-muhammad-al-maqdisis-efforts-to-arrange-prisoner-exchange-deal-to-free-jordanian-pilot.html) (accessed 22 April 2015).

86 Author interview, 2015.

87 'Jordan Executes Sajida al-Rishawi after Pilot Murder', Al Arabiya News [online], 4 February 2015 (http://english.alarabiya.net/en/News/middle-east/2015/02/04/Jordan-to-execute-jailed-would-be-bomber-jihadists-security.html) (accessed 22 April 2015).

88 Lamiat Sabin, 'Who Is Sajida Mubarak Atrous al-Rishawi, the Female Suicide Bomber at the Heart of "Isis" Japanese Prisoner Swap Plan?', *The Independent* [online], 24 January 2015 (http://www.independent.co.uk/news/world/middle-east/who-is-sajida-mubarak-atrous-alrishawi-the-female-suicide-bomber-at-the-heart-of-isis-prisoner-swap-plan-10000572.html) (accessed 22 April 2015).

89 'Japan Outraged at IS '"Beheading"' of Hostage Kenji Goto', BBC News [online], 1 February 2015 (http://www.bbc.co.uk/news/world-middle-east-31075769) (accessed 30 April 2015).

90 Roya TV, Jordan, interview with Maqdisi, 6 February 2015; transcript translated by MEMRI and published on 8 February 2015.

91 Quoted in 'Sheikh Abu Muhammad al-Maqdisi's Efforts to Arrange Prisoner Exchange Deal to Free Jordanian Pilot'.

14: Killing the caliphate

1 Author interview, anon., 2014.

2 Author interview with firemen, 20 October 2014; there's a short report about the attack on the mosque from Agence France-Press, on NDTV, *Fresh Attack at Baghdad Shiite Mosque Kills at Least, 11,* 20 October 2014.

3 NDTV, *Fresh Attack at Baghdad Shiite Mosque Kills at Least 11*, 20 October 2014.

4 Al-Hayat Media Center [IS], Inside Ayn al-Islam [as Kobani is also known], IS propaganda film presented by John Cantlie.

5   Anne Barnard and Karam Shoumali, 'Kurd Militia Says ISIS Is Expelled From Kobani', *New York Times*, 26 January 2015.

6   According to London-based Syrian Observatory for Human Rights; see Kunal Dutta, 'Kobani "Back in Kurdish Hands" after Isis Militants Desert City', *The Independent,* 27 January 2015.

7   Katrina Montgomery, '180,000 Refugees from Kobani Mark the Biggest Department in the Biggest Refugee Criris, Ever', Syria Deeply, 9 October 2014.

8   Confidential sources, April 2015.

9   Confidential sources, 2015.

10 Martin Chulov and Kareem Shaheen, 'Isis leader Abu Bakr al-Baghdadi "Seriously Wounded in Air Strike"', *The Guardian*, 21 January 2015.

11 Mark Piggott, 'Isis: 'New leader' is former physics teacher Abu Alaa Afri replacing paralysed al-Baghdadi', *International Business Times,* 23 April 2015.

12 Confidential sources, 2015.

13 See Chapter 6 / Charles Lister from the Brookings Institute mentions an Aouf Abd al-Rahman al Arfi [sic] in his compilation of Islamic State senior leaders, Brookings Doha Center Analysis paper, 1 December 2014. Other than that there is precious little mention of Afri until he assumed temporarily the role of 'emir'.

14 BBC, Islamic State deputy leader 'killed in Iraq air strike', 13 May 2015.

15 Confidential sources, 2015.

16 Kieran Corcoran, 'ISIS Terror Chief "Believed Dead": Iraqi Military Confirm Warlord WAS Injured in US-led Airstrike as Speculation Grows Feared Jihadist Perished in Attack, Reuters and Mail Online, 10 November 2014.

17 Ruth Sherlock and Magdy Samaan, 'Islamic State Leader Abu Bakr al-Baghdadi's Close Aide Killed in Airstrike', *The Telegraph*, 9 November 2014; Abu Suja's death was confirmed by his relatives to the Iraqi security advisor and analyst Hisham al-Hishami whose contacts within IS were widely considered second to none

18 Ibid.

19 *The Guardian*, Isis leader incapacitated with suspected spinal injuries after air strike, by Martin Chulov, 1 May 2015.

20 Al-Furqan Media Center, Islamic State, Audio message by Abu Bakr al-Baghdadi, posted 14 May 2015 by the Middle East Media Research Institute (MEMRI) Jihad and Terrorism Threat Monitor, 'In New Audio Speech, Islamic State (ISIS) Leader Al-Baghdadi Issues Call to Arms to All Muslims'.

21 See Chapter 1.

22 Author interview, 2014.

23 Author interview, 2014.

24 'Islamic State 'Seizes Syrian "Oil Field", Al Jazeera, 3 July 2014.

25 Sneha Dhanker, 'ISIS Takes Over Baiji, Iraq's Largest Oil Refinery', *International Business Times*, 18 June 2014.

26 Author interview with Hoshyar Zebari, October 2014.

27 Author interview, 2014.

28 'Iraq PM Rebuts US Criticism of Security Forces', AFP, 25 May 2015.

29 Author interview, 2015.

30 Martin Robinson, '"The Dawn of a New Era Has Begun"': ISIS Supporters Hand Out Leaflets in London's Oxford Street Encouraging People to Move to Newly Proclaimed Islamic State, Mail Online, 13 August 2014.

31 Sam Webb, 'ISIS on Oxford Street: Two Men in Court Accused of Handling Out Pro-Terror Leaflets in Central London', *Daily Mirror,* 22 April 2015.

32 'Militant Muslim Warns Royal Wedding Terror Attack is Highly Likely' Mail Online, *Daily Mail*, 1 April 2011.

33 Dominic Glover, 'ISIS Hate Preacher Anjem Choudary Hopes to Quit Britain for "Freedom" of Islamic State' International Business Times, 7 November 2014.

34 Author interview, 2015.

35 Richard Spillett, Rebecca Camber and Ian Drury, 'The Schoolgirl Jihadi Brides, Three Girls from One British School Fly Off to Join ISIS: Police Face Questions over How They Were Able to Board Turkey Flight, Mail Online, *Daily Mail*, 21 February 2015.

36 Confidential source 2015.

37 Carol Anne Grayson (Radical Sister) blog, 'Alan Henning: Open Letter from Abu Muhammad al-Maqdisi, a Sha'riah Ruling and an appeal from a revert sister', (https://activist1.wordpress.com/2014/09/22/alan-henning-open-letter-from-abu-muhammad-al-maqdissi-a-sharia-ruling-and-an-appeal-from-a-revert-sister/), 22 September 2014.

38 Tim Golden, 'Jihadist or Victim: Ex-Detainee Makes a Case', *New York Times*, 15 June 2005.

39 For more details see The Story of Cerie Bullivant, February 2010, https://www.liberty-human-rights.org.uk/sites/default/files/control-orders-case-study-cerie-bullivant.pdf

40 Press conference 26 February 2015, see https://www.youtube.com/watch?v=MngUaaOIVqg

41 'ISIS Releases New '"We Will Burn America Video"', 13 April 2015.

42 Dabiq, Issue 9, 'They Plot And Allah Plots', by John Cantlie, 'The Perfect Storm, What started as an explosive moment in Iraq has now suddenly turned into a global phenomenon that the West and the democratic world as a whole is ill-equipped to deal with', pp.77, al-Furqan Media Centre, Islamic State.

43 Author interview, 2014.

44 Author interview, 2015.

45 Author interview, 2015.

15: Masters of Mayhem

1 Shaikh [sic] Abdullah Azzam, 'Defense of the Muslim Lands: The First Obligation after Iman', master's thesis, Al-Azhar University, Cairo, circa 1971, tr. 'Brothers in Ribatt'.

2 See Chapter 1.

3 See Chapter 2.

4 See Chapters 1 and 2.

5 'Foreword', Dabiq 4, 2014, p. 4.

6 Ibid.

7 Bill Roggio, 'Iraq Report, Al Douri Flips on al Qaeda', Long War Journal [online], 22 August 2007 (http://www.longwarjournal.org/dailyiraqreport/2007/08/iraq_report_al_douri_flips_on.php) (accessed 16 October 2015). The early 2004 report was originally posted on the SITE website.

8 See Chapters 10 and 11; Douri's death in Tikrit in 2015 is mentioned in Chapter 14.

9 Official Spokesman for the Islamic State, 'Indeed Your Lord Is Ever Watchful', Dabiq 4, 2014, p. 8.

10 John Steinbeck, East of Eden, Chapter 42.

11 Joel Hunter, 'Alan Kurdi Death: A Syrian Kurdish Family Forced to Flee', BBC News [online], 4 September 2015 (http://www.bbc.co.uk/news/world-europe-34141716) (accessed 12 October 2015).

12 Helena Smith and Mark Tran, 'Germany Says It Could Take 500,000 Refugees a Year', The Guardian, 8 September 2015.

13 'The Danger of Abandoning Dārul-Islām', Dabiq 11, 2015, p. 22.

14 Glad Tidings of the Subjects with the Gold Currency, available at Jihadology

[online] (http://jihadology.net/2015/09/02/new-video-message-from-the-islamic-state-glad-tidings-of-the-subjects-with-the-gold-currency-wilayat-al-furat) (accessed 12 October 2015).

15   See Chapter 13 for more details about the IS currency.

16   Sarmad al-Jilane, 'Water in Raqqa Province is "Undrinkable"', Raqqa Is Being Slaughtered Silently [online], 18 September 2015 (http://www.raqqa-sl.com/en/?p=1401) (accessed 12 October 2015).

17   Ibid.

18   Confidential sources, October 2015.

19   See Chapter 7.

20   Confidential sources.

21   Under Queen Zenobia Antoninianus, much of the East seceded from Rome in the 260s. Her 'Palmyrene' empire came to an end with her capture by the Roman emperor Aurelius in 271 and she died in Rome some time later.

22   Kristin Romey, 'Why ISIS Hates Archaeology and Blew Up Ancient Iraqi Palace', National Geographic [online], 14 April 2015 (http://news.nationalgeographic.com/2015/04/150414-why-islamic-state-destroyed-assyrian-palace-nimrud-iraq-video-isis-isil-archaeology) (accessed 12 October 2015).

23   'Islamic State "Demolishes" Ancient Hatra Site in Iraq', BBC News [online], 7 March 2015 (http://www.bbc.co.uk/news/world-middle-east-31779484) (accessed 12 October 2015).

24   'Palmyra's Baalshamin Temple "Blown Up by IS"', BBC News [online], 24 August 2015 (http://www.bbc.co.uk/news/world-middle-east-34036644) (accessed 12 October 2015).

25   'Destroying the Shirk Temple of Bel', *Dabiq* 11 (2015), p. 33.

26   Louisa Loveluck and Magdy Samaan, 'Isil Murders Scholar Who Hid Treasures of Palmyra', *Daily Telegraph*, 20 August 2015.

27   Ben Hubbard, 'Syrian Expert Who Shielded Palmyra Antiquities Meets a Grisly Death at ISIS' Hands', *New York Times*, 19 August 2015.

28   AFP, 'Afghan Taliban Admit to Covering Up Mullah Omar's Death', Al Arabiya News [online], 31 August 2015 (http://english.alarabiya.net/en/News/middle-east/2015/08/31/Afghan-Taliban-admit-covering-up-Mullah-Omar-s-death-.html) (accessed 12 October 2015).

29   'Foreword', *Dabiq* 11 (2015), p. 4.

30   Ibid.

31   The story of the so-called 'Pope Joan' of the thirteenth century is widely considered to be a fantasy.

32   Judit Neurink, 'ISIS Leader Abu Bakr al-Baghdadi Repeatedly Raped

US Hostage Kayla Mueller and Turned Yazidi Girls into Personal Sex Slaves', *The Independent*, 14 August 2015.

33 Polly Mosendz, 'Umm and Abu Sayyaf: U.S. Forces Kill Senior ISIS Leader, Take Another Alive', *Newsweek*, 16 May 2015.

34 See Chapter 10.

35 Jonathan Eyal and Elizabeth Quintana (eds), *Inherently Unresolved: Regional Politics and the Counter-ISIS Campaign*, Royal United Services Institute, September 2015.

36 Author interview, 2015.

37 Yara Bayoumy and Mohammed Ghobari, 'Iranian Support Seen Crucial for Yemen's Houthis', Reuters [online], 15 December 2014 (http://uk.reuters.com/article/2014/12/15/us-yemen-houthis-iran-insight-idUKKBN0JT17A20141215) (accessed 12 October 2015).

38 See Chapter 13. Urfa was the scene of the bungled kidnapping by IS of Abu Issa, leader of the Raqqa Rebels.

39 Security sources, September 2015.

40 See Chapter 11.

41 BBC News, Battle for Sinjar: Kurdish forces enter IS-held town in Iraq, 13 November 2015.

Index

INDEX

INDEX

INDEX

INDEX